ACKNOWLEDGEMENTS

Harriot Mellon was a prolific letter writer but, unfortunately, comparatively few of her letters have been preserved. All the known papers relating to her private and business affairs are in the archives of Coutts Bank in the Strand, and I have been fortunate enough to gain access to them. She kept all the letters written to her by Thomas Coutts before and during his marriage to her, but he, for obvious reasons given their extra-marital relationship, did not preserve her personal ones to him in the ten years before they married. There are, however, business letters, leases, bills and other papers relating to Harriot's personal fortune, and to the private life and affairs of Thomas Coutts and his family. They were apparently deposited there by Harriot after she became a partner in the bank, either in the first year of her widowhood in 1822 or on her marriage to the Duke of St Albans in 1827.

I am extremely grateful to Barbara Peters, the now-retired archivist at Coutts Bank, to Tracey Earl the current archivist, and to her assistant Philippa Davenport, for searching out documents and allowing me space in their office to work on them. Harriot said that she found it very difficult to examine her own motives and behaviour, and avoided doing so; it is therefore not surprising that there is no evidence of her writing a journal. Nonetheless, she is a fascinating and complex person, and much can be learned from her surviving correspondence, and from what others wrote about her.

I am grateful also to the libraries which provided other research materials: the British Library; the Theatre Museum Library of the Victoria and Albert Museum in London; and the Deering Special Collections Library at Northwestern University, Illinois.

Above all, my thanks go to my husband, Harold Perkin, for his constant aid and support both academically and personally.

THE MERRY DUCHESS

Joan Perkin

ATHENA PRESS
LONDON

THE MERRY DUCHESS
Copyright © Joan Perkin 2002

All Rights Reserved

No part of this book may be reproduced in any form
by photocopying or by any electronic or mechanical means,
including information storage or retrieval systems,
without permission in writing from both the copyright
owner and the publisher of this book.

ISBN 1 84401 015 5

First Published 2002 by
ATHENA PRESS
Queen's House, 2 Holly Road
Twickenham TW1 4EG
United Kingdom

Printed for Athena Press

THE MERRY DUCHESS

Contents

Acknowledgements		v
Introduction		ix
I	The Child of Nature	13
II	The Country Girl	26
III	The Rivals	41
IV	The School for Scandal	55
V	The Follies of the Day	68
VI	The Way to Keep Him	82
VII	The Wedding Day	97
VIII	The Devil to Pay	110
IX	The Constant Couple	127
X	The Agreeable Surprise	144
XI	She Would and She Would Not	158
XII	A Bold Stroke for a Husband	171
XIII	The Romp	185
XIV	The Doldrums	200
XV	The Will	213
Bibliography		227
Index		232

INTRODUCTION

The Wheel of Fortune[1]

> *What a strange eventful life mine has been, from a poor little player, with just enough food and clothes to cover me, dependent on a precarious profession, without talent or a friend in the world! To have seen what I have seen, seeing what I see. Is it not wonderful? Is it true? Can I believe it – first the wife of the best, the most perfect being that ever breathed, his love and unbounded confidence in me, his immense fortune so honourably acquired by his own industry, all at my command… and now the wife of a duke.*[2]

Harriot Mellon's life is one of the most astonishing success stories of the eighteenth, nineteenth, or indeed any other century. It was a story of social mobility from the very bottom to the very top of society that few men in that or any other age could emulate. Born in 1777 the almost certainly illegitimate child of a poor Irish seamstress who became wardrobe mistress to a troop of strolling players, then regarded by the law as 'rogues and vagabonds', and earning her living from five or six years of age as a child actress, she rose in her profession by her talents and charm to stardom at the Theatre Royal, Drury Lane. Unusually, she invested her not inconsiderable income, far larger than most craftsmen, parsons or lawyers could then earn, in a small landed estate. This she did without the usual practice of actresses at that time of sleeping her way to the top. Her close colleague Dorothy Jordan for example had thirteen children by various lovers, including ten by the royal Duke of Clarence, later King William IV. That is, at least, until she met an old man over twice her age who offered his protection and set her up as his protégée. Whether Thomas Coutts, the royal banker and one of the richest men in Britain, slept with her in their apartment in Little Russell Street, off Drury Lane, is unclear.

---

[1] *The Wheel of Fortune.* An anonymous play in which Harriot appeared as Emily Tempest in September 1801.
[2] Letter from Harriot, Duchess of St Albans, to Sir Walter Scott, 1827.

But what is clear, and altogether surprising in that age of rakes and mistresses, is that, when his invalid wife died in 1815, he secretly married Harriot.

Thomas's daughters all married into the aristocracy, becoming the Marchioness of Bute, the Countess of Guilford, and Lady Burdett, wife of the famous radical M.P., Sir Francis, respectively. They had befriended Harriot when she was only their father's 'little friend', but were furious and tried to have the clandestine marriage annulled. Yet the lovers, he nearly seventy-nine and she thirty-seven, renewed their vows in public and lived happily together for a further seven years. The daughters and their families, especially the snobbish and greedy Sir Francis Burdett, snubbed Harriot and treated her so badly that Coutts determined to make them pay.

Such marriages between rich lovers and famous actresses were not quite unknown. The third Earl of Peterborough secretly married the singer Anastasia Robinson in 1722, and then publicly in 1735; and the twelfth Earl of Derby married the actress Elizabeth Farren in 1797. Thomas Coutts, who funded half the aristocracy and the profligate royal dukes and could have had a peerage for the asking, was certainly in their league. What was more surprising yet, however, was that, when he died in 1822, he left Harriot his whole fortune, including his majority partnership in the Bank.

Harriot became the richest and merriest widow in England. She had already established herself, at her grand house off the Strand and her country house, Holly Lodge, in Highgate, as one of the great hostesses of London society. Aristocratic ladies might sneer behind her back at her low origins and nouveau riche extravagances, but their husbands, and especially the Prince Regent and the royal dukes, were only too ready to leap at her invitations to dinners, soirées and fêtes champêtres, as their eager letters affirm. She also acquired a reputation, not too welcome to her aristocratic neighbours, of pampering the poor with food and clothing at her back door. For this and other social sins, such as flaunting her unfashionable connections with the stage and giving charitable handouts to her old thespian friends down on their luck, she was cartooned and vilified in the satirical prints and the popular press.

Meanwhile, as this book will show, she was not the sleeping partner and parasite upon the bank that contemporaries thought. She was a very active partner in the enterprise. Her collaborators would not make a large loan of any kind without 'consulting Mrs Coutts', and she laid down who should and should not become a partner. She kept such an eagle eye on the business that she once spotted a shortfall of £10 in her account of many thousands. During her fifteen years as senior partner the capital of the bank doubled. For a child brought up without any formal education whatever, she was a formidable business woman.

Finally, to crown her rise into the highest ranks of society as well as wealth, in 1827 she married a man half her age, the eager wooer and somewhat simple-minded Duke of St Albans. Although he was a descendant of perhaps the most famous of social climbing actresses, Nell Gwyn, and Charles II, his family were just as incensed as the Coutts daughters, and treated Harriot with contempt. They too were to pay for their lack of courtesy and foresight, and Harriot was to cut them out of her Will, except for the duke, who got no capital but a limited income for life.

To add a final, fascinating twist to her amazing life, when she died in 1837, just as the young Princess Victoria came to the throne, she left her whole fortune, though not the partnership in the bank, to her youngest step-granddaughter, Angela Burdett. That young woman, under the name Harriot insisted on, was to become Baroness Burdett-Coutts, the greatest philanthropist of the Victorian age. Even then, Harriot was to control her fortune from beyond the grave. When the long-celibate Angela, at the age of sixty-seven, married her American-born secretary, against Harriot's expressed injunction against marrying a foreigner, she lost most of the fortune to her elder sister, Clara Money. Nevertheless, through Angela's many charities, the child of fortune, Harriot Mellon, the little player girl, became at second hand fairy godmother to the Victorian poor.

Harriot, Duchess of St Albans, friend of George IV, the royal dukes, Sir Walter Scott, and most of the greats of her time, was far more renowned in her own age than she is now, if indeed she is remembered at all. Her contemporaries Dorothy Jordan, Sarah

Siddons, Emma Hamilton, Georgiana Duchess of Devonshire, and the unfortunate mother of feminism Mary Wollstonecraft earned repeated biographies, but Harriot the Merry Duchess and Lady Bountiful deserves a memorial at least as much as they. This is her story, told in all its richness and complexity.

Chapter I
THE CHILD OF NATURE[1]

For a woman destined to marry, first, one of the richest men in Britain and secondly, a duke of royal descent, Harriot Mellon came from an unpromising background. She was born in London on the 11 November 1777, of an Irish seamstress who had worked in a company of strolling players, the lowest level of the theatrical world. The year of her birth was disputed, as was the spelling of her name and the marital status of her mother, but her theatrical upbringing was never in doubt.

Harriot's mother Sarah, whose family name is unknown, was the only surviving child of a poor Irish smallholder and his hardworking wife. Sarah received no formal education and had never seen play-acting until she was fifteen years old, when the Kena company of strolling players came to her village overnight and put on an adaptation of Shakespeare's *Romeo and Juliet* in the barn of a local farmer. For Sarah, the moving drama of a hopeless love was a glimpse of a different world, and she longed to be with players.

Within months her father died, worn out by hard work and poverty. She and her mother went to Cork, where Sarah took a job as a milliner's assistant. Milliners made good profits, but gave mean wages to their employees, so Sarah's future prospects were not rosy.

Disease was widespread among the Irish poor, and epidemics were frequent. Sarah's mother fell ill during one of these and died within months of arriving in Cork, so Sarah was left alone. Some time later she met in the street Mrs Kena, wife of the manager of the company of players that had stirred her imagination in the

---

[1] *The Child of Nature*. A play by Elizabeth Inchbald in which Harriot played Amanthis in 1796.

village. She decided to try to join them and lead a more adventurous life. Mrs Kena would not recruit an inexperienced actor, but she said Sarah's dressmaking would be very useful to the company, and she could go on stage sometimes as 'one of the crowd'.

When Sarah joined the Kena company, strolling players were legally regarded, along with beggars and footpads, as rogues and vagabonds. The law punished 'all night walkers and other idle persons', meaning all persons wandering abroad without lawful reason or means of support. This covered wandering scholars, minstrels, fortune-tellers, gypsies, tinkers, peddlers, and beggars, but it also included any poor persons found wandering out of their respective parishes without means of support, who could under the Settlement Act of 1660 be arrested and sent back to their home parish – even as far as Ireland if that is where they came from. Offenders, including strolling players, could be stripped naked and whipped until their bodies were bloody, before removal to their place of settlement by the parish officers. Failing that, they could be sent to a House of Correction or the common gaol for three months' hard labour. Each village in Merrie England had a stocks and a whipping post, providing targets for the villagers' brickbats. Every county town had a gallows or 'Tyburn tree' for public hangings of lawbreakers of the two hundred capital offences under the Black Act of 1725. When Oliver Goldsmith wrote, 'laws grind the poor and rich men make the law',[2] he was stating an obvious fact, which was only mitigated in the last years of Harriot's life.

Strolling players were especially vulnerable. They had to get permission from local worthies before they could perform at all. On the complaint of any respectable citizen a local magistrate could imprison them or at least stop their performance. Sometimes strollers were tolerated for one night, but were hunted from the parish in the morning by threats of the stocks.[3] Their enemies said that the strollers would arrive without money, borrow a barn, props and clothes to make a show, and then, if

---

[2] Oliver Goldsmith.
[3] J. Genest, *Some Account of the English Stage from 1660–1830*, 1832.

their takings were small, make off during the night without paying their debts for board and lodging. Angry landladies sometimes anticipated their flight and seized their belongings whilst the actors lay in bed, leaving them to escape in what clothes they could find.

In London and most larger towns there was no prejudice against players, but in other areas the hostility was amazing. The actress Anne Mathews wrote of Yorkshire,

> Leeds at the end of the eighteenth century was considered little less than Botany Bay [the penal colony in Australia] for actors... The extraordinary, nay frightful prejudice cherished made the periodical stay amongst them a matter of serious dread, especially with the females of the theatre[4].

Wakefield was not much better, and the locals singled out visiting actors for especially ruffianly sport. Actors had to be strong, courageous and ready with repartee to deal with such attacks.[5] Strolling players who made it to a more respectable level of established theatres, as Harriot Mellon eventually did, would have learned already how to deal with heckling, hissing and unruly audiences.

However, for Harriot's mother the life of a stroller provided a bewitching life, with plenty of glamour and delight. Actors dazzled people with their self-confident dash and panache, and for a fleeting moment they were the talk of the town. They were never in one place long enough to get bored. Not all strollers were talented, yet there was a peculiar magic by which they could metamorphose an old barn, stable, or out-house, into a prince's palace or a peasant's cottage, or a Grecian temple. Their poor costumes forgotten, they could by words enchant the minds and soften the hearts of the severest audience. The power to lift the imagination and sway the feelings was what made acting so emotionally rewarding to the performers, and the drama a pastime in which so many people revelled.

Many strolling players were imprudent and extravagant. They

---

[4] Anne Mathews, *Memoirs of Charles Mathews*, 4 vols. 1838.
[5] Tate Wilkinson, *The Wandering Patentee*, 1795.

lived in a world of fancy, artifice and gaiety. They had no settled prospects in life before them. They were like everyone else, a mixture of good and bad. Jealousies were common, but so was the need to support and assist each other. Yet the life was not a bad start for an acting career, as Harriot Mellon later found. Three of the most distinguished tragic actresses ever to appear on the London stage – Mrs Siddons, Miss Brunton and Miss O'Neill – were daughters of managers of strolling companies and learned their trade on the roads.[6]

Harriot's mother was a poor actor but she was a good wardrobe-keeper and money-taker. Manager Kena soon admitted he had never before had his receipts so honestly managed. What Sarah did not realise, however, was that Kena was a typical 'pro' in that he worked very hard when he wanted money, but directly his pocket was full he disbanded the company and enjoyed himself until every penny was gone. Then he would start again, form a new company and earn more money. Some time after Sarah joined the troupe, they went on tour in Wales, and made so much money that Kena dismissed his actors in order to have a good time. Grateful, however, for Sarah's excellent management, he paid her travelling expenses back to Ireland.

Disappointed that her strolling days seemed to be over, Sarah took up work again in the milliner's shop. She was a good worker and the milliner was glad to take her back. The milliner, however, was a Wesleyan Methodist and strongly opposed to play-acting, so Sarah had to pretend she had been away travelling as companion to a lady. She was not averse to changing the story of her life in order to make it sound more respectable. Now aged twenty-two, attractive, rosy-cheeked and dark-eyed, Sarah was soon the object of admirers in Cork. Among them was a Lieutenant Mathew Mellon, of the Madras Native Infantry, on sick leave in Ireland for a change of air. Sarah always later said she and Mathew were married in January 1777 and together moved to London, where Harriot was born later that year. No evidence of this marriage has ever been found. It was common enough for a young officer, footloose and fancy-free, to pursue an attractive young girl, love

---

[6]Boaden, 1831; Brian Fothergill, *Mrs Jordan: Portrait of an Actress*, 1965.

her and then leave her when the regiment moved on. Young milliners in particular were regarded as fair game, since many of them were part-time prostitutes. If the truth is that she had never been married, but seduced and abandoned, it is understandable that she would not have wanted her child to be branded a bastard, but she always insisted she was a widow.

Harriot always believed that her parents had been married. She described her mother when young as 'extraordinarily beautiful, with a fine oval face and regular features'. From association with actors Sarah had learned more polished manners and speech, though she was said to be violent when angered. People later described her as clever, artful, scheming and inordinately fond of money, though when she could afford to she gave money to the sick and indigent. Harriot always said it was from her mother that she learned to help those less fortunate than herself.

Left without means to support herself and her child, Sarah Mellon had to find work, and when she heard that the Kena company was in the area of London where she was living it seemed almost a miracle. She went looking for them, and found they were about to start a country tour, picking up stray actors they chanced to meet on the road. Knowing how useful Sarah had been before, Kena willingly took her and the baby along with them.

Harriot learned early in life the hardships, struggles and temptations that come from poverty. Until she was in her teens, she knew no other world than the sordid and makeshift one of the wandering players. Higher-ranking theatre companies looked with horror and contempt at the strollers who eked out a precarious living by touring the towns and countryside, staying anywhere that might provide an audience and food and shelter for the night. They trudged along in all sorts of weather, at all seasons of the year. Often when they arrived in a town they looked a pitiful sight, a motley crew dressed in ragged clothing, tired, footsore and covered in dust or mud. There were older actors, married couples, and often pregnant women among them, yet during the year they might have to cover hundreds of miles on foot, or begging rides on farm or coal carts. Their scenery and wardrobe were not elaborate or heavy, and when their funds were too low to hire a vehicle each man and woman took a portion of the props on his/her back as they trudged on to the next town or village. When Harriot was a baby and toddler, her mother had to carry her, wrapped in a shawl, on her back, as well as her share of the props.

The company needed to advertise its arrival, but having little money to spend they prepared a few handbills, which they distributed to passers-by in the town, or nailed to trees and walls. Sometimes a young boy in the company carried a drum, which he banged to announce their arrival. 'Roll up! Roll up! The greatest show on earth!' the actors would shout, marching in step to the drumbeat. But this was not considered respectable, and some troupes added a note to the bottom of their printed bills, 'N.B. The Company does not use a drum.' Such little snobberies divided groups whose fortunes differed by no more than a pin. Strolling players relied on the goodwill of a farmer, or the owner of an inn, to provide a place for them to perform, usually in a large room or barn where the group set up their own stage. Their plays were tailored to the taste of their audiences. Shakespeare was made easy for the uneducated: *A Midsummer Night's Dream* was turned into *The Fairies*; *King Lear* was given a happy ending. How long they stayed in a particular place depended on how many plays they could perform, how recently another band of strollers had been there, how much money they earned, and how the locals treated them.

When Harriot was five years old her mother married Thomas Entwisle, a talented violinist who was the sole musician in the Kena company, at the parish church at Brampton on the Roman Wall in Cumberland, where the strollers happened to be in July 1782. Harriot said later that she was never called Harriot Entwisle. Sarah was twenty-seven years old, and still extraordinarily pretty, though she had begun to drink heavily and could not control her temper. Thomas was eighteen years old. Marriage between fellow strollers was common, since people were thrown together continuously and had a similar outlook on life. It was also not uncommon for a young working man to marry an older woman in the same trade; journeymen often married their master's widow. Thomas was an unpretentious young man. Some said he was simple, but that probably meant he did not put on airs. The son of a hard-working family in Wigan, Lancashire, he had received a good, plain education, and in this had the advantage of Sarah, who was almost illiterate. But they were both given to drinking and carousing, habits which grew worse as the years passed. Anne Mathews, wife of the famous actor Charles Mathews, knew Sarah and Thomas well from a time they were in the same company. She liked Harriot, but disliked her parents intensely, and described their marriage as 'the union of a woman of coarse and uninformed mind, and a man of vulgar and sottish habits.' She said Thomas was 'far superior to his lady in point of education' though he was 'on a parity in matters of taste and pursuits'.[7]

Nonetheless, Thomas was always kind to Harriot, and she was fond of him. When she was young and they were too poor to ride in a cart or wagon, he used to carry her from place to place. When money was available, he insisted that she at least should ride, even if he and her mother did not. He also insisted that Harriot get some rudimentary education, at dame schools or charity schools in towns where they stayed for a few days or weeks. She was taught reading, writing and arithmetic, which was more than most poor girls received at the time.

Sarah Entwisle loved her daughter, but as a disciplinarian she was sometimes extremely cruel. Anne Mathews said Sarah was 'one of those teaching parents who beat a child for having fallen down and hurt itself... Her favourite threat, when any one stood between her and her maternal wrath, was – with certain expletives which we omit – 'Let me get at her! let me get at her! and I'll be the death of her.'[8] On one occasion Harriot was so frightened of her mother that she ran away and slept in a charcoal-pit, amongst charcoal used in the Lake District for making iron. She reappeared in the morning, black from head to foot. Despite this occasionally harsh treatment, Harriot never rebelled against her mother, and indeed retained great affection for her when she became rich.

The Kena company toured Wales soon after Sarah and

---

[7]Anne Mathews, op. cit., 1838.
[8]Anne Mathews, *Tea-Table Talk, Ennobled Actresses and other Miscellanies*, 2 vols. 1857, p.64.

Thomas married, but this time they did not make much money so the Entwisles decided to try their luck again in Lancashire. At Preston they met with manager Thomas Bibby, and joined his company, Sarah as wardrobe mistress and Thomas as leader of the orchestra (such as it was). This move not only improved the family fortunes, providing a more regular income, but also their standing in the profession. Everyone knew the pecking order in the theatrical hierarchy, as they knew their place in every other walk of life, and Bibby had more prestige than Kena.

The following year, 1787, Harriot began her acting career. The Bibby company arrived at Ulverston in the north of Lancashire, a seaport town on the southern edge of the Lake District and known, locally at least, as the 'Metropolis of the North'. Ulverston Theatre was a roomy barn belonging to the White Hart Hotel, and was better fitted up than most. The price of admission was 1 shilling for the gallery, and 1 shilling and 6 pence for the pit. These were large sums for ordinary people to find, when northern farm labourers commonly earned about 9 or 10 shillings a week. So for an audience the theatre relied on the better-paid craftsmen, shopkeepers, farmers, apothecaries, doctors and lawyers, as well as the local gentry. Sarah and Thomas Entwisle earned about 17 shillings and sixpence a week between them from theatre work, as much as a skilled artisan; Thomas augmented this with music lessons and Sarah dyed silks and cleaned feathers and lace.

The Entwisles stayed in Ulverston for a considerable time, taking lodgings with a clog-maker who made Harriot a pretty pair of clogs, which her mother thought too undignified for a child actor. They paid a few pence a week to send Harriot first to Town Bank School, and later to Miss Calvert's school. Harriot was said at that time to be a laughter-loving, playful, and thoroughly idle little scholar who disliked a school book. She was constantly getting into trouble and being punished with extra lessons, or kept in school after the others had gone home. One day Miss Calvert asked her, 'Does your tongue never lie?' (meaning 'lie still?') to which Harriot slyly answered, 'No, ma'am, it never lies, for that would be naughty.' She could learn a lesson by reading it through twice, a skill which stood her in good stead when she had to learn her parts in plays. She never doubted that she would go on the stage, speaking often to her young friends of 'when I am a fine London player'. Of course, if she had never made it to the London stage, no one would later have remembered her childish words. Out of school hours, Miss Calvert taught her poetry and took her to church so that she could learn the responses and how to behave properly. The other children in school were inclined to look down on her as a stroller child and sometimes called her a gypsy or a tinker, but they were jealous when she began to appear on the stage, even in non-speaking parts. Harriot had learned to sing and dance prettily, and her stepfather took her to different public houses in the area, to dance hornpipes whilst he played the fiddle. Harriot would collect money for him, since the topers would always give more money to a pretty, curtsying child than to a tippler like themselves.

Harriot's stage career began with walk-on parts, but on 16 October 1787, the playbill for the Ulverston theatre announced that after the main items there would be the farce of *The Spoiled Child*, with the following cast:

Old Pickle	Mr Farquharson
Tag	Mr Bibby
Miss Pickle	Mrs Blanchard
Maria	Miss Valois
Little Pickle	Miss Mellon (her first appearance)

This play, which became the most popular in the company's repertoire, consists of stock situations of uproarious farce and mistaken identity. Bibby had cast her in a piece that exactly suited young Harriot's abilities, and she scored a big success as the pert, obstreperous child. The romp, hardly above the level of a charade, was pure fun for Harriot, and she went through it without the slightest bashfulness. She wore a laurel green tunic made by her mother, and with her bright eyes, pretty complexion, and dark curls topped by a fancy riding-cap, she made a lively picture. People said she had a very clear, piping, musical voice, and an infectious laugh that suited the youthful high spirits required for the role. Bibby was delighted with her resounding success and in addition to her weekly wage of a few shillings gave her a present of ten shillings, which her mother immediately pocketed. For Harriot's next part Bibby cast her as Priscilla Slowboy in T.A. Lloyd's *The Romp*[9]. This was another play with songs, a musical entertainment of a very childish kind, but it was popular with audiences and used to fill the theatre. The play mirrored the times, which were hardly refined in the late eighteenth century.

Priscilla Slowboy was a hoyden part in which the young lady uttered very daring expressions which contrasted with the innocence of the young actress playing the role. Harriot always said she had been too young for the part in 1787, but according to the Entwisles' landlord she was 'a fine, well-grown girl, looking two or three years older than her real age, and having a sweet, clear utterance, which was heard throughout the theatre; she had a nice address, and played as if she had acted all her life; but, of course, she could only take very young characters.' For her part as Priscilla, her mother fashioned a quantity of black wool into a headpiece; over this she put Harriot's own hair, 'pomatumed' and powdered until the edifice added four inches to her height and more years to her age. The pomatum (pomade) was made with candle-ends, melted by the fire. In order to give her breadth to correspond to her new height, she wore a pink 'calimanco' (calico) petticoat which could stand by itself. But then, because she was looking too broad, height was added again by high-heeled shoes. Twenty years after first playing this part, Harriot was criticised by *The Monthly Mirror* as only being able to play such childish roles as Priscilla Slowboy, but these mock-innocent characters were the ones with which audiences identified her and which they loved. As the company moved around the North of England in the next few years, Harriot began to take older parts, such as Gillian in *The Quaker*,[10] a comic opera by Charles Dibdin.

Harriot's mother was ambitious for her daughter, wanting her to have a better life than herself. She knew that acting was one of the very few professions in which a woman without personal fortune or education could succeed and obtain independence

---

[9]*The Romp*, T.A. Lloyd.
[10]*The Quaker*, Charles Dibdin.

without, if determined enough, sacrificing respectability. Sarah Siddons and Eliza Farren were two outstanding examples (more will be said of them later). It was Sarah's dream that Harriot should become an actress on the London stage, and she was determined that she should learn the necessary accomplishments to pass for a fine lady, both on the stage and in the company of the well-to-do who patronized the theatres. So she made sure that Harriot did not get into bad company or adopt a lax moral attitude, for she hoped that Harriot would make a good marriage. Harriot's strict upbringing stood her in good stead when she later mixed socially with fashionable patrons. The actress Mrs Abington said, somewhat spitefully, that Harriot never tried sufficiently hard to imitate females of the first rank. It is true she was not completely accepted by peeresses even when she became a duchess, though their husbands were not too snobbish to accept her invitations on their behalf.

Another watershed in Harriot's life was 1789. During the summer she was playing at Otley in Yorkshire, and heard that the famous Dorothy Jordan was coming to the theatre in Harrogate. Harriot and her mother walked eight miles to Harrogate, to see Mrs Jordan perform one of her most famous breeches parts, as Sir Harry Wildair, the rakish hero of George Farquhar's play, *The Constant Couple*.[11] Patrons liked women in the roles of young men, because they showed their legs and displayed their figures to advantage. Normally, it was considered daring to show as much as an ankle, though actresses always made sure they did. Harriot later became famed for her breeches roles herself, and often stood in for Dorothy Jordan at Drury Lane.

After the performance, Harriot and her mother needed to stay the night in Harrogate, but all the beds had been let. Harriot was invited to share the bed of Miss Hilliar, a young actress with whom she 'vowed eternal amity', who later married Thomas Dibdin, the actor, playwright and manager.[12] Harriot's mother was not so fortunate, and had to sit up all night on the stage throne, with the property man watching her to see that no accident

---

[11]*The Constant Couple*, George Farquhar.
[12]Thomas Dibdin, *Reminiscences of a Literary Life*, 1836, vol.1, pp.109–10.

occurred, so she was understandably in a bad temper by the time they walked back to Otley the following morning. Harriot's friendship with the Dibdins continued throughout their lives, and Tom Dibdin recalled that:

> On another occasion during the same summer [1789] they came again to Harrowgate [sic] on the arrival of some London performers, and after the play was over they supped with the narrator [Dibdin] who had invited several of the Harrowgate company to meet Miss Mellon and her mother. During the evening the observant girl gave such clever, spirited imitations of some of the acting she had just witnessed, that a very young comedian who was present remarked to her, 'Your talent will one day place you on the London boards, and then do not forget to use your interest towards procuring a situation for me!'
>
> 'It will not be wanted', Miss Mellon replied, 'for you look as if you were destined to be a London manager, and then you will be more likely, if willing, to serve me.'[13].

According to Dibdin, both predictions were fulfilled, though he did not name the actor-manager.

Harriot was a very attractive young woman by this time. An amusing and scandalous book called *The English Spy*[14] by Bernard Blackmantle (a pseudonym) says of her:

> Little Harriet [sic] was a child of much promise playing all the juvenile parts in Bibby's company. From this time her fame increased rapidly, which was not a little enhanced by her attractive person, for even among the cotton lords of Manchester, a fine-grown, raven-locked, black-eyed brunette, arch, playful, and clever, could not fail to create sensations of desire.

At the end of 1789, the Bibby company moved to Blackburn in Lancashire. Harriot's mother asked Bibby to increase Harriot's salary, and when he offered to raise it only to four shillings and sixpence, the Entwisles left and joined the Stanton company in Stafford. Here, Sarah earned 14 shillings a week as wardrobe

---

[13]Thomas Dibdin, op. cit., p.110.
[14]*The English Spy*, Bernard Blackmantle, 1825

keeper, Thomas Entwisle 21 shillings as musician, stage-keeper and property man, and Harriot 10 shillings and 6 pence for playing juvenile parts. Harriot's wages were as much as a labourer's, but her mother took all her money, since it was usual for parents to consider their children's earnings as part of family income. In the Entwisles' case, their total income of £2. 5s. 6d. a week compared very favourably with that of manual workers, who were classed as 'self-supporting' if the family earned 12s. a week (£31 a year).[15]

In the larger world, earth-shaking events were taking place at this time. In July 1789 the French Revolution broke out and the Bastille fell. Charles James Fox, the Whig leader, remarked, 'How much the greatest event it is that ever happened in the world! and how much the best!' His friend Edmund Burke, on the other hand, hated 'the multiple tyranny of the masses' and saw the Revolution as 'rebellion against all the laws of religion and morality'. But for ordinary people like Harriot and her parents, these events seemed far away from their lives. The most important thing for them was to survive in a harsh world by their own efforts. Their own luck was about to take a turn for the better.

---

[15]Patrick Colquhoun, *A Treatise on Indigence*, 1806.

Chapter II
THE COUNTRY GIRL[1]

Life In The Provincial Theatre

Harriot Mellon took a big step in her career when she joined the Stanton company of 'travelling comedians' in Stafford in 1789. She began to play comedy roles such as Beatrice in *Much Ado About Nothing* and Lydia Languish in *The Rivals*, and worked with more accomplished actors. Mrs Davenport, afterwards for thirty-six years a respected actress at Covent Garden, was in the Stanton company when Harriot joined, and Stanton's actress daughter, Mrs Nunns, befriended Harriot and gave her acting lessons. In country theatre, without elaborate scenery, all eyes were on the actor, whose face and movements had to express the story. The audience was usually a boisterous, unruly crowd, generous to its favourites but cruelly savage to those who failed to please.

At first, the Entwisles had tiny lodgings, clean but poorly furnished, in a cottage belonging to a shoemaker, paying him two shillings and sixpence a week rent. Sarah always tried to make sure they did not stay in garrets or cellars, or share their rooms with others, as the poorest players did. She got an instructor to teach Harriot reading, writing and arithmetic, in return for violin lessons which Thomas Entwisle gave to a relation of the tutor. Harriot was not enthusiastic about the lessons, but was later, as banker, to find them invaluable. Her mother sent her on Sundays to the parish church at Ingestre, four miles from Stafford, telling her that among the farm labourers her shabby dress would be less noticeable than in town. On the way to and from church, Harriot used to talk or play ball with the local children, but if her mother

---

[1] *The Country Girl*. A comedy by William Wycherley, in which Harriot played Lucy in 1796.

found this out she beat her, saying such behaviour was 'a disgrace to the high blood' (Lt. Mellon's), in the girl's veins. Harriot continued to fear her mother's temper, and early in 1790 she was beaten by her so severely that she ran away and did not return for her performance in the theatre that evening. She wandered all night in freezing weather, only half-dressed, and then managed to get to Mr Stanton's house. He protected her from her mother's wrath, and made Sarah promise to treat her daughter more kindly in future – to little avail, however.

Stafford was a market town in the heart of England. The only large town in a wide agricultural area, it was not a quiet place; the noise of iron-shod wheels on the stone setts of the streets was ear-shattering, and there were the constant cries of hawkers and tradesmen. It was always very busy on Wednesday, the weekly market day, and more so at the occasional cattle market. Harriot was fascinated by the Swan Hotel, the chief coaching inn. She used to stand and look at the coaches, full of passengers inside, the outside heaped with people, boxes, bags and bundles, and fantasise about the day she would take a coach to London on her way to be a fine player. A more sombre aspect of the town was the gaol at the north-east end. Sarah used to give money and food to the prisoners – many there because they were debtors – putting what she could spare in the basket they hung out for the purpose.

Harriot knew of the wretched living conditions of the poor, who in Stafford lived in shanties and cellars and could scarcely afford a fire. She heard of many an industrious labourer, with a wife and five or six children, who were obliged to exist in one damp room with a dirt floor. She also knew that some of the artisans and craftsmen had well-appointed houses made of stone or brick, and could afford not just necessities but novelties. They wore clothes of good cloth, and their wives and daughters had dresses of chintz, straw hats on their heads, and scarlet cloaks on their shoulders.

Harriot also learned a lot, while she lived in the Midlands, about the old customs, magic and folkways that held sway in the countryside. She later said that as a child she believed in a literal hell and eternal punishment, the devil, hobgoblins and ghosts, as well as guardian angels, and she remained very superstitious for the rest of her life. In that age of reason polite society was not supposed to believe in witchcraft any more, and they rejected folklore as silly, cruel and vulgar, but Harriot later met plenty of gentlefolk who were as superstitious as she, and who hovered when ill between physic and folk remedies, between which there was not much to choose.

When Harriot went to Stafford in 1790, licensed drama was officially confined to the two London theatres, but since 1768 the county magistrates had regained their right to allow local performances, and this had caused a huge boom in theatre building across the country. Hundreds of theatres were active around Britain, though many had no resident company and were used only for part of the year. A stock company would use one town as a base from which to tour the circuit theatres in the area, and such travelling companies made good money with 'blood and thunder' drama, farces, ballads, recitations, pantomimes and tragedies all jostling on the same playbills, so there was something for everyone.

Many of the plays of the seventeenth and eighteenth centuries now make dull reading. The brilliant works of Sheridan and Goldsmith stand on crowds of smaller shoulders. Colman gave the theatre two excellent comedies, as did Macklin the actor. Mrs Inchbald was a popular writer of sentimental comedy. Murphy had a particular comic sense of his own, and Holcroft wrote workmanlike dramas. Mrs Cowley, Burgoyne, Foote, Kelly, Cumberland, Reynolds and Moore all wrote stock comedies, as well as romances and domestic tragedies. Few of these plays were consistently good, though many contained scenes or dialogue of true comic or genuine tragic spirit. Minor plays of any period were of poor quality, and these were no worse than most.

Based on the circuit playhouse in the county town of Stafford, the Stanton company had a higher position in the theatrical world than Bibby's. The company ranged from there around a large and prosperous area of farming and craft industry. The Stafford theatricals were for many years held in the Town Hall, which stood on pillars with the open market underneath. In 1790 it was suggested that the Town Hall be pulled down, and Stanton decided that a permanent theatre was needed. A subscription for building by shares was started, and the theatre was built by 1792. It was a brick edifice scarcely higher than a single-storied house, with an iron grating a foot under the roof to admit air and light and disperse the inevitable smells for which theatres at that time were notorious. The price of admission was 2 shillings for the pit – there were no boxes – and one shilling for the gallery. A full house produced about £45 per night.

While the new theatre was being built, the company moved twenty miles to Leek, a small silk town, where Thomas Entwisle earned extra money by giving piano and violin lessons to local children. Lack of money, mainly due to heavy drinking, caused Sarah and Thomas to quarrel endlessly. He would play his violin in local pubs and suchlike places until the small hours, then oversleep and miss early rehearsals for the theatre. Harriot had constantly to make excuses for him, but she could not escape from the family quarrels, which were accompanied by broken glass and earthenware. She often had to borrow tin stage-cups so they could have breakfast. Sarah said a player's sixpence did not go as far as a townsman's groat (4d.), because the players were charged more for everything. In good inns actors paid dear for luxuries, and in bad ones they were fleeced and starved. So although the townspeople abused actors for running into debt, they were unhappy if the company failed to return at the appointed time to spend again and bring in monied visitors to see the plays.

The Stafford theatre was keenly supported both by the local professional people and by the well-to-do county families who came in from their country houses to attend the Quarter Sessions of the Justices of the Peace, and to flock to the balls and routs of the local Season which served as a marriage market for their daughters. Only the very rich could afford the journey to London and the expenses of the Season there, so these local festivities were the highlight of most people's lives. Some of the provincial ladies found plays such as *The Country Girl* – a risqué piece in which a sly rake pretends to be a eunuch in order to seduce the ladies without alarming their husbands – too rude and vulgar. They were not as tolerant as London audiences, though their manners were no better, as Harriot found on one occasion in

Lichfield when a lady of fashion occupied the stage box and received parties of militia officers during the evening. At every tragic scene in the play, the lady and her military escort broke into screams of laughter. At last the leading actor stopped his performance, saying he would not go on until the lady finished her conversation. Overcome with confusion, the lady was hissed out of the theatre. But then her friends demanded the dismissal of the actor. The manager refused, and for several nights the militia constantly interrupted the performance, until a visiting general who wanted to enjoy the play in peace intervened to stop their rudeness.

On the other hand, it was usually good fortune to play in a town which was the headquarters of the militia, for the actors would automatically receive the patronage of the officers and their wives. A 'Bespeak' from the gentry, that is, a prior request for a particular play, meant social approval plus the chance to fill the more expensive seats, while a Bespeak from a senior officer brought in many of the regimental officers and their womenfolk. It was a regular part of actors' duties to call on the local gentry and humbly request a Bespeak. They would send one or two members of the company on ahead to the next town on the circuit, to get from the local mayor or magistrate a licence to play, then find a printer, distribute bills and call personally at the houses of the local gentry to solicit custom. Harriot was often one of the supplicants.

Travelling companies were like small kingdoms, in which the manager was the monarch. Mr Stanton was a man of considerable energy: he would print his own playbills and help to distribute them, then help take money at the door of the theatre; a little later he would appear on stage as a major or minor character, and between the acts he would conduct the orchestra. From time to time he was actively engaged as a scene-shifter, lamp-dresser or prompter. Two of his daughters were successful on the London stage, and his eldest son, John, starting as a scene-painter, became manager of the Stockport theatre. Some people said Stanton was greedy about money, made blunders, and was stupid to the point where he became the butt of the whole company. But in spite of some bickering, Harriot said there were no serious disagreements between him and his actors, though she admitted that most of them were in debt to him and so were obliged to remain loyal.

Harriot always paid tribute to Mr Stanton's unfailing kindness to her. She said there were two equal hazards for young actresses: the unwelcome sexual advances of the manager, and the jealousy of the manager's wife. Many managers used their power to allocate good parts to young actresses, to strengthen their attempts at seduction. Actresses were proverbially short of cash and often in debt, so a manager would come forward with a handsome loan, then demand repayment in kind. If his advances were resisted he would threaten to have her arrested and put in prison for debt, a terrifying prospect. What aroused the passion of a manager's wife was not so much fear of losing her husband's affections as of losing the leading roles she considered to be hers by right in favour of her husband's paramour. Harriot said she experienced neither of these hazards with the Stanton company, and for this she was always grateful. A contemporary description of Harriot reads, 'Miss Mellon and Mrs Nunns (a daughter of Mr Stanton) were the best actresses we ever had in Stafford. She (Harriot) could show a little temper sometimes at the theatre, and was uncommonly particular about her dresses. She had her own way very much with the manager, and was made much of by him, as well as by his eldest son, who was said to be attached to her'.[2]

Nonetheless, the acting profession had as many jealousies as any other, and the Stanton company was no different. Woe betide a new member of the company who challenged the standing of an established actress. In an overcrowded profession this might mean verbal quarrels if not physical blows. Players were jealous when a rising actress got a benefit night earlier than they thought warranted. Rival actresses were jealous of each other's elegance of form in breeches parts, when they could show off their legs in male costume. They would place themselves at strategic points offstage, endeavouring to put the performing actress off by whispering, pointing and making disparaging remarks. Sarah Mellon was not above playing such tricks on Harriot's rivals; she would stand near the stage door and go through a pantomime of

---

[2]Charles Pearce, *The Jolly Duchess*, 1915, pp.41–42.

horror and disgust as she watched the rival act, casting her eyes to heaven and throwing her apron over her head.

In 1792 when the new Stafford theatre opened, Harriot's salary was raised to 21 shillings a week; Thomas Entwisle got the same, and Sarah 14 shillings. Their weekly family income came to £2. 16s., much higher than that of ordinary workers, augmented by Entwisle's earnings from music lessons and playing the fiddle at local dances. They were able to take better lodgings, in the home of a painter in Diglake, Stafford. Harriot was always fond of the landlady there, Mrs Walker, and in later years annually sent her tea and sugar, gowns, a winter cloak and a shawl.

In the five years Harriot spent in Stafford, the Stanton family became very attached to her and regularly invited her to parties in their house. Her mother was not invited, but escorted her to and from the house. Harriot was embarrassed for her mother, but Sarah was delighted that her daughter was accepted into respectable local society. Well-to-do friends lent Harriot clothes to wear both on stage and for private parties, and her mother looked after them so carefully that she was often given them later as presents. On one memorable occasion Harriot needed clothes for a breeches role, playing Peggy in *The Country Girl*, and the housekeeper of a wealthy baronet living nearby offered to lend her the wedding clothes of her old master. The baronet was a small man, and his clothes, a light amber-coloured silk coat, pale blue stockings, shoes, ruffles and buckles, fitted Harriot nicely. They were at least thirty years old but, having been worn only once, were in perfect condition. Harriot got great applause for her performance, but unfortunately the owner of the clothes, who had not given permission for the loan, was in the audience. A long argument took place but, no harm having been done, he forgave his housekeeper and got his wife to make Harriot a present of a handsome dress. Harriot and the housekeeper could both have been charged with stealing the clothes and sent to prison – stealing property to the value of 10s. was a capital offence – but all's well that ends well.

Personal friendship between the manager and the leading actors with prominent local families could make the difference between the company's success and failure. Three or four carriages at a performance denoted good patronage. Sarah Entwisle knew that the Stanton family was on visiting terms with all the best families in the towns where the company played, and she hoped that Harriot would be noticed and taken up by them. To her delight, so she was – surprisingly, since actors were looked on askance in Staffordshire – but Harriot had a spotless reputation. In Burton-on-Trent she became friends with the wife of a rich coach-maker, Mr Deakin, and stayed at their house whenever the company played there. She remembered their best parlour as well proportioned, with a black boarded floor covered with a Lisbon mat, the pictures curtained to keep off the flies, a handsome clock on the mantelpiece, a tortoiseshell cabinet filled with china, a fire-screen of embroidered silk, a kidney-shaped writing table, cherrywood armchairs, and mezzotints in black Brazilian frames. Later she found that the élite considered a best parlour, rather than a drawing room, slightly vulgar, a tradesman's notion, but at the time she was dazzled by its opulence. In Market Drayton she often stayed with the vicar and his wife, Mrs Stubbs, and slept with one of their daughters. This family was 'shabby genteel' but quite delightful, and so well-read she enjoyed their conversation.

The family of Mr Wright, the Stafford banker, also petted Harriot as 'the player girl', and his daughters took a delight in dressing her for her stage characters with gowns, gloves, and shoes, and lending her their jewellery. She had an open invitation to go to their house on any evening she was not performing, and there she met all the principal families of the area. The well-to-do middle class at home played card games such as 'whisk' and 'vingt-et-un', a form of rummy or poker. They drank spruce beer and mead, mostly home-brewed, and also port and brandy. The social part of the day began after dinner, which was between 3 and 5 P.M. According to a contemporary, Harriot was described by 'a very estimable patroness at Stafford' as being 'very handsome, very lively, highly amusing, and perfectly ladylike, though not what is termed accomplished; she sang pleasantly and was an admirable dancer.'[3] 'Accomplished' meant having the social

---

[3] Charles Pearce, op. cit., p.41.

accomplishments of a young lady, including embroidery, playing the piano, dancing, ornamental penmanship, and French or Italian conversation. Another contemporary said,

> Miss Mellon was a great favourite among the principal families and with all the young people of both sexes… The mother was a gay, pretty woman, but very rough with her daughter occasionally… They were in straitened circumstances because her stepfather was disposed to drinking and low company. Miss Mellon's situation between the two, who disagreed exceedingly, was greatly pitied, so that even among the poorer classes (especially the shoemakers with whom Stafford abounds) she was an excessive favourite and greatly respected.[4]

Everyone knew that her home was very uncomfortable, and she was encouraged to spend her free time with respectable friends rather than with her mother and stepfather.

Harriot was amazed by the handsome doors and sash windows of the middle-class homes she visited in Stafford. She always remembered one brick terraced house where the floors were of Dutch oak, the rooms all wainscoted and painted in a costly manner. They had marble chimney pieces, each with a mirror over the mantelpiece, as well as a marble slab in front to catch the ashes and a brass fender with tongs, poker and shovel. They had fires in nearly all the rooms, and used the parlour every day. The chairs were of walnut, some with leather, damask or embroidered seats; she had previously only sat on chairs with cane or rush bottoms. The house had mahogany tables and walnut chests of drawers, handsome glasses on top of the dressing-tables, Axminster and Wilton carpets, and wallpaper on the walls.

Her well-to-do friends owned ceramic tableware made by Spode, Royal Derby, and the Wedgwood factory, only twenty miles from Stafford. They drank tea, coffee and chocolate, and ate white wheaten bread and other delicacies to which Harriot was unaccustomed. She observed how everyone strove to outdo their neighbours, and how the tea-table conversation lingered over the last detail of their material possessions, especially the newest and

---

[4]Charles Pearce, op. cit., 1915, p.42.

most fashionable. All this was exciting for a girl quite unused to luxury.

Harriot's fashion-conscious friends often visited local stately homes to find out the latest motifs, fabrics, wallpapers and furniture. England's stately homes were private domiciles, but the proud proprietors threw them and their grounds open to respectable visitors, strangers included. There was no official fee, but the servants expected 'vails', a sizable tip for their complacence. Some even sold teas, prints, guide books and souvenirs to visitors, like their modern successors. The wealthy liked pedestal tables, cerulean chairs, coats of arms with gilded beasts as supporters, bits of Egyptian ornament, and exotic bric-a-brac. They consorted well with the muslin gowns and high waists of the turn of the century 'Empire line', lending the correct classical tone to a society which prized elegance without disdaining ease. The rich festooned their houses and grounds with exotica – pet monkeys, parrots, goldfish, fuchsias, acacias, veronicas from the Falkland Islands, camellias from Japan, and jade ornaments from China. They ate such delicacies as pineapples, sardines, kippers and Stilton cheese, and cucumber sandwiches made of slices of bread and butter cut as thin as poppy leaves. At tea they toasted bread before the fire and soaked it with butter. Harriot used to think that if ever she were rich, she would have all these wonderful things in her own house. She did, and more.

Provincial towns like Stafford put on London airs. John Palmer's new flying coaches from 1784 rushed London fashions to the regions. Their eyes on the capital, genteel provincials suppressed their dialects and affected London catchphrases, slang and euphemisms. The ladies with whom Harriot mixed in the Midlands became for her models of how a well-brought-up young lady should think, feel and behave. Social finesse and etiquette helped to secure entrance and advancement in a world of social nicety. To Harriot's amusement, they told her that 'Life is a stage on which good actors will shine.' Good manners were said to be the art of putting at ease people with whom one conversed. Great value was placed on sociability, the ability to mix and sink political, religious and family differences in any company, without opinionising or exposing too much of one's inner self. True taste was not to be flash or racy but modest and decent, yet lively enough to be interesting and entertaining to one's friends.

Harriot never completely mastered the finesse of this etiquette, though she took to heart the advice not to expose her inner self and afterwards was rarely able to be completely open about her true feelings; she even shrank from examining her own motives and behaviour. She was indeed too much of a child of nature to behave in so artificial a manner. However, she accepted her fine friends' values, since good-heartedness came naturally to her, reinforced by her mother's discipline. Her Stafford friends, especially the Wright family, remained close to Harriot for the rest of her life.

In a way, Harriot anticipated in her outlook and behaviour the 'moral revolution', the transformation of attitudes towards sex, bawdy talk, and brutal and cruel sports, that Francis Place remarked in the 1820s before a parliamentary committee.[5] This change coincided with Harriot's theatrical career, beginning in the late eighteenth century and reaching completion by the time Queen Victoria came to the throne and gave it the name of Victorianism. It affected the theatre by suppressing bawdy plays like *The Country Wife* and *The Beaux Stratagem* and led to a hiatus in English drama before its revival in the 1880s. Before that moral revolution, the free and easy morals of the English, especially the aristocracy, were renowned. It took time for the change to spread throughout society, but respectable Harriot still had to cope with the shady reputation which actresses carried in the early nineteenth century.

The moral revolution began even before the French Revolution. In 1787, the year of Harriot's stage debut, William Wilberforce, M.P., friend of Prime Minister William Pitt and leader of the Evangelical 'Clapham Sect', persuaded the King to issue a Royal Proclamation urging the aristocracy to show an example to the people by attending Church (of England, naturally) and improving their behaviour. Wilberforce then formed the Proclamation Society, which set out to reform the

---

[5] Harold Perkin, *The Origins of Modern English Society*, 1969, Chapter 8.

manners of the great. In 1802 this was absorbed into the more powerful Society for the Suppression of Vice, which came down heavily on Sabbath breaking, swearing, brothel-keeping, and using false weights and measures. Influenced by John Wesley and the Methodists, he was assisted by Hannah More, whose pamphlets 'Thoughts upon the Importance of the Manners of the Great'[6] and 'An Estimate of the Religion of the Fashionable World'[7] became bestsellers. To the chagrin of the thespians, Shakespeare was emasculated and re-written years before Thomas Bowdler, in 1818, took out his scissors to eradicate the bard's 'barefaced obscenities, low vulgarity, and nauseous vice'. The aristocracy did not change their ways, but were forced to become more discreet, and flaunt their amours and mistresses somewhat less than before.

During her years at Stafford, Harriot was the belle of the theatre circuit, and might easily have become some rich man's doxy. But she had been strictly brought up and so guarded by her mother that she had no difficulty resisting all the offers from the swarm of rich young suitors smitten by her dark eyes and raven hair. Because she never misbehaved she was received socially by the best families. Yet since she was an actress, some young bloods made the mistake of thinking she would be an easy conquest. Once she was staying in the country with a woman friend whose father was a miller. The miller's landlord and his friend (a pair of dandies) called at the house and asked to see the young woman. Harriot would not leave her room, and sent a message that it was an insult for men of superior rank thus to suppose she would appear at their bidding, to be stared at without respect. The miller scolded Harriot, and apologized to Mr Jervis, the magistrate at whose house the young men were staying, for Harriot's behaviour. Mr Jervis so disliked actors that he had never granted a licence for a theatrical performance in his jurisdiction. But when he heard how resolutely Harriot had dismissed the young men, he and his wife called on her and took such a fancy to her that they invited her to stay with them, to show the neighbours they were not prejudiced against all actors. Harriot persuaded him to grant a

---

[6]Hannah More, 'Thoughts upon the Importance of the Manners of the Great'.
[7]Hannah More, 'An Estimate of the Religion of the Fashionable World'.

licence for the play in which she appeared, and to attend the performance. Harriot's chastity no doubt stemmed from a prudent concern for her reputation, but her mother's warnings and violence may also have crushed her romantic feelings towards importunate young men. Perhaps also she was one of those rare women who used her natural charm to seduce whole audiences rather than to woo, or succumb to, individuals of the opposite sex.

In October 1794 Harriot Mellon got the greatest opportunity of her life so far – the chance to perform before the famous playwright, Richard Brinsley Sheridan, manager and part owner of the Drury Lane Theatre in London. Sheridan, as Member of Parliament for Stafford, was that year appointed steward of the Races, the crowning event of the town's social year. Horse racing, the sport of kings and long an exclusively aristocratic pastime, was becoming big business and so popular that grandstands were built to segregate the rich from the crowds. Betting attracted both rich and poor. The race stewards were expected to bespeak a play and a farce for a gala night at the theatre, and they suggested Hannah Cowley's *The Belle's Stratagem*, a feminine tit-for-tat to Farquhar's more famous *The Beaux Stratagem*, plus Lloyd's farce *The Romp*. Mr Stanton produced the plays, and Harriot, who was not quite seventeen years old, played the major parts of Laetitia Hardy and Priscilla Tomboy.

Sheridan said afterwards he was very pleased by Harriot's performance, and that it was a pity her talents were confined to so small a theatre. Her friends the Wrights, who accompanied Sheridan to the theatre, spoke warmly to him of her disposition, conduct and industry, and suggested that Sheridan should engage her for Drury Lane. The banker thought this was the way things were usually done in the theatre, as in business, and that Sheridan's reply that he would think about it was more than mere politeness. Mr Wright also knew Sheridan well enough not to rely entirely on a vague promise, and next evening he persuaded his friends the Misses Williamson, daughters of the Chairman of Quarter Sessions, to invite Harriot and Sheridan to tea. When the manager repeated his promise, her friends thought the matter was settled. Sheridan left for London and nothing more was heard from him, though Mr Wright wrote to him twice on the subject in the next two months. While waiting for a reply, Harriot took a profitable benefit night at the theatre, which brought in £50. With the proceeds, her mother bought her some clothes, and at Harriot's request gave some money to the debtors at Stafford prison, but left some over for the London trip. The winter of 1794–1795 was very severe, food prices rose, and the poor of Stafford suffered such misery that a committee was formed for their relief. An amateur play was put on for charitable purposes, and for no pay Harriot played Sophia in a June 1795 production of *The Road to Ruin*.[8] The title must have seemed ironic to the poor, but it did raise some funds for their relief.

Sheridan's long connection with Stafford ended sadly. He was M.P. from 1780 to 1806, and had once wittily toasted the shoemaking town: 'May the trade of Stafford be trod under foot by all the world'. When in 1812, after the Drury Lane fire and his financial losses, he stood again for election but was unable to buy votes at the usual 5 guineas apiece, he came bottom of the poll. The voters of Stafford, like many others before the Great Reform Act of 1832, were a mercenary lot, and the town only just managed to escape disenfranchisement in the 1830s for flagrantly corrupt practices.

The Stanton company's final performance for the 1794–1795 season on 22 May was O'Keefe's farce *The Dead Alive*, in which Harriot played the pert chambermaid. She persuaded Mr Wright to contact Sheridan again, and the playwright vaguely promised an engagement for the following September. The Entwisles decided to move to London, in readiness for the expected contract at Drury Lane, and went there by coach at the end of June 1795.

This was a year of privation and discontent. After a bad harvest and record bread prices, there was increased unrest in the great towns of England, and a crop of repressive legislation. War had broken out with the French Revolutionaries and, alarmed by the 'Jacobins', the Radical Parliamentary Reform movement led by the London Corresponding Society and opposed in turn by the pro-Church and King mobs, Parliament suspended Habeas Corpus and passed the Treasonable Practices Act forbidding

---

[8]Thomas Holcroft, *The Road to Ruin*.

public meetings of more than fifty people, and banned the writing, printing, preaching or speaking of sedition against the Crown. The opposition Whigs complained with some justice that Britain was ruled by a despotic government.

By the end of the year Napoleon Bonaparte crushed the Jacobins in Paris with his famous 'whiff of grapeshot', and saved the five-man Directory led by Danton. Years of French victories on land began, with Napoleon beating the combined forces of Prussia, Austria and Russia, while the British Navy held the sea. Like most Britons, Harriot Mellon detested Napoleon, and maintained her hatred of the French to the end of her life, to the extent of affecting her future aristocratic relations.

Meantime, however, Harriot's career was to take a gigantic leap to the London stage, where she would play a starring role first on the boards and then in high society itself.

Chapter III
The Rivals[1]

London Life and The Theatre

When Harriot and the Entwisles arrived there in 1795, London had a population approaching one million. It was not only the largest city in England, nearly as populous as all the other towns put together, but was the largest city in the known world. It was the power-house of politics, the Court, law, the arts and sciences, the capital of finance, the greatest port for overseas trade, and the centre of fashion and all the luxury trades. London set the ton (*sic*) which all the provinces aspired to. Three-quarters of the population still lived in the countryside or in towns no bigger than villages, but most of the aristocracy and leading gentry found their way to London for some portion of the year, to attend parliament or the Court, the law courts, and to take part in the pleasures of the 'Season', that round of dinners and balls, gaming and sport, concerts and exhibitions, shopping and gossip, that constituted the social life of the élite.

Fashionable London was still a physically small city, comprising the square mile of Mayfair, bounded on the north by Grosvenor Square, on the south by St James's Park, on the east by Covent Garden, and on the west by Park Lane. An address in that area was a symbol of status. The West End was a genteel ghetto, laid out in elegant streets and squares that were kept paved, cleaned and repaired, lighted by oil lamps at night, and guarded by watchmen and the Bow Street Runners. Beyond St Paul's the city lay outside the fashionable perimeter, left to lawyers, shopkeepers, bankers, and merchants who often lived over or within sight of

---

[1] *The Rivals*, R B Sheridan's play in which Harriot appeared as Lydia Languish in September 1795.

their chambers, shops, banks, and warehouses. East of the city lay the docks and the slums of the dockers, sailors, and street traders. West of Mayfair elegance was beginning to spread, towards Bayswater and the still rural village of Paddington on the edge of the built-up area. Beyond lay the green fields and market gardens of rural England accessible by the new turnpike roads that charged tolls not only for coaches, wagons and riding horses but for pedestrians both rich and poor.

London town was a microcosm of English society. Wealthy merchants and bankers vied with the nobility in their houses, food, furniture, manners and carriages, some on their way to joining the landed gentry, and were emulated in their turn by the middling ranks. Josiah Wedgwood aimed his sales through royalty and the aristocracy at those beneath them: 'The Great People have had these Vases in their Palaces long enough for them to be seen and admired by the Middling Class of People, which class we know are vastly, I had almost said, infinitely, superior in number to the Great.' Middle-class social life was an imitation, if not a caricature, of the haut-monde. Merchants and lawyers went to the coffee houses, few of which admitted women, to discuss politics. Edward Gibbon said the pleasures of town life, the daily round from the tavern to the play, from the play to the coffee house, from the coffee-house to the whore-house, were within the reach of every man who was regardless of his health, his money and his company! The lowest orders lived mainly in the street, where peddlers and barrow boys, flower girls and milkmaids, patterers and ballad-mongers, rat-catchers and chimney sweeps, and vendors of every kind with their street cries, milled around in a maelstrom of bustling humanity.

Wealth, privilege, arrogance and leisure flourished in upper-class English society in the late eighteenth and early nineteenth centuries. Brutal sports and crude practical jokes were popular with both upper and lower classes, though the prudent middle classes kept their distance from such pastimes. Dorothy Marshall, the eminent historian of eighteenth-century England, wrote that the aristocracy's 'indifference to the pain of others and sexual laxity were accompanied by a verbal coarseness and frank acceptance of bodily functions which the middle class of the time, and later generations, found deeply shocking.'[2] Noblemen cultivated manners and affectations similar to the jockeys, prize fighters and stagecoach drivers with whom they consorted. Illustrious prize-fighters were backed by glittering publicity: the sport was termed 'the fancy' and had a patois of its own. It was popular because, like horse racing, it was tailor-made for gambling. Thousands of guineas were staked on big bouts, and successful fighters became rich, set up their own gymnasia, and gentrified bruising into the art of pugilism. Men about town, known as Bucks or Corinthians, rode races like jockeys and supported bare-fisted pugilists, some even becoming pugilists themselves. Their chief diversions were drinking, hunting, horse breeding, driving phaetons (the sports cars of the age) like maniacs, cock-fighting, wenching, keeping mistresses, and above all gambling.

England was gripped with gambling fever. People bet on political events, births and deaths, dog fights, bull baiting, the arrival of particular ships – any happening subject to Lady Luck. The state ran a lottery from 1709 to 1824, national institutions from the British Museum to Westminster Bridge being partly funded out of the proceeds. Gaming was also the life blood of London clubs such as Almack's, White's and Boodle's, and astronomical sums of money changed hands. Georgiana, Duchess of Devonshire, married to one of the richest men in Britain, ran up such huge gambling debts, borrowed partly from Coutts' Bank, that she dared not tell her husband, until he was forced by her creditors to pay them.

London's concentration of humanity demanded entertainment. Showmen supplied 'diversions for the curious', ranging from Mrs Salmon's Waxworks which offered scenes of shepherds and shepherdesses 'making violent love' to Burford's Panorama in Leicester Square showing views of Niagara Falls and Pompeii. The St Martin's Lane Appollonicon performed 'by mechanical powers' overtures, songs and duets four times daily, admission 1 shilling; and the Exeter Change in the Strand housed a menagerie, the roar of whose animals frightened the horses in

---

[2]Marshall, 1975, p.114.

the street.

Vauxhall Gardens, south of the river at Westminster, and Ranelagh, at Chelsea were two of at least sixty-four pleasure gardens, where Londoners of nearly all classes could take tea, listen to concerts, watch the fashionable, keep assignations, and consort with ladies of the town. Horace Walpole mock-complained of Ranelagh, 'The company is universal: from his Grace of Grafton down to children out of the Foundling Hospital – from my Lady Townshend to the kitten'.[3]

Above all, the acme of entertainment was the theatre. There were many theatres in London, for every level of society. Most of them were unlicensed but thrived as 'places of public entertainment' under the Theatres Act of 1752, by which local magistrates could license theatres annually for music and dancing as long as they did not confine themselves to straight drama, which was feared by the government as a vehicle for criticism and satire. In effect, this came to mean that they could produce almost any kind of play as long as it was accompanied by music or ballet, if only between the acts. The 'burletta', a 'drama in rhyme, which is entirely musical', evolved into the ballad opera, a play with songs like John Gay's *Beggars' Opera*.[4] Serious drama without music or dance was confined to two theatres, one at Drury Lane and one at Lincoln's Inn Fields (the patent of which was transferred to Covent Garden in 1732), which enjoyed the monopoly of spoken drama in the capital until it was abolished by the Theatres Act of 1843.

The Lyceum began as 'an academy and exhibition' in 1765, which failed and became a theatre putting on any kind of show, from musical plays to circuses and boxing matches. At Sadler's Wells, Astley's, the Royalty Theatre, and the Royal Circus, there were freaks, midgets, women gladiators, and contortionists. In 1826 there were nine major theatres in the West End besides scores of back street 'penny gaffes' where urchins and teenagers, costers and prostitutes could watch bawdy comics and 'flash dancing' (leg shows). Even the leading theatres dedicated to

---

[3]Walpole, 1891.
[4]John Gay, *Beggars' Opera*.

serious drama catered for a variety of tastes. Their programmes were long and immensely varied. They would include a main piece two or three hours long – Shakespeare or Dryden perhaps, an interact ballet, a farce, and perhaps a song or two to round off the evening. Anything less was likely to cause a riot. The theatre was also used for propaganda for both Government and Opposition. In the fall of 1794, in the midst of the Church and King riots against the 'Jacobins' (parliamentary reformers), Mrs Mattocks electrified the house with an epilogue upholding 'the good old constitution', to prolonged applause and cries of 'God save the King!'[5] Conversely, in 1795, a year of starvation and misery, a line in Otway's *Venice Preserved*[6] – 'Cursed be your Senate – Cursed your constitution!' – evoked prolonged, uproarious applause, and the play had to be withdrawn under government pressure.

The Drury Lane and Covent Garden theatres were the height of fashion and everyone who was anyone was seen there. The boxes were filled with royalty and aristocracy. The middle classes in the stalls and the hoi polloi in the gallery would stare at the celebrities and applaud more than the play the comings and goings of the King and Queen and the princes, the leading politicians, war heroes and famous beauties. The fictional Bob Tallyho, a typical Buck or Corinthian, in *Real Life in London* observed that:

> The theatre is a sort of enchanted island, where nothing appears as it really is, nor what it should be. In London, it is a sort of time-killer or exchange of looks and smiles. It is frequented by persons of all degrees and qualities whatsoever. Here Lords come to be laughed at – Knights to learn the amorous smirk and a-la-mode grin, the newest fashion in the cut of his garments, the twist of his body, the adjustment of his phiz [face].[7]

On the other hand, Leigh Hunt thought there was previously greater involvement in the drama. In the 1830s he wrote about the

---

[5] *The Times*, 1 October 1794.
[6] Otway, *Venice Preserved*.
[7] *An Amateur*, 1821–1822, vol. I, p. 209.

beginning of the century:

> ...people of all times of life were much greater playgoers than they are now... Nobility, gentry, citizens, princes – all were frequenters of the theatre and more or less acquainted personally with the performers. Nobility intermarried with them; gentry, and citizens wrote for them: princes conversed and lived with them.[8]

Certainly, many leading actors were celebrities and on intimate terms with aristocratic patrons. Some actresses married noblemen or became mistresses to them. Yet in his *Life of Goldsmith*[9] Forster made clear the ambiguous status of actors: 'Even men of education were known to have pursued David Garrick, when on country visits to noblemen of his acquaintance, with dirty, clumsily-folded notes passed amid the ill-concealed laughter of servants to the great man's guest and addressed to 'Mr Garrick, Player'.[10] They wished to make his acquaintance without drawing attention to their condescension.

Despite their elegance and high-toned clientele, both patent theatres could be as boisterous and rowdy as the rest. The actors had to quieten the hubbub and chatter before they could begin, and if they did not please they were assailed with cat-calls, stamping of feet, drumming of walking sticks, followed by orange peel and empty bottles. According to Bob Tallyho, on his night at Drury Lane,

> The Gods in the gallery issued forth an abundant variety of discordant sounds, from their elevated situation. Growling of bears, grunting of hogs, braying of donkeys, hissing of geese, the catcalls, and the loud shrill whistles, were heard in one mingling concatenation of excellent imitation and undistinguished variety. At the interval, when the admission price was reduced by half, a crowd would rush in jumping over boxes and obtaining seats by any means, regardless of politeness or even of decorum – Bucks and Bloods warm from the pleasures of the bottle, dashing Belles

---

[8] Leigh Hunt, ed. R. Ingpen, *Autobiography*, 1903, ed: p.152.
[9] J Forster, *Life and Times of Oliver Goldsmith*, 1855.
[10] J Forster, op. cit., 1855.

and flaming Beaux, squabbling and almost fighting, rendered the amusements before the curtain of a momentary interest.[11]

Holcroft, the actor, said in 1798 that,

> Our theatres at present... are half filled with prostitutes and their paramours: they disturb the rest of the audience, and the author and common sense are the sport of their caprice and profligacy.[12]

Riots were fairly common. In 1809, following the famous 'Old Price' riots over the raising of admission charges after a disastrous fire at Covent Garden, John Kemble was forced to restore the old prices, but this left him permanently financially crippled. Two years later the theatregoers in the Pit took offence at the Indian and Paisley shawls which the fashionable set draped over the box ledges. A cry of 'Shawls off the boxes!' was kept up and eventually those in 'the Gods' rained down apple cores on the offenders and forced the removal of the shawls. All this was in an atmosphere as rank as a stable or cesspool: there were no public lavatories in the theatres, there were no assigned seats except in the boxes, and anyone who left had almost to fight to get back to their place. The result was an unsanitary house and an appalling smell. To add to the fun the audience decided how the actors should behave and speak. Kemble once tried to introduce what he took to be authentic, that is archaic, pronunciation into Shakespeare ('ojus' for odious, 'hiddjius' for hideous, and so on), until the audience vociferously forced him to stop. It was in this theatrical world of elegance and tumult that Harriot Mellon hoped to make a name.

When Harriot and her parents arrived in London they went immediately to Drury Lane and called on Sheridan. The famous playwright-manager and Whig politician was often drunk, always in debt, a manipulator given to using people for his own advantage, making hollow promises, and lying when he needed to. He had clearly forgotten his promise to engage Harriot, and probably never expected to see her again. What to do? They decided to stay in London and write to their Stafford friends for

---

[11]*The Amateur*, 1821–1822, p.206.
[12]Thomas Holcroft, *Memoirs*, 1816.

help.

Meanwhile, they rented a house in Southwark, an hour's walk from Drury Lane, at £10 a year, and for the first time they had a home 'with furniture of their own'. It was near St George's Fields, an almost wild park with large ponds where hunters shot snipe in the winter and strollers promenaded in the spring and summer. Harriot was offended when people sneered at her 'rusty black gowns', 'poor cotton stockings' and 'bonnets such as were worn two years before'. She began to feel that they had been foolish to leave Stafford.

At the end of the summer, Mr Wright the banker wrote to Sheridan, pointing out 'the position Miss Mellon was placed in through relying on his promises'. Anxious not to alienate an important constituent, Sheridan invited her to call again, and asked her to read the parts of Lydia Languish and Mrs Malaprop from his play *The Rivals*. She diplomatically answered that she dared not do so in front of the great author and asked him to do her the honour of reading it himself. He read her nearly the whole of the play, until she picked up his style and agreed to read the parts of Lydia and her aunt. Sheridan was impressed and offered her an engagement at 30s a week. It was a tough contract: she had to deposit a large sum from which the management could deduct fines for indiscipline, lateness or absence from rehearsals and performances. Breaking the contract could result in being arrested for debt. It was a poor start, compared with, say, Mrs Jordan, who began on £4 a week, rising to £12 within twelve months, but Sheridan also found her stepfather a place in the band, though he could offer nothing to her mother. Delighted with the offer, she did not know how lucky she was. Drury Lane was in debt, having been rebuilt on too lavish a scale and opened still unfinished outside in 1794. It was described by Mrs Siddons as a 'wilderness of a place', with a proscenium 43 feet wide and 38 feet high, seven times the height of the performers, and Harriot, used to small provincial theatres where her head almost touched the curtain, said she felt a 'mere shrimp' on its stage.

Harriot came to Drury Lane at one of the greatest periods in the history of the London stage. Actresses, moreover, had opportunities open to few other women with nothing to live by but their looks and talent. They could earn far more than any other respectable woman in the few trades open to females: domestic service, needlework, shopkeeping, or assisting as cheap labour in the crafts, where women were excluded from apprenticeship. A star could earn £30 a week, as much as a labourer in a whole year. As an ingénue from the provinces Harriot was lucky to be there at all. She could not compete with Sarah Siddons, sister of the famous John Philip Kemble, or Dorothy Jordan, or at first even with the established second-rank actresses who supported them. Mrs Siddons was the queen of tragedy, discovered by David Garrick, who brought her from Cheltenham to London in 1775. Though her debut was not a success, Sheridan gave her another chance seven years later at Drury Lane, where she broke all records. 'Siddonian idolatry' reached fever pitch and George III and the Prince of Wales, the peerage and the public flocked to the performances of 'the divine Sarah'. Audiences developed an insatiable appetite for tragedy, and some of them were known to swoon at her Lady Macbeth.

Dorothy Jordan, on the other hand, was the queen of comedy. The theatre rang with happy laughter at her fresh, high-spirited humour in such roles as Peggy in Wycherley's bawdy *The Country Girl*, a transvestite role in which she played a boy for part of the time and showed off her admirable figure. Her private life was tragic. As an actress at the Smock Lane Theatre in Dublin, she was seduced in her teens by James Daly, the lecherous manager, and had a child by him. Escaping to Drury Lane, she lived for five years with Richard Ford, son of one of the proprietors who was physician to the royal family, and had two children by him. When the father would not allow Richard to marry her, she was taken up by the Duke of Clarence, fourth son of George III and later King William IV, and by him had ten children. She continued to act and earn money to help pay the debts of her royal protector, and was cartooned with the duke pushing a bassinet surrounded by children. The selfish duke cast her off in 1811 when he unsuccessfully pursued in marriage a rich but reluctant heiress. Robbed by two of her sons-in-law who embezzled her bank account, she died in poverty in 1816.[13] As King, 'Sailor Bill' as he was called from his days in the Navy, had a fit of remorse and in 1831 commissioned Sir Francis Chantry to make a marble statue of Mrs Jordan with two of her small children; this was recently recovered from the basement of Buckingham Palace and a plaster cast of it was put on exhibition at Kenwood House, Hampstead in 1995.[14]

Eliza Farren, another Drury Lane star, was besieged by importunate suitors but had 'an anxious and scrupulously watchful Mamma' who protected the honour of her 'matchless daughter' from the blandishments of the Earl of Derby until she was forty, when his ailing wife died and he married her. Sarah Entwisle played much the same role of duenna with Harriot, and her tough love and rigid morality unwittingly paved the way for a romantic fairy story beyond even her dreams of worldly success.

In 1795 Harriot was about eighteen years old, a fine-grown young woman with a brilliant complexion and dark eyes and hair, inclined to the youthful plumpness which was then fashionable. 'The young men used to look under her bonnet with unrestrained expressions of impatient admiration,' to no avail, since despite her stage persona which was sexy and flirtatious, she was not sentimental, had much prudent common sense, and under her mother's watchful eye maintained a spotless reputation. Other actresses fell into temptation, the green room was full of scandal, and Mrs Siddons termed Drury Lane a 'sink of iniquity'. Leaving aside Mrs Jordan's liaisons, Mrs Bland was having an affair with her fellow actor Mr Caulfield, Mrs Wells, who had the effrontery to look down on Mrs Jordan, was the mistress of Captain Topham, a well-known beau, while Mr Dodd made a pass at every new female in sight. By contrast, a fellow actor said of Harriot,

> She was a good humoured, pleasant creature in the theatre at that time, and mixed with this pleasantness a decision admirably calculated to repel any disagreeable attentions. This I remember

---

[13] A. Aspinall, *Mrs Jordan and her Family*, 1951, p.xii.
[14] I Dejardin, *The Images of Mrs Jordan, Mrs Jordan: The Duchess of Drury Lane*,1995, p.52.

she proved to old Dodd, who was (though a capital actor) a man of unbounded vanity and of very indifferent character, and who received two or three severe checks from Kemble for frivolities with regard to the younger actresses. Miss Mellon at once put an end to this annoyance in a prompt and spirited manner, and she spoke aloud too. Everybody was pleased except Dodd, who, I believe, never forgave her…[15]

Harriot commenced her career at Drury Lane as Lydia Languish in *The Rivals*, on 1 October 1795. She was billed as 'a young lady from the Stafford theatre'.[16] A critic wrote: 'Her appearance was striking, her voice musical, her action powerful when not checked by fear, and there were some tones of archness at times which practice may increase, so it would be unfair to call last night a failure though she did not succeed'.[17] According to Lingard, she was paralysed by nervousness on this first appearance, and it was considered prudent for a time to keep her on stage, but in less significant parts such as Lady Godiva in O'Keefe's *Peeping Tom*[18] and Lucy in *The Recruiting Officer*.[19] In December she played more substantial roles, and in these productions she watched Mrs Jordan play four of her best parts. Harriot studied minutely the methods by which that consummate mistress of comedy charmed the audience. In January she played Lydia Languish again, this time to a much better reception from audience and critics.

In March 1796 she got a stroke of luck. The theatre announced: 'The Publick is most respectfully informed that, on account of the sudden indisposition of Mrs Jordan [probably yet another confinement], Miss Mellon will undertake the character of Amanthis in *The Child of Nature*,[20] and the management humbly solicits their indulgence'. As a child of nature herself, the part was made for her, and critics duly indulged her: 'in many points she closely approaches the celebrated original', but it was difficult for anyone to outshine the galaxy of Drury Lane stars. A fellow actor

---

[15]Charles Pearce, op. cit., 1915, p.9.
[16]J Genest, op. cit., 1832.
[17]Charles Pearce, op. cit., 1915, p.58.
[18]O'Keefe, *Peeping Tom*.
[19]*The Recruiting Officer*.
[20]*The Child of Nature*.

rhapsodised about them,

> Miss Farren was then, despite the smallpox, the reigning toast; she was an elegant woman. Mrs Jordan was in her bloom, and she was a fascinating one; Mrs Goodall was delightful; and Miss De Camp set half the young fellows mad; nay, Mrs Bland was voted a charmer by many – the coarse signora had admirers; to say nothing of the majestic Siddons, the Cleopatra – like Mrs Powell, and that most graceful and lovely of all syrens, Mrs Crouch. These ladies had such a style, you could class them as divinities.

The same actor wrote of Harriot at this period,

> Miss Mellon was merely a countrified girl blooming in complexion, with a very tall, fine figure, raven locks, ivory teeth, a cheek like a peach, and coral lips. All she put you in mind of was a country road and a pillion!... I remember her as Lady Godiva because I went to the front to see Jack Bannister playing Peeping Tom. The lady had very little to do, and the part is generally given to some fine-looking woman; I presume her personal appearance was the solid ground of her selection, though she was always inclined to embonpoint. There was no one in the theatre who would go on for so slight a part except Miss Mellon. It was [later] understood that she should play some of the secondary parts formerly assigned to Miss De Camp and Mrs Gibbs. Very little was expected of her, and she rather disappointed Kemble, who had no great opinion of new comers. Miss De Camp increased in public favour so rapidly that it was deemed inexpedient to send her on for any but important parts. Miss Mellon, therefore, had many characters which, though not exceedingly prominent, were better than she had probably expected.[21]

Harriot had to learn the tricks of the theatre trade, and change them when they did not suit her. It was the fashion for London actresses then to use white face paint, which made them look like simpering china dolls. The comic actor Dickey Suett said she looked a fright with such paint on – her nose too broad, her cheeks like two muffins, almost ready to act the clown, and he

---

[21]Charles Pearce, op. cit., 1915, p.99.

told her to wash it off her nice, brown, merry face. She did, and it came off in stringy lumps like vermicelli, which Dickey said made her look as if she had been baking muffins, so she left it off ever after.[22]

Early in 1796 she was in a production of *Vortigern and Rowena*,[23] a spurious Shakespeare play by William Henry Ireland. It was so bad it caused a riot, and Harriot was said to have turned pale as death, trembled like an aspen leaf, and seemed about to faint. She said that she had never seen such condemnation of a play before, and expected the audience to leap on the stage, demolish the scenery, and physically attack the actors. But in her first season she played a host of parts and proved herself, in the actor Michael Kelly's opinion, a valuable acquisition to the Drury Lane dramatic corps, 'a handsome girl and much esteemed'.[24]

Her modest London fame gained her profitable work in the summer, too, when the metropolitan theatres were closed and the leading players toured the chief provincial cities. The leading stars could command high fees: according to Tate Wilkinson, manager of the York circuit, Mrs Siddons earned £1,000 for seventeen nights' work in 1786, and Mrs Jordan cleared £900 for her appearances in Bath and Birmingham in the summer of 1809. Liverpool audiences demanded London stars for the whole summer, and could be difficult if their expectations were not met: years earlier, when Kemble and Mrs Siddons were still unknown, they were hissed, booed and pelted off the Liverpool stage. Mrs Siddons eventually prevailed over the clamour, but her brother was hissed for the whole season.

In June 1796 Harriot went to Liverpool, along with her parents, to appear at the Theatre Royal and, despite its reputation, she became a great favourite. She was paid £2 a week plus a half-benefit night, more than she earned at Drury Lane (but not clear of expenses). There she played leading roles which she had understudied in London, and as a London actress advised the manager on casting and scenery. She appeared in fifty plays over

---

[22]Margaret Cornwell Baron-Wilson, *Memoirs of Harriot, Duchess of St. Albans*, 2 vols. 1839, pp.295–96.
[23]William Henry Ireland, *Vortigern and Rowena*.
[24]Michael Kelly, *Reminiscences*, 1826.

the summer, a marathon of memorization, which she seems to have done willingly, mimicking the performances of Mesdames Jordan, De Camp and Farren, and improving her acting through the enthusiasm of the audiences.[25] The magazine *The Age*,[26] later her most vicious critic, described her at this time as 'the belle of the provinces... a luxuriant-looking woman of brilliant talent, great archness of manner, black eyes and raven hair'.

Mrs Siddons visited Liverpool for a fortnight's engagement that summer, and introduced Harriot to the company as 'her young friend'. This made Harriot a person of importance, and she was overwhelmed with attention. The following season, according to Lingard, Mrs Siddons presented Harriot to the Green Room as follows: 'Ladies and gentlemen, I am told by one I know well [almost certainly Stanton's son at the Stafford Theatre, her youthful admirer], that this young lady, for years in his father's Company, conducted herself with the utmost propriety. I therefore introduce her as my young friend.' She was henceforth admitted to the first Green Room reserved for the leading players, where wealthy patrons of the theatre came and went. This was to have some significance for Harriot's future, not only on the stage but in society.

Lingard insisted that Thomas Coutts was present at that introduction, and slipped five guineas into her hand, saying 'That's for your benefit, when you have one.' When Harriot asked, 'Who is that kind old gentleman? He is pale and sickly, and looks almost as poor as I', Mrs Siddons replied, 'That is an honourable man who throughout his life has been partial to artists and the arts. Though his scratch wig is the worse for wear, and his old coat white at the seams, that is the banker, old Tom Coutts; be civil to him, for he is the richest man in England.' If true, and Lingard says he got it from Harriot herself, it took Coutts nine years to get to know her better [Lingard, n.d.]. However it began, the eventual friendship was to change her life, and set in train an astonishing rise to the pinnacle of worldly wealth and fame.

---

[25]*Fine Acting*, or a sketch of the life of Miss H M of Drury Lane Theatre and T C, Esq, Banter 1815.
[26]*The Age*.

Chapter IV
THE SCHOOL FOR SCANDAL[1]

Harriot at Drury Lane

When Harriot Mellon returned to Drury Lane Theatre after her summer triumphs in provincial theatres, she had to go back to playing secondary roles, and for doing this without complaint she was considered by her fellow-actors to be 'a good trooper'. One of them wrote anonymously,

> I recollect on the reunion of the company after the vacation [summer 1796]… hearing several actors and actresses… speak of having met Miss Mellon in the provinces… and that at York and Liverpool she became a great favourite. Our great folks spoke very highly of her indeed – Bannister, Mrs Crouch and others – and she was often praised for her goodnatured readiness to play for any one in cases of illness, etc. On such occasions (if very sudden) the higher performers would say, 'I saw her play it very well at such a place'. These things made her very popular with the management, for she was indefatigable, and after flaunting as the fine lady in the absence of some greater actress she returned to the secondary business she was accustomed to play with a good grace and a good humour. Old Wewitzer was a great friend of hers, so were Miss Leak, Miss De Camp, and Mrs Jordan, who were so situated in the theatre at that time that their kindness amounted to a sort of patronage.[2]

As a result of these friendships, the 1796–97 season at Drury Lane brought Harriot into more prominence. Since Mrs Jordan was to be absent until November, Harriot took over her parts of Amanthis in *The Child of Nature*, a play by Mrs Inchbald, and Nell

---
[1]Sheridan's famous play, in which Harriot played Lady Candour in January 1815.
[2]Charles Pearce, op. cit., 1915, p.101.

in *The Devil to Pay*,[3] by Charles Coffey. Critics said her performances 'came very close in several points to her admirable original'.

The actress Anne Mathews said that Harriot at that time had 'dark, bright eyes, and deeply fringed lids; a delicate nose and well-shaped mouth, with white and regular teeth; clear and blushing skin, and fine black hair, waving in natural curls'. But, Mathews said, she was not a great actress; 'a heavy frown and a sunny smile' were her only expressions, though 'a modest dropping of the eyelids from time to time while speaking had a most loveable effect upon the recipient'.[4]

Another, anonymous, actor said,

> Miss Mellon was a remarkably handsome brunette, but did not look a bit like an actress. She was more like one of the genuine beauties of a quiet village two hundred miles from town. It was, I suppose, this rusticity that made her for a long time unnoticed. I don't mean unnoticed merely as an actress, for with our company she was of course prepared for that, but unnoticed as a beauty. She had really more claim to the title than (two or three excepted) most actresses of the day.[5]

Beauty was then judged in terms of sophistication and artifice rather than natural, healthy good looks, and Harriot's behaviour was that of a high-spirited gamine rather than a lady.

When the 1796–1797 season was over, Harriot was well established at Drury Lane. During the summer she and her parents moved from the spartan accommodation in Southwark to 17 Little Russell Street, Covent Garden, opposite Drury Lane theatre. They first rented the second floor, then later took over the first floor as well, and eventually the whole house. Little Russell Street is now Russell Street and the character of the neighbourhood is much changed since the late eighteenth century, when it was a favourite residential quarter for actors and actresses. These early years in London were happy for Harriot.

---

[3]Charles Coffey, *The Devil to Pay*.
[4]Anne Mathews, *Memoirs of Charles Mathews*, 4 vols., 1838.
[5]Charles Pearce, op. cit. 1915, pp.99.

Anne Mathews said she and her husband often went to parties in her new home, and described one of them,

> Miss Mellon's dances were annually looked forward to with delight... At the entrance of the room duly appeared the hostess, radiant with smiles and genuine hospitality, to welcome her willing guests... in a corner of this narrow room leaned Mathews, not then a lame man... he would watch for a lucky minute when the hand of his hostess was free to seize it and lead her off through the meanderings of 'Money Musk' or 'Sir Roger de Coverley'... These were in truth joyous days and nights.[6]

During the summer of 1797 Harriot was again at the Liverpool theatre. One evening she played a weeping heroine in debt to a callous creditor who threatened to send her to prison,

> 'Then I have no hope – I have not a friend in the world,' she cried. 'What! will no-one go bail for you to save you from prison?' asked the creditor. 'I have told you, I have not a friend on earth,' she sobbed. 'But just as I was uttering these words,' Harriot later recalled, 'my eyes were attracted by the movements of a sailor in the upper gallery who, springing over the railing, was letting himself down from one tier to another until finally reaching the pit, he bounded clear over the orchestra and footlights and placed himself beside me in a moment, before I could believe the evidence of my senses.'
>
> 'Yes, you shall have one friend, at least, my poor young woman,' cried the sailor, 'I will go bail for you to any amount. And as for you' (turning to the frightened actor), 'if you don't bear a-hand and shift your moorings, you lubber, it will be the worse for you when I come across your bows.'

The audience thought it was all part of the show, and applauded wildly. It was impossible to resume the play, however, so the orchestra played 'God Save the King' while the curtain dropped. The chivalrous sailor was only persuaded to relinquish his care, as Harriot reported, 'by the illusion being still maintained behind the scenes; the manager, pretending to be an old friend of mine, arrived unexpectedly to rescue me from all difficulties with a

---

[6]Anne Mathews, op. cit., 1838.

profusion of theatrical banknotes.' The sailor then went quietly home under the care of his friends.

Harriot's benefit night in Liverpool that year was unusually large; her stepfather had written to all his friends and relations in his native Wigan (a town not far away), asking them to patronise the theatre on the appropriate night. She made £110 for her half benefit on 28 August, playing Peggy in *The Country Girl*.

Returning to Drury Lane for the 1797–1798 season, Harriot had her salary increased to £2 a week. During the season she took part in Frederick Reynolds' successful play *The Will*, or *The Man of Straw*.[7] In his Memoirs Reynolds wrote in 1827:

> Cicely Copesley, the game-keeper's daughter in my comedy, was performed by Miss Mellon with considerable effect. I little thought at that time that I was to become the vassal of this young, handsome Cicely Copesley. Mrs Coutts is my 'Lady of the Manor', for under her I hold a small copyhold estate near Chelmsford in Essex, and by an old feudal law (which though obsolete is still unrepealed) she might compel me, gout and all, to attend and serve at her next Highgate public breakfast in armour.

When Harriot read this in 1828, friends urged her to claim her feudal rights, but she laughed and replied, 'In any other case I might be rigid, but from him I would be happy to accept 'the Will' for the deed.'[8] That season Harriot also played Cherry in George Farquhar's *The Beaux Stratagem*, and was so much liked that a popular engraving was made of her in the character, which sold well.

She played in Liverpool from June to September, 1798, and took an entire benefit for herself; after paying expenses she cleared £240, on top of her salary.[9] Harriot now had considerable earnings, and a prudent disposition to save and invest, as well as being generous to her parents and friends, as is clear from business papers relating to the period before her marriage [Coutts Bank Archives]. Before she met Thomas Coutts in 1805 she

---

[7]Frederick Reynolds, *The Will*.
[8]Margaret Cornwell Baron-Wilson, op. cit., 1839, p.220.
[9]Margaret Cornwell Baron-Wilson, op. cit., 1839, p.244.

already had a bank account and substantial savings with Thomas Wright of Henrietta Street, Covent Garden (a long-established firm connected to her patron, Mr Wright of Stafford). It was with a cheque on this account that she bought an estate in Essex in 1801.

Success did not lead Harriot to ignore friends she had made earlier in life. Mr Gibson, a violinist at the Ulverston theatre when she had played there nine years earlier, had been the Entwisles' landlord. He said that in 1798 he saw Harriot in Liverpool with a bevy of ladies, and he tried to avoid what he thought would be an embarrassing meeting for her. But Harriot said, 'My good Gibson, I shall not allow you to shun me in that way. I have told these ladies how kind and indulgent you were in my childish days, therefore they know I am anxious to see you.' She asked him about friends in Ulverston, and invited him to dinner with her parents to catch up on the news. Gibson said that at age twenty-one Harriot was 'very striking, from the brilliancy and contrast of her complexion, eyes and teeth; her features were little altered from childhood'; he was impressed by the sweet, low sound of her voice, so childlike in its tone. At dinner she was candid about her disappointments, her hopes deferred, and the disadvantage of being without patronage.

Back at Drury Lane in January 1799, Harriot turned down an offer to appear at Covent Garden in a 'pantomime and dramatic spectacle' at twice her Drury Lane salary. She refused because it would have closed the doors of Drury Lane against her for ever, and she preferred less money and more respectability. Philip Astley tried to persuade her to go with his troop to Dublin, to star in the theatre he planned to erect there, but she refused that too. However, she made a bad mistake in performing for one night (for a friend's benefit, and without her name on the play bill), in a production by strolling players at the George Inn, Epsom. Someone told the Drury Lane manager, and she was fined for misbehaviour. She was lucky not to have her engagement cancelled, so the management must have considered her an asset.

Harriot played several parts early in 1800 as stand-in for Mrs Jordan, who was absent for one of her many pregnancies. She was in the theatre the night in May when there was an attempt on the life of George III; he had just entered the Royal Box when a man named Hadfield raised a pistol and fired point-blank at the King. The bullet missed him by an inch. The King remained cool, staying at the front of the box and bowing to the audience, which went wild with enthusiasm.

The following season at Drury Lane, John Kemble had got over his earlier disappointment with Harriot's acting, and he played Penruddock to her Emily Tempest in *The Wheel of Fortune*. A critic wrote: 'Miss Mellon... gave to the part a high degree of interest from her captivating sprightliness. However, she should never attempt seriously to cry; the audience, accustomed to her merry face, thought she was jesting, and hailed her tears with laughter'.[10] Yet when Harriot played Berinthia in Sheridan's *The Trip to Scarborough*,[11] *The True Briton* said she had 'a polished style and was an accomplished representative of all elegant comedy' and praised the point and precision with which she delivered the dialogue.

In January 1802 Harriot played Nell in Charles Coffey's *The Devil to Pay*. This was one of Mrs Jordan's most famous parts, and Harriot was lucky to succeed in it as well as she did, helped by playing opposite an excellent Jobson in the actor Bannister. *The Thespian Dictionary*[12] commented of Harriot that year,

> The vivacity of her manner was much admired, and the advantage of a pleasing countenance and figure gave it additional effect. Since the period 1793–4 she had been gradually rising in the public favour, and now ranks among the principal comic supports of the theatre. During the summer seasons she has constantly performed in the principal theatres of the kingdom... where...she met with the most distinguished tokens of kindness and approbation.

When Harriot played Constantia in *The Chances* at Plymouth one summer season, she had to say, 'Now, if any young fellow would take a liking to me, and make an honest woman of me, I'd make

---

[10]Margaret Cornwell Baron-Wilson, op. cit., 1839, p.278.
[11]*The Trip to Scarborough*.
[12]*Thespian Dictionary*, 1802.

him the best wife in the world.' One evening, a young midshipman sitting athwart the boxes called out in great rapture, 'I will! and I've two years' pay to receive next Friday'.[13]

In 1802 Harriot was earning £5 a week. It seemed a good salary but she found out later that others at Drury Lane earned far more: John Kemble got 40 guineas [a guinea was 21 shillings] a week during the season when he acted; as manager he got 14 guineas a week throughout the whole year; his annual salary thus exceeded 2,000 guinea; Mrs Siddons got 40 guineas a week, or 1,200 guineas for the season, plus provincial earnings; Mrs Jordan earned almost 1,000 guineas for the season, plus provincial earnings. Miss De Camp, Mrs Mountain, and Mrs Bland each got £12 a week in season, Mrs Pope £11 a week, Mrs Young and Mrs Powell each £10 a week. Others were less fortunate: Mrs Crouch's salary was reduced by one half, from £14 to £7 a week, in consequence of her 'having been somewhat disfigured by the overturning of her carriage'; Mrs Grimaldo got £4 a week; and Mrs Sparks £3 a week in the season only. A number of players earned less than Harriot, but the majority received more than she.

In January 1803 Harriot took over the part of Mistress Page in *The Merry Wives of Windsor*,[14] replacing Miss Pope who was ill. Sir William Beechey painted a full-length portrait of her in this character, which was published as an engraving. Harriot kept the dress she wore for the part for many years, and the performance was a treasured highlight of her career.

Having established herself as a favourite with the public, Harriot had a 'ticket night' by which she sold tickets to her friends, gave half the money to the manager, and retained half for herself. Apparently the house was well filled. Nearly all the theatre critics of the time saw her as a second Mrs Jordan. *The Dramatic Censor* in 1804 said, 'Miss Mellon has appeared this season as the successor of Mrs Jordan in the lower walks of comedy. Her Estifania, though an avowed copy of her predecessor, is, notwithstanding, entitled to commendation.'

This connection between Harriot and Dorothy Jordan was

---

[13]Margaret Cornwell Baron-Wilson, op. cit., 1839, p.291.
[14]*The Merry Wives of Windsor*.

remembered after their deaths. 'As an actress,' wrote *The Gentleman's Magazine* in October 1837, 'Miss Mellon was in the school of Jordan, but by no means a servile imitator. She wanted the versatility and rapidity of the great original, but she had some points that Mrs Jordan did not. She might be described in Byron's words – 'Being rather large, and languishing, and lazy, yet of a beauty that would drive you crazy'.[15] But in a contest with the great Mrs Jordan, Harriot could not possibly win.

Though busy with her stage life, Harriot was asked to coach aristocrats in their amateur theatricals, principally at Strawberry Hill, the late Horace Walpole's old residence, which he had passed on to the Hon. Mrs Damer, who built a private theatre there. Private theatricals were a major amusement of the upper classes. Gentry families such as Jane Austen's staged plays in their homes, as did the rich in their great houses, and texts of plays were bestsellers.

Walpole's friend, Miss Berry, found among his papers a comedy by Boissy, an early eighteenth-century French dramatist, and she produced an English adaptation of this at Strawberry Hill, called *Fashionable Friends*, in which she, Mrs Damer and the Earl of Mount Edgcumbe took part. Harriot Mellon helped coach the actors, but said there was never such a stupid task as drilling fine people in acting; they could never quite forget their rank and dignity, so playing an ordinary being made them awkward and gauche. She thought it more amusing to help coach the Kentish Bowman's Lodge at Dartford Heath, a club which practised archery as well as amateur theatricals. Once when Harriot was acting with 'the fine folk', she missed an evening's performance at Drury Lane, and *The Messenger* complained about Mrs Humphries playing Mrs Harlowe in *The Old Maid* saying 'the part should have been played by Miss De Camp or Miss Mellon, for the piece deserves the best comic performers that the theatre will afford.' Harriot thought it was worth missing a performance to get such praise.

Anne Damer was a distinguished sculptor and the centre of a brilliant social and intellectual circle. Between 1797 and 1811

---

[15]Margaret Cornwell Baron-Wilson, op. cit., 1839, p.305.

Strawberry Hill was an exclusive salon, and as a guest there Harriot acquired many useful social contacts and greater social poise. There were hidden dangers of course in mixing with people who accepted her for her talent, not her birth, as Harriot discovered when she later married into the peerage. Aristocratic society loved taking part in amateur theatricals, and welcomed professional actors to aid their performances, but to enter the profession themselves was not to be thought of. Actors were tolerated for the amusement they provided, but were generally kept in their place like doctors and lawyers and other ancillary professions and never allowed to forget their inferior social position. But in visiting their homes Harriot could watch, listen to, and study the manners of the great folk for imitation on the stage.

The French wars seem to have made little difference to the lives of the rich, though in 1800 bread cost 1s.5d the quartern loaf, coal was priced at six guineas the caldron, turkeys cost 16s. and capons 8s.6d. All meat was at a price prohibitive to the lower classes. After the Peace of Amiens (1802) Napoleon refused to evacuate Malta and by May 1803 England was again at war with France. But life went on gaily for the aristocracy. Miss Berry gave this account of festivities that year,

> Three or four balls at Devonshire House kept the young people in motion; there have been also, several morning dances, followed by a breakfast, by way of practising quadrilles. Lady Elizabeth Foster brought some pretty music from Paris, and some of the young ladies just come forth proved themselves excellent dancers [Berry, 1844].

In 1804 Napoleon declared himself Emperor of the French and once more threatened to invade England. October 1805 brought news of the Battle of Trafalgar, which ended the invasion threat and proved the turning point of the long global war, and the account of Nelson's death. In January 1806 there was a great state funeral for him, everyone wearing crepe scarves and black cockades with 'Nelson' inscribed on them. But the war in those days was far from total, and London's round of pleasure was scarcely interrupted.

Some time around 1804, Harriot had a romantic disappointment which put her off similar ventures. An apparent gentleman named Barry, newly arrived from the West Indies and with a good appearance and manners, was introduced and paid her attentions. Her mother did not approve, thinking him insufficiently exalted for her daughter, and asked what means he had of supporting Harriot if he took her off the stage. He talked of family connexions and said he was heir to an aunt of good property. Nevertheless, Sarah Entwisle maintained a careful watch on her daughter and did all in her power to prevent her meeting Barry. Harriot was very unhappy, and confided in her friend Eleanor Goddard. Eleanor knew Barry, and happened to know that the story of a rich aunt was a fabrication, and deduced that he hoped Harriot would keep him from her earnings from the stage. Sarah, it seemed, was right. Harriot, who was not afraid of being poor, might have accepted a suitor without money if he had been honest, but she would not put up with deceit. She refused Barry's offer of marriage, and would soon have reason to avoid such young covetous suitors.[16]

In 1804 Thomas Entwisle was sacked from his job with the orchestra at Drury Lane for continual drunkenness, and thought he would try his fortune selling sheet music in Cheltenham, a fashionable watering-place to which holiday crowds flocked 'to idle away time, ogle the exquisite, haggle marriage matches for their daughters, and above all to gamble.' Sarah and Thomas left London together, opened a music shop in the High Street in Cheltenham, and to gain further income let off the furnished upper part of their large house. It was an amicable parting of the ways for Harriot and her parents, whom she continued to support financially, and she decided to have her friend Sally Stephenson to live with her in Little Russell Street as a companion, which she was later to regret.

When the season ended in June, Harriot went to stay with her mother in Cheltenham, performed at the theatre there for five nights, and took a benefit in July. She then went on to Liverpool and made a lot of money from her performances there. Whenever

---

[16]Margaret Cornwell Baron-Wilson, op. cit., 1839, p.307.

she performed in the provinces she secured good benefit nights, since she was treated as a first-rate London actress. People liked her unaffected good nature, cheerfulness and hard work, and she always collected hundreds of pounds. In September she returned to Cheltenham, where a great patroness of hers, Viscountess Templetown (Lady Mary Montague, daughter of the Earl of Sandwich), 'bespoke' the plays for Harriot's second benefit, allowing her to advertise her patronage, and persuading wealthy friends to attend the performance.

At this stage, Harriot and her mother were still on good terms, since she provided everything Sarah asked for her home and comfort. When Thomas Entwisle was ill in the summer of 1804, Harriot was affectionate and caring, but her parents grew greedier for money, and often visited London to press for more. Harriot was not always willing to give it, and this caused endless arguments and unpleasantness. Sarah was also angry that Harriot did not seem to be reaching the top of her profession. In September 1804 she played Lady Ruby in *First Love*[17] and Polly in *The Land We Live In*,[18] but was comparatively idle professionally for the rest of the season. Seldom seen, she was for a time almost forgotten and unappreciated, being kept by management for filling in parts when people were sick during the 1803–1804 season.

Harriot's misfortune was to alternate between great and trivial parts in plays at Drury Lane, which meant her career was not advancing. She was good-natured and willingly took insignificant parts when asked, which made her popular with management and fellow actors, but injured her development as an actress. More ambitious actresses would have refused minor roles once they began to play major ones. Harriot herself argued that, without patronage, she had no means of getting regular big parts, yet by her own efforts she was slowly making her way up in the public's estimation, and also getting higher praise from the critics.

Fortunately for Harriot, a wonderful opportunity arose when Tobin's *The Honeymoon*[19] was read to the company assembled in

---

[17]*First Love*.
[18]*The Land We Live In*.
[19]*The Honeymoon*.

the first Green Room at Drury Lane. Mrs Jordan decided to have nothing to do with it, and Harriot was given the leading role, becoming the first to play Volante in January 1805. The part was exactly suited to her powers and she at last established herself in the eyes of the public as a major talent. *The Weekly Messenger* said, 'Miss Mellon has one of the best female characters; we except not Miss Duncan's; there is more archness and comic sprightliness in the part, and it was admirably suited to her talents.' *The Morning Post* commented, 'The character of Volante is most aptly suited to Miss Mellon's lively acting, and we never saw her to more advantage.' A coloured engraving of Harriot as Volante, after a portrait by Sir William Beechey, was brought out and sold rapidly. On the strength of her popularity she ventured that season to take a benefit on her own account, on 21 May playing Mistress Ford in *The Merry Wives of Windsor*; under the rules of the theatre she was not allowed to play Volante for a benefit. Afterwards she found herself with considerable savings. Her mother, realising that Cheltenham was increasing in fashion, persuaded Harriot to invest her benefit money in a house there, to be let furnished to provide an income for her parents. It was built at Cambray, but Mrs Entwisle could not get as much rent as she wanted. So she asked Harriot for even more money, and got it.

Harriot's new-found fame also brought her into contact with Colonel McMahon, the Prince of Wales's 'jackal' (aide), and Harriot asked him to find a post for her stepfather. McMahon suggested the position of postmaster at Cheltenham; Entwisle knew nothing about postal work, but nonetheless was appointed. It was a disaster. Entwisle's carelessness led to serious complaints; there was a scandal when a young man failed to receive a letter telling him his father was dying, and was unable to get home in time to see him alive. He drew up a petition for Entwisle's dismissal and got many upper-class people to sign it. Asked for her help, Harriot at first said events must take their course, her stepfather having behaved so badly, but eventually she begged her new friend Thomas Coutts, the banker, for help, and he used his influence with the postmaster-general to have Entwisle severely reprimanded but not dismissed.

It was in Cheltenham in 1805, as will appear, that Harriot met and became friendly with Thomas Coutts. Whether or not it was their first meeting, this closer encounter was to change both their lives. After that, she was on the London stage for ten more years. When her acting career came to an end, she had long been, as the *Dictionary of National Biography* delicately described it, 'intimate with Thomas Coutts the Banker, said to be the richest man in London'; 'intimate' in those days did not have its modern sexual connotation, but the further point, that 'the connection, which was generally known, caused much unfriendly comment', was a considerable understatement.

What, however, do we know about that rich old man who became Harriot's protector and was to be her first husband? He was an extraordinary man of independent mind, an intimate friend of royalty and the aristocracy yet impervious to common opinion, and at the same time a product of the values, attitudes and sexual mores of late Georgian and Regency England, as we shall see in the next chapter.

Chapter V
THE FOLLIES OF THE DAY[1]

Thomas Coutts and his Social Circle

Thomas Coutts, who became Harriot Mellon's protector and later her first husband, was a banker. Not just any banker, but the royal banker who made large loans to the king, the royal dukes, and half the aristocracy, and was one of the richest men in England. Born in 1735, he was the fourth son of John Coutts, a wealthy timber-merchant, banker, and Lord Provost of Edinburgh.[2] His mother died when he was a year old. He was brought up by his maternal grandmother, Lady Stuart, and went to the high school in Edinburgh. The eighteenth century was the age of commercial capitalism, when techniques of exchange became faster, cheaper and more reliable. The paper-money economy grew. Certain forms of money making were more honourable than others, principally large-scale overseas trade and finance, in which his father's firm John Coutts & Co. was involved, rather than domestic wholesale or retail business. Two of Thomas's brothers were buccaneers: Patrick, the eldest, was engaged in mysterious activities in France, for which he was for a time jailed as a spy. His brother John was sent to Rotterdam as a partner in the firm of Robertson, Coutts and Stephens, and he too became involved in dubious affairs, helping to supply Scottish smugglers and trading in tea and whisky. However, his brother James was Member of Parliament for Edinburgh, and he worked for, and later took over, Campbell's bank in the Strand, London, which had been founded by a goldsmith in 1692. In 1761 he asked Thomas to join him and the bank was renamed Coutts Bank. The partnership was not a

---

[1]A play by Thomas Holcroft, in which Harriot played Cherubin in 1796.
[2]Low, 1892.

happy one, and it was dissolved in 1775. Thomas was undoubtedly the directing genius and master of the bank, insisting that he and his heirs should retain 'the supremacy... of the House as well as the half share of the Bank'.

The Coutts banking house stood on the site of the former Exchange. Here Thomas built his strong rooms, a depository for his bank funds and books and for security of his customer's plate, jewels, etc. he lived 'over the shop'. The upper portion of the house in the Strand, as rebuilt in 1769, was a spacious and splendid building. The drawing room and dining room had Adam mantelpieces and were furnished with rare and costly cabinets. The drawing room was eventually, and still is, decorated with the famous Chinese wallpaper sent to Thomas from China in 1792 by Lord Macartney, the first British ambassador there, as a souvenir; the wallpaper illustrated the growth and manufacture of the tea plant.

Thomas was an excellent man of business. Starting with a modest capital of £4,000, he eventually acquired a fortune of £900,000, not counting residences in London. His advice was sought by the greatest in the country, and he became one of the most influential men in England. The business he transacted involved little investment, apart from his considerable 'Stock in partnership in the Strand.' He subscribed to Government loans – Long Annuities, Naval Annuities, the 'Voluntary Loan', etc. – only when Prime Ministers asked him to do so; he was always doubtful of their security, though the interest was good; and he made gloomy prophecies concerning the future of the national finances. Industrial investments never tempted him. To a friend he wrote, 'I am sorry to see... that you are engaged in coal and lime; for I never knew a gentleman make anything of either, nor of farming.' He was right in the sense that more money was always made in finance and commerce than in industry or agriculture.[3]

Speculation in land he rarely touched, though as we shall see later he advised Harriot Mellon before their marriage about good properties to buy. He said he never bought an estate (as did the majority of very wealthy men, who hoped thereby to improve

---

[3]Rubinstein, 1981, p.185.

their social standing) because he needed a lot of ready cash to fund his bank, and anyway he did not want the trouble of attending to it. His business acumen was founded, he said, 'in the power of obliging my customers with loans of money.' He had a shrewd knowledge of when to open his purse and when to keep it closed. Lending money was at that time a very risky business. For though great fortunes were quickly made in India and in the West Indies, they were lost even more swiftly at the gaming tables, when men like Charles James Fox and Lord Sandwich and some women like Georgiana Duchess of Devonshire threw away great estates in a single evening.

Thomas followed his inclinations, usually being well informed about the assets of his noble friends and clients and the security against which money could be loaned to them. Early on in his career, he heard that a certain nobleman had applied for a loan of £30,000 and been refused. He sent a message to the nobleman saying that if he called at Coutts Bank he could have what he required. When his lordship appeared, Thomas put into his hand thirty one-thousand-pound notes and refused to take any security other than a note of hand. So pleased was the nobleman that he recommended Coutts to his friends, and told the King of the incident. The King then became a patron of Coutts Bank. Not only was Coutts the royal banker, but the King also employed him on confidential missions abroad. Thomas was appointed a Gentleman of the King's Privy Chamber, an unusual honour which gave him direct access to the sovereign, and he later destroyed evidence of his many services to George III, saying, 'I was much in His Majesty's confidence, which I never did anything to forfeit, and I never mentioned any circumstances of his affairs to any one, and have left no trace of them behind.'

However, Thomas did not let his friendly relations with royalty affect his independence. Through no fault of Coutts, the King vented his displeasure on him, as Sir Francis Burdett's father-in-law, following the rowdy election in Brentford in 1802 and demonstrations in front of Kew Palace where the King was in residence, by transferring his bank account to Drummonds. At the same time Lord Hawkesbury (later Prime Minister Lord Liverpool), acting on his own authority, withdrew the Secret

Service Fund and other official accounts from Coutts bank. Thomas could not question the King's personal decision, but he appealed to Pitt, the Prime Minister, about Hawkesbury's action, and most of the official accounts came back to him.

The Government seems to have given Thomas a roving commission to check the expenditure of all the Royal Dukes. 'The damndest set of millstones round the government's neck' was what the Duke of Wellington called the King's sons.[4] At Christmas 1792, Thomas set out in writing the terms on which he was prepared to lend £60,000 to the Prince of Wales, known as the First Gentleman in Europe:

> I wish to begin and end my proposals on the business by a condition that appears so essential to my comfort in the prosecution of the plan, that unless it can be positively fixed and uniformly and steadily observed, I would rather choose to decline engaging at all in this matter. What I mean is that no account of His Royal Highness, or one of those concerned for him in his affairs, shall ever be overdrawn at my shop.

The particulars of the property assigned as security were set out in 196 pages, and the terms were accepted by the Prince. Coutts regained his position as banker to the Privy Purse when the Prince of Wales became Regent, and so continued when the Prince came to the throne.

Thomas was a close friend of the Duke of Clarence, who wrote about personal as well as business affairs. For example, in 1797 the Duke wrote that Mrs Jordan was 'one of the most perfect women in the world', and how much he owed her, since there were times when Mrs Jordan's financial contribution from her stage earnings made the difference between his solvency and disaster. He spoke of Mrs Jordan having recently loaned him £2,400, which he was to repay as he thought proper (but probably never did). In 1818 he wrote about his forthcoming marriage to Princess Adelaide, saying, 'I really believe... I have a fair prospect of success', and in this he was right. The Duke remained a client of the bank when he became William IV, and until his death.

---

[4]Edna Healey, *Coutts & Co: The Portrait of a Private Bank*, 1992, p.129.

The Duke of Kent was the closest of the royal dukes in friendship with Thomas. The duke neither drank, swore nor gambled, and like Thomas he was a strict disciplinarian but capable of many acts of kindness. He was unpopular with his father for many reasons: because he was a Whig in politics, and because of his liaison with a French lady, Mme de St Laurent, his wife in all but name for twenty-eight years. He lived abroad for some years for reasons of economy, but returned to England after the death in 1817 of the heir to the throne, Princess Charlotte, when the royal dukes were ordered to marry and produce a legitimate heir. His mistress was cast off, and she first entered a convent in Paris, but later went to Canada and married a French nobleman. In 1818, the duke married a German princess, Victoria Mary Louisa, widow of the duke of Saxe-Coburg-Saalfeld, encouraged like his brother Clarence by the offer of an increased income from the government. Their child, the future Queen Victoria, was born in 1819, but eight months later the duke died of pneumonia.

Most of the Bank's profit during Thomas's lifetime came from the interest on money borrowed. A list of distinguished customers would fill many pages: dukes and earls, cabinet ministers and ambassadors, generals and admirals, advocates and landowners, painters and sculptors, writers and actors, all came to him for help. Sheridan asked for support for Drury Lane Theatre. Retired servants of the state wrote for help, because their pensions were far in arrears. Lady Chatham, for example, pleaded frequently for money for her ailing husband, the elder Pitt, worn out in the service of his country. Time and again Thomas used his influence to persuade the Government to pay its debts, though sometimes he had to use near-blackmail – threatening to expose the Government's inefficiency. Still more pitiful were unhappy heirs whose estates had fallen into the hands of Chancery. There are many entries in Thomas's notebooks saying of a client, 'Not to be pressed because it was lent out of compassion.'

On principle, and as a matter of prudence, Thomas meddled little in politics. By tradition and descent he was a Tory, and by temperament he was on the side of privilege and authority, but he had political sympathy with the Whigs. He hated all wars as a waste of money, and was on the side of the American colonies, since the moneyed class, whose patriotism was balanced by common sense, deplored a ruinous conflict with America that could only end in loss and disaster. The Duke of Clarence reproached him for his 'little England views': 'I am astonished to hear you, a man of business, deprecating a Colonial war: this country is nothing without commerce, and what is commerce without Colonies?' But Thomas believed, with Adam Smith, that more trade was done with free countries than with colonies, and constantly affirmed his belief that trade and a strong Navy to keep the trade routes open go hand in hand.

Coutts took no part in party politics, but corresponded with almost every eminent politician. Amongst monied men he was looked up to as an oracle. It was only by loans from his bank that many a statesman was able to maintain his position in public life. He was consulted by borough mongers on the raising of loans for bribes, and was privy to their distribution. He knew what went on behind the scenes, especially after the Earl of Guilford (eldest son of the late Prime Minister, Lord North) became his son-in-law in 1796. However, when offered a seat in Parliament in 1784, without condition or expense, Coutts refused it because he would not opt for one party or the other. Lady Hester Stanhope, niece and housekeeper for her uncle, William Pitt the younger, in the last three years of the Prime Minister's lifetime, confirmed in her Memoirs that it was suggested Thomas be made Lord Coutts, but the Marquess of Bute, amongst others, prevented this. Ironically, Bute, grandson of George III's first prime minister, later became Thomas's son-in-law. Coutts had no personal acquaintance with Charles James Fox, leader of the Whig opposition and a noted gambler and rake, and little or no sympathy with his opinions, but for some reason he was willing to lend him £5,000 in September 1787, and another £5,000 the following July. Repayment was not pressed for.

On the other hand, Thomas could be strangely mean about a small debt. One of his friends attended a lavish banquet at the Coutts home, and then the next day went to settle business at the counting house. He owed Thomas one penny change, but said he would not pay it. Thomas said he must have the penny, and when the friend protested that dinner the previous night must have cost the host £100, he replied, 'True, but it is by being rigidly correct in matters of business that I am able to give you a dinner!'

Punctual in starting work at the bank, within a minute of St Martin's clock striking nine Thomas stepped into his office, a slight figure in shabby but formal dress. He insisted on discipline and efficiency. He planned every hour of the daily routine of every clerk, from the juniors, who were expected to work on Sundays, up to the chief clerk. After closing the door to customers, every clerk had to make up his accounts and strike a balance, which had to tally to the farthing. Thomas was described as sedate in his deportment, punctual to an extreme of nicety, frugal and sparing in his personal expenditure, careful of his health, and still more careful of his reputation. What drove him on in his stressful life? Not a desire for wealth for its own sake, but it seems a desire for prestige and the power to secure patronage for his friends. As 'a person of the first respectability' wrote of him in 1819:[5] 'the whole of Mr Coutts's public conduct through life plainly evinces, that he was more attached to independence than to wealth, that he stood but little in awe of public opinion, and that his mind was encumbered with few prejudices.'

For most of his life, Coutts scorned luxury, his tastes being simple, and he was not overly impressed with society life, knowing too much about it from the inside. He was already a rich banker, living in St Martin's Lane, when he married the maidservant of his brother James. Thomas was 28 and Susannah 30 years old on 18 May 1763 when they married at St Gregory's Church in London, by special licence from the Archbishop of Canterbury. She was a native of Preston in Lancashire, daughter of a small farmer, and had been in domestic service before coming to London. The brothers James and Thomas quarrelled over the marriage but continued in business together for some years. The elevation of Susannah from housemaid to mistress of the house was kept secret before the event. A few days before the marriage she was 'scowering' the stairs of the house in the Strand, and

---

[5] *Authentic Memoirs*, p.9.

because it had been raining she asked one of the resident clerks, who had just come in, to take off his shoes before going upstairs. He got in a rage and instead left a trail of dirty marks as he climbed the stairs. Then he heard the angry Betty (as Susannah was familiarly called) say, 'Before long, I'll make you pull off your shoes and stockings too, if I choose it!' After the marriage took place, the clerk expected to lose his job, but the new bride never mentioned the matter and always treated him well, which shows she had a good heart.

Very little is known about the marital relations of Thomas and Susannah, but apparently they always lived in harmony, first at St Martin's Lane, later in apartments over the bank in the Strand, and eventually in the great mansion on the corner of Stratton Street and Piccadilly. Susannah never relaxed her frugal disposition and did not entertain in a grand style, but she had the qualities Thomas most admired – simplicity, common sense and competence.

Susannah's enemies said she was illiterate and uncultivated, but she must have been entrusted with some knowledge of her husband's business affairs, because once when Thomas granted a further advance to 'a fair and high-born customer', he alleged his wife's intercession as his excuse for relenting against his better judgment. Susannah's daughters loved her and Thomas never complained that he lost out by his unfashionable marriage. They had four sons who died in infancy, and three daughters, all born in St Martin's Lane. Each girl received an expensive education, at a school in Queen Square, and later at an exclusive convent in Paris.

All the daughters married aristocrats: Sophia, the youngest, married the radical baronet and landowner, Sir Francis Burdett, in 1793; Susan married George Augustus, third Earl of Guilford, in 1796; and Frances married John, first Marquess of Bute, in 1800, as his second wife. In the eyes of the world, Thomas's daughters made brilliant marriages. Yet in none of his sons-in-law did he find a man fit to take over the bank. Sir Francis Burdett was reckless and impetuous, a radical in politics who had inherited considerable property from his elder brother, from his grandfather and from an aunt, providing an income of £20,000 a year. The Earl of Guilford was handicapped by ill-health, although he was a good speaker in the House of Lords. The Marquess of Bute was a great territorial magnate, and had held posts at embassies abroad, but he was never intimate with Coutts. Of all the sons-in-law, Sir Francis Burdett was to prove the most troublesome, as will be seen.

High society in the late eighteenth and early nineteenth centuries was openly tolerant of sexual freedom and robust pastimes. A wealthy man could afford a home, a wife, a family, a club, and two social lives, one shared with his wife, the other independent of her and shared with a mistress or series of lovers, who might be his social equal or of lower social status, and might be wholly or partially 'kept' or 'protected' by the man. The upper-class wife had similar sexual freedom to that of her husband, after marriage and the production of 'an heir and a spare', particularly if she had economic independence through control of her own fortune and income, though her love affairs were with men of her own social class.[6]

The alternative London social world inhabited by wealthy men and their mistresses was known as the demi-monde, a half-world beneath the larger beau monde and ruled by the fashionable courtesans whose personalities and style, more than beauty alone, commanded large sums of money, independence and a certain respect. The progress of Georgian harlots was not always tragic, despite Hogarth's famous print sequence. There was a growing discourse about sexuality as a fact of personal relations. Tolerance of extra-marital affairs was common in a large section of society, certainly more extensive than the libertine elite. In this relaxed society, neither state, Church nor public opinion was very vigilant in policing the morals of the affluent in town or country, or of the urban lower orders.

Yet, towards the end of the eighteenth century, as was shown in Chapter 2, moral reform and the restoration of puritan values became a clarion call for certain people. The middle ranks, the professional and business men and some of the intelligentsia, had always been censorious in their public morality, if not always in

---

[6]Joan Perkin, 1989, chapter 4.

their private behaviour, but now there was yet another revival of moral righteousness in what came to be called the moral revolution.[7] The Evangelical movement offered the rising middle class a stern, personal creed by which they could stabilize their lives, minimize insecurity, and win the respect of their fellows. Their main aim was to impose their own middle-class morality on the aristocracy and the lower orders. Respectability, a word first said to have been used in 1785, began its meteoric career.

Like his Scottish Calvinist forebears, Thomas Coutts even as a young man was always respectable. He never seems to have been a rake or young buck, and there is no evidence that he ever frequented brothels, or kept a mistress until at the age of 70 he became the 'protector' of Harriot Mellon. Though he had left school early, Thomas became a man of wide-ranging culture with a large collection of books and pictures, as the inventory of his possessions made after his death shows. His daughter Fanny claimed that he always carried a volume of Shakespeare in his pocket, and that if one began a Shakespearean quotation, he could always finish it. He loved the theatre, taking long leases on boxes at Drury Lane and Covent Garden, and giving generously to the rebuilding of both theatres after fire destroyed them. He was considered to have the best box at Drury Lane, one which the Prince of Wales coveted. Leasing a box was not only a means of supporting the theatre, but also good business, since many of his distinguished customers were delighted to be loaned it for a play or an opera.

With a discerning eye for real artistic talent, Thomas guided Sir Joshua Reynolds through a difficult financial affair. Thomas Lawrence, the darling of the fashionable world, had more commissions than he could undertake, but was hopeless with money and always in debt, so Coutts supported him for many years. Thomas also commissioned the old sculptor, Joseph Nollekens, to make a statue of him. He generously supported the brilliant and eccentric Swiss, Johann Heinrich Fuseli, first as a poet and man of letters and later in his avant garde painting career. But he also backed losers, and even the successful lost him more

---

[7]Harold Perkin, The *Origins of Modern English Society*, Chapter 8, 1969.

than he gained. Time and again he rescued Haydon, an artist tortured by a demonic drive to create enormous canvases, yet obsessed by a sense of failure. No one really knows the extent of Thomas's private charity. He was naturally kind-hearted, with an understanding of the artistic temperament and sympathy for sensitive souls in a harsh world.

Apart from making friends with the most influential men of his time, Thomas Coutts also had a talent for dealing with women – old and young – who found him a sympathetic listener. He dealt kindly with the mistresses of his distinguished customers, discreetly setting up trusts for them and their illegitimate children. He befriended Mrs Fitzherbert, morganatic wife of the Prince of Wales; the actress Dorothy Jordan, mistress of the Duke of Clarence; and Mme de St Laurent, companion of the Duke of Kent. Rarely shocked by eccentricity, he was the friend of Lady Hester Stanhope, who after her uncle Prime Minister Pitt's death, travelled to the Middle East and lived a strange life in a disused convent on a remote mountainside; she took as her lover a young man, Michael Bruce, who agreed to make her an allowance of £400 a year, payable by his father via her 'old friend' Thomas Coutts, who also handled a government pension which her uncle the Prime Minister had given her. Lady Hester wrote that Coutts was not like other bankers, and Georgiana, the gambling Duchess of Devonshire said to him, 'You are my father,' as did many other ladies, when he helped them out with their problems. A mixture of romance and caution, love of the exotic and yet of simplicity gave him his special quality. He had strict personal standards, but a ready acceptance of human frailty, so that he was not only a banker but a trusted friend. Many times when the rules of business conflicted with his wish to be kind to friends, friendship won.

As Thomas Coutts got older, he became a remarkably shabby dresser, despite his wealth. He was described as 'a tall, thin, spare figure' and it was said that his ill-fitting clothes bore the appearance of being 'rubbed at the seams'. He was often taken for an indigent person, and he told the following story, and similar ones, with great amusement: for exercise he used to walk daily to a chemist's shop some distance from his office in the Strand, to get a tonic to improve his appetite. He was so quiet and unassuming, always making way for others who came into the shop, that no one guessed he was a rich man. A kind-hearted bystander who chanced several times to be in the shop at the same time as Coutts, thought he was a gentleman in reduced circumstances, and prepared a sum of money to give to him. The day he intended to give the money, Coutts did not appear in the shop, and the stranger asked the chemist how he could get in touch with him, saying he wanted to help him. The chemist was amazed, and said Thomas Coutts certainly needed no money, but the next day he told the story to the old banker.[8]

This, then, was the rich old man, almost seventy years old, who became enchanted with Harriot in 1805. He had seen her before, on his frequent visits to the Green Room at Drury Lane theatre, but it was when Harriot was on tour at the theatre in Cheltenham, where Thomas was a summer visitor, that they really got to know each other. She needed money to help her parents, and proposed to devote the proceeds of her benefit night at the theatre to them. Being an elderly invalid gentleman, Thomas did not join in society parties at the spa, but he passed many hours daily taking exercise in the Long Walk. Harriot's mother discovered from his servant that 'notwithstanding his impecunious appearance', this was one of the richest men in London, but that he was very unhappy because he thought his wife was going out of her mind. Sarah Entwisle realised that the 'old, pallid, sickly thin gentleman in a shabby coat and brown scratch wig was the great Mr Coutts, who managed the finances of the Royal Family and commanded everything he liked.' She persuaded Harriot to write and ask him to take a box at the theatre for her benefit night; when he did not reply immediately, Harriot said she thought 'the moping, thin old creature was too full of his own troubles to care about those of other people.'

However, one day on the Long Walk he introduced himself to Harriot, telling her that he had seen her at Drury Lane, and apologised for not having replied sooner to her letter. He went on to say that he had heard at every turn in Cheltenham admirable

---

[8]Anonymous, *Life of Thomas Coutts*, 1822, p.8.

accounts of her laudable, filial efforts. Coutts had sent Harriot five guineas, and in an accompanying letter he commended her industry, good reputation and perseverance, hoping his trifling present would prove to be 'luck-money'. So it proved, and Harriot always refused to part with the five, shining, golden guineas fresh from the Mint which she put in a separate purse and managed to keep out of the rapacious hands of her mother. On the day of her marriage to Coutts she produced them for him to see, and she showed them again at the bridal party to celebrate her second marriage, when she became a duchess.[9]

Coutts had become very lonely later in his life, his wife an invalid and his daughters married, and he seems to have neglected himself. According to Sarah Entwisle, Coutts complained to her one day of numbness in his arms and pain in walking. Sarah, an ex-wardrobe mistress who was a skilled needlewoman, suggested that his sleeves might be too tight, and that his shoes and stockings were not fitting comfortably. She told him to bring her one of his flannel waistcoats and a pair of stockings. When she saw the samples of the rich man's wardrobe, she nearly laughed out loud: the waistcoat had been worn, patched and washed so often that it had shrunk into 'a little yellow hard thing, like a washed glove'. The worsted stockings were equally hard from frequent washings, and had been darned in lumps over and over again, so that Coutts was in pain when walking in them. Two days later, Sarah produced a dozen newly-made flannel waistcoats and a dozen pairs of new stockings. Thomas said Mrs Entwisle had clearly understood a problem that he had been too busy to solve for himself, and frequently referred to this change in the comfort of his clothing.

However shabby-looking Thomas Coutts was, Sarah Entwisle marked him down as a patron for her daughter from the first time she met him, and she encouraged their friendship. She was anxious to advance Harriot's position in the world, and had previously guarded her moral conduct by never letting her go out alone with a man. But Harriot was now twenty-eight years old, and no acceptable offers of marriage had been made, so we can

---

[9]Margaret Cornwell Baron-Wilson, op. cit., 1839, p.339–40.

speculate that her mother had decided that a rich protector was a good bargain.

Thomas Coutts always asserted publicly, in letters to his friends and daughters, and in his private letters to Harriot – none of which he had reason to believe would ever be made public – that his relationship with Harriot before their marriage was 'pure and unsullied'. Only the couple themselves knew the truth of this. The journalist Westmacott, who later wrote scurrilous accounts of Harriot's relationship with Coutts, nonetheless affirmed that prior to their meeting in 1805, during the years 'when the green room of Drury Lane was frequented by the élite of the land, from the accomplished Prince of Wales to the highly polished Colonel Mellish, from Beau Brummell to the wits Jeykill, Tickell and Sheridan', Harriot was an object of admiration to them all but was 'inaccessible'. Her worst enemies could find no gossip even about flirtations. Westmacott thought the actor Ralph Wewitzer was her 'sole mentor and advisor', and speculated that it was he who arranged the terms on which she 'surrendered to old Coutts'. There is no proof of what 'surrender' meant. But between 1805 and 1807 the friendship ripened into a genuine love affair between Harriot Mellon and Thomas Coutts, and it was to last until death parted them.

Chapter VI
THE WAY TO KEEP HIM[1]

A Ten-Year Love Affair

From motives of prudence or affection or both, Harriot Mellon preserved most of the letters she received from her 'protector', Thomas Coutts. As long as Thomas's wife lived, he could not marry her. If he had died before his wife, Harriot might have needed proof that his generous gifts to her had been voluntary, if his family had claimed otherwise. Such careful thought for the future was characteristic of Harriot, though she was also very sentimental and throughout her widowhood she always carried with her a casket containing the letters from Thomas, reading them over and over again for comfort. None of the letters were signed in full: only a few were dated in full. There are a few dating from 1805, but seventy exist for the years 1811 to 1814. Coutts did not keep Harriot's letters, presumably because he did not wish them to fall into the hands of his partners or family, though she wrote to him as frequently as he did to her.

The letters give glimpses of Thomas's home life and the misery caused by his wife's insanity, but they mainly concern relations with Harriot. The earliest letter is touched with affection and apprehension, but is not really a love letter. Dated 25 September 1805, it reads in part as follows,

> I beg you will indulge me with a few lines, conveyed as you did the last, as I am sincerely anxious to hear how you have settled your residence for the winter; also whether your health is perfectly recovered... I am very uneasy not hearing from you. I saw in the Papers that a Lady belonging to the Theatre was about to have a coronet added to her name: it may be You! None

---
[1] A play by Arthur Murphy, in which Harriot played Lady Constant in 1803.

deserve any pre-eminence so well. I hope it will not be a painful pre-eminence.[2]

Already, Thomas was jealous of the possibility that Harriot had other admirers. Two months later, on 11 November 1805, he sent her a birthday letter addressed to 'My dearest Harriot', and although it contains so much financial advice it is nonetheless a love letter. He began by saying that 'preserving so pure a mind with so much natural gaiety and vivacity of temper in the midst of temptations and in a profession which exposes a young and beautiful woman to more danger than any other, is almost a miracle.' By this time, however, he knows all about her business affairs, and is ready to give her advice.

Evidence of Harriot's sound financial status before she met Thomas Coutts is in her business papers. Correspondence between 1801 and 1803 includes a Copy of an Act for settling the customs of the manor of Cheltenham[3] and a copy of Court Rolls clearing up title to land there which Harriot bought for her mother's use.[4] In 1801–1802 she spent £243 on new furniture. A receipt dated 15 November 1803 shows she then received £210 from 'reduced 3% annuities'.[5] Harriot had been investing part of her theatrical earnings and already had a fair amount of income from this, but Coutts regretted that she was not yet financially independent, and promised to help her become so. His letter continued in businesslike terms:

> You have 3500 Reduc'd 3 p.ct producing £105 per annum
> 3500 Cons [Consolidated Fund] 3 p.ct £105 per annum
> 235 Long Anny [Annuity] £235 per annum.
> Total £445 per annum.
>
> The Property Tax doubled next year will take away £44.10s & leave you clear £400.10s.
>
> You have determined, as to the £105 in the 'Reduced', to leave the interest to be accumulated and laid out as it comes due in more of the same Stock; and I wish you should understand and

---

[2] Coutts Bank Archives, 2370.
[3] Coutts Bank Archives, 4910/4.
[4] Coutts Bank Archives, 4910/1 & 2.
[5] Coutts Bank Archives, 2425.

practice management in this way, till you add £105 to your income, in order that you may have a clear Five Hundred Pounds a year. I shall now enable you to purchase £200 p. ann. in the Long Annuities, the income of which you may apply to expenses or how you think fit. As to the £105 in the Consoles 3 p.ct, I certainly think you may freely apply it to procure for yourself any addition you wish for to the present comforts of your life.[6]

In the 1805 birthday letter, Thomas also recommended that, should Harriot marry, she should beforehand 'make over your fortune to trustees, and by your marriage contract secure it to be your own, and the income to be received by yourself as if you had still remained single.' This is not advice one would generally expect to see being given by a man to a woman he hoped to marry. But Coutts knew that the English rich had developed, for the protection of their womenfolk against the provisions of Common Law (under which a woman's property on marriage became her husband's), a system of private law known as Equity which made it possible legally to tie up a woman's fortune so that a prospective husband could not get his hands on it. [Joan Perkin, 1989] Thomas approved of this device, and by it Harriot ensured control of her own money in each of her two marriages.

For almost two years from November 1805 there survive no letters between Thomas and Harriot in the archives, but in the summer of 1807 she was away on tour in Swansea and he was detained in London, by business and his wife's health. If only, he wrote on 31 August, he could step away for half an hour's conversation with Harriot, he could put up with London in August. As it is, faute de mieux he 'takes a look at her dear room', reports the progress as to repairs and decorations, and 'I kiss the paper you are to look upon and beg you to kiss it just here. Your dear lips will then have touched what mine did touch just now'.[7] A birthday letter to Harriot in November said, 'I possess the greatest treasure… the heart of a virtuous affectionate woman'.[8] Further letters were written at long intervals, when Harriot was

---

[6]Coutts Bank Archives, 2371.
[7]Coutts Bank Archives, 2372.
[8]Coutts Bank Archives, 2375.

on tour in the provinces or Thomas had taken his wife on holiday.

Coutts had his family obligations, and could not see Harriot as much as he would have wished, but she had her own family and friends. Now and again her mother stayed with her in Little Russell Street, and sometimes Harriot visited Sarah or stayed with friends. Harriot always had a chaperone such as Sally Stephenson to ensure her respectability. She indulged Sally but later quarrelled with her. Another companion was Eleanor Goddard, niece of Mr Graham, the respected Bow Street magistrate who had the management of Drury Lane Theatre and whose wife became Harriot's patroness. Eleanor became Harriot's companion on condition that she was never brought into the Green Room or dressing room of the theatres – Harriot had another woman to accompany her in her professional duties.[9] Eleanor stayed for nineteen years, leaving because she had become an invalid. Harriot afterwards allowed her a handsome income, and in her will Eleanor was one of the annuitants.

The fact that Harriot had a chaperone did not stop gossip. For example, *The Age* newspaper reported that Harriot's apartments in Little Russell Street were 'very mean' until 'she first blazed forth upon the town by starting a very splendid equipage, a barouche and four horse, and astonished her cockney neighbours, who could not understand how she had acquired this very sudden increase in fortune'. But they could all guess that she had a protector.

By 1806 Harriot's business letters contain correspondence about land she was renting.[10] In October, 1809, Coutts mentioned that he intended to go and look at the house she had bought in Worthing.[11] In February 1810 Sir Henry Tempest offered the lease of Holly Lodge, Highgate – built sometime around 1807 – for 48 years for £3,800 (it had cost him £4,075) or to rent it for 21 years at £300 per annum.[12] On 1 March 1810, Harriot took the lease on the house and nearby property for 48 years, paying by cheque drawn on her account with Wright's Bank; the lease was

---

[9]Margaret Cornwell Baron-Wilson, op. cit., 1839, p.242.
[10]Coutts Bank Archives, 4910/8/11.2, 3 & 11.
[11]Coutts Bank Archives, 2376.
[12]Coutts Bank Archives, 2439.

renegotiated in 1811 for 94 years. In 1815 the land was measured as 41 acres, 2 rods and 4 perches.[13] Harriot purchased three farms at Woodham Walter in Essex in August 1811: Place Farm and Loppice Wood (135 acres), Sheepens Farm (136 acres) and Tobits Farm (100 acres).[14] In an undated letter, Sir Henry Tempest told Harriot his valuation of two of these farms had been too high at £4,500; he said £4,000 should have been the maximum.[15] Regarding one of these purchases, Coutts wrote to Harriot on 16 March 1813,

> The delay respecting the Essex estate is really intolerable… You mention a sum of money You are it seems call'd upon to pay of £270 (I Presume when the conveyance is finally completed). I do not remember to have heard of this before – one thing however I am sure of, viz that you should never pay the money until you see the Engagement by which you may justly be call'd upon… and also you must be satisfied that it is a fair and just demand – and finally they must give you a receipt in full of the same…[16]

Harriot learned much from Coutts's businesslike attitudes. In June 1813 she bought Whitehouse Farm, in Essex, for £3,458. 16s. 5d.[17] In August 1813 she bought at auction land and cottages in Cheltenham for £2,424. 4s.[18] In September 1813 she bought the Manor and Farms at Woodham Walter for £30,000,[19] and in December 1813 she bought the lordship of the Manor of Woodham Walter for £95.14s.2d.[20] The farms were let out to tenants, and details of Harriot's farming income were kept carefully.[21] In 1813, Sir Henry Tempest wrote to Harriot saying that she had told him to pay £20,000 or guineas for an estate; he had got it for £18,000 and he complained that now Harriot was querying the one and a half per cent commission he was making

---

[13]Coutts Bank Archives, 4922/17.
[14]Coutts Bank Archives, 4910.
[15]Coutts Bank Archives, 4910/9/14.
[16]Coutts Bank Archives, 2385.
[17]Coutts Bank Archives, 2431.
[18]Coutts Bank Archives, 2432.
[19]Coutts Bank Archives, 4912/10/2.
[20]Coutts Bank Archives, 4910/6.
[21]Coutts Bank Archives, 4910/12.

as go-between.[22] Tempest thought she was being a skinflint: she just thought she was being careful.

Harriot had repair work done on her house in Little Russell Street, spending almost £1,500 in 1812, and around £2,000 in 1813, as well as buying more furniture.[23] On 20 January 1813, Mr Grant, who was supervising the work, queried some of the repair bills and had the bill reduced from £543 to £500; the tradesman wrote to him saying Miss Mellon was always a prompt payer of bills and he was anxious not to lose her as a client.[24] On 6 October 1812 Harriot paid quarterly taxes as follows:

window duty £14.8s.9d; House duty £11.6s.8d;
male servants duty £3.2s.0d; duty on carriages with 4 wheels £6;
horse duty £1.8s.9d; dog tax £1.1s.0d,
a total of £37.7s.10d.[25]

She was also paying £25 a year property tax; £7.15s.0d. for fire damage and life insurance; and £9.6s.3d government duty on 31 Henrietta Street.[26]

Between 1805 and 1815 Thomas Coutts settled on Harriot large sums of money, enabling her to buy properties and furnish her houses, and he loaded her with presents of plate and jewels. When Thomas died in 1822, Harriot's private fortune, over and above that of her husband's estate, was said to be at least £200,000, larger than most gentry families. Harriot's lavish lifestyle before her marriage, and her regular high investments – for example in June 1813 Harriot purchased £10,000 3% Consuls[27] – must have been funded by Coutts, though such dealings were kept in his very secret accounts which are not open to view.

The story of Harriot winning a fortune with a lottery ticket appeared for the first time in *The Satirist* of 17 September 1808: it reported that since she had obtained a prize in the lottery, 'the

---

[22]Coutts Bank Archives, 4910/10/13.
[23]Coutts Bank Archives, 7532–7568.
[24]Coutts Bank Archives, 7564.
[25]Coutts Bank Archives, 7921/1–17.
[26]Coutts Bank Archives, 7921/4.
[27]Coutts Bank Archives, 22429.

stage was looked upon as a secondary object, and rather used as an ostensible than a necessary profession'. The amount she had won was not specified, but Harriot said she drew a prize of £5,000. Anne Mathews said Harriot often speculated on the lottery, and that Coutts used this as a stratagem for augmenting her income. Among Harriot's papers there is a lottery ticket for the First Lottery of 1815, to be drawn in November, on which Harriot wrote, 'I shall get a prize signed H. Coutts'[28] (a hint of a present?), so she was still buying lottery tickets after she married, though there is no indication of what she won on that occasion. The story of the lottery ticket was revived by Percy Wyndham in 1822. His scurrilous tract said the lottery ticket was a fraud, that £10,000 was the price of an assignation, and that the broker who arranged the terms was the actor, Ralph Wewitzer. In the even more scurrilous *A Tale of the last Century: The Secret Memoirs of Harriott Pumpkin*,[29] Harriot was alleged to have said of Coutts's proposal to be her protector, 'What would the world say of me?' and Wewitzer is alleged to have replied, 'That you are a sensible woman. Damn your reputation – are you bent upon fagging all the days of your life, and become a poor old woman at your death?' Coutts allegedly also suggested it be reported she had won £10,000 in a lottery, to lull suspicions as to where her new income was coming from. This story was to dog Harriot for the rest of her life. Clearly, however, an actress of the second rank was not rich enough from her earnings to entertain sumptuously, gain credit for charity on a large scale, and keep her own carriage, as Harriot did. So the gossip of the Green Room supplied plenty of copy for the journalists, in an age full of the scandals of the rich and famous.

What difference did Harriot's relationship with Thomas Coutts make to her professional career? Certain it is that she continued to act full time until her marriage. The Drury Lane season began on 20 September 1805 with Harriot playing Volante in Tobin's *The Honeymoon*,[30] the part which had made her famous earlier in the year. During 1806, an artist made a drawing of

---

[28]Coutts Bank Archives, 15468.

[29]*A Tale Of The Last Century: The Secret Memoirs of Harriott Pumpkin*, 1825.

[30]Tobin, *The Honeymoon*.

Harriot in the character of 'The Comic Muse', which was afterwards engraved and published. Though it is somewhat melancholy, it was said by contemporaries to have been a good likeness. The costume was decorous, the robes having sleeves halfway down to the elbows and the drapery fastened high and close round the shoulders. Yet her mother lectured Harriot on the painter's imprudence in publishing 'such an improper picture'.

By 1806 Harriot Mellon was a stage celebrity, but she was overwhelmed by the 'Master Betty' craze which dominated the theatre at the time. The precocious boy actor was as marvellous in comedy as he was in tragedy. Harriot was praised for her appearance as Miss Biddy in *Miss in Her Teens*,[31] but appearing in it alongside Master Betty as Captain Flash was barely to be endured, she said!

Harriot had no luck in December 1806 with her leading part of Melisinda, in Charles Lamb's play *Mr H.*,[32] a part written specially for her. The piece was thoroughly damned and lasted only one night. The thinness of the plot, the waning of the curiosity as to the meaning of the name *Mr H*, and the lame and impotent conclusion, proved too much for the patience of the audience.

The run of ill luck continued with her part in a play by Andrew Cherry called *A Day in London*,[33] which ran for only three nights. On 2 June another new play, *Something to Do*,[34] was produced with Mrs Jordan, Miss Mellon, Elliston and Mathews, and this, as John Genest reported, was 'damned'. She had another leading part in Henry Siddons's piece, *Time's a Telltale*,[35] which ran for nine nights in October, 1807. Of this performance *The Monthly Mirror* said it was 'superlatively lame and silly' and remarked unkindly, 'The part of Lady Delmar was very useful for Miss Mellon, who... is only seen to advantage in ladies' maids'. However, Harriot was not the only actor to have a bad time in the 1806–1807 season. Drury Lane had a list of failures that year

---

[31] *Miss in Her Teens*.
[32] Charles Lamb, *Mr H*.
[33] Andrew Cherry, *A Day in London*.
[34] *Something to Do*.
[35] Henry Siddons, *Time's a Telltale*.

which included two tragedies, four comedies, one opera and three farces!

In September 1808, Covent Garden theatre was burned down, and in February 1809 Drury Lane Theatre also burned to the ground. Despite water appliances and the iron curtain for which so much had been claimed, a theatre that had cost £129,000, and still was not completed, was reduced to ashes. It was a staggering blow to Sheridan. The theatre was insured for only about a quarter of the sum which he and his partners had invested in it. Harriot gave thirty of her fellow actresses a warm bath cloak each, and other clothing, to help make up for the costumes they had lost, but some people unkindly called these cloaks 'the Mellon livery'.

The Lord Chamberlain agreed to allow the Drury Lane company to use the Lyceum theatre until a new theatre could be built. There Harriot had another unfortunate part in a short-lived farce called *Sharpset*.[36] However, in the summer of 1809 she was in Plymouth and had great success at the theatre there, for her patron, Lady Duckworth, was the wife of the port admiral. But new rivals were coming into prominence at Drury Lane, and Harriot was not called on as often as before. A letter from Thomas dated 1 November 1809 mentions her not being well, and says, 'You must be kept quiet and you must give up the stage – you should do it decidedly at once'.[37] But Harriot had a mind of her own and did not give up her career. The printed Articles of Agreement between the Theatre Royal, Drury Lane, and Harriot Mellon, dated 24 July 1812 show that she was given a three-year contract, and was paid £11 a week for the first season and £12 a week for the second and third seasons.[38]

Drury Lane Theatre opened again on 10 October 1812 with an address written by Lord Byron and delivered by the actor Elliston. The play was *Hamlet*[39] and the farce *The Devil to Pay*,[40] with Harriot playing Nell. Because of her increasing size she was

---

[36]*Sharpset*.
[37]Coutts Bank Archives, 2377.
[38]Coutts Bank Archives, 15774.
[39]*Hamlet*.
[40]*The Devil to Pay*.

forced to abandon some of the younger roles she had been playing, and she became a target for the caricaturists. A Cruikshank engraving dated 1 December 1812 is a satire on the management of Drury Lane theatre; on the extreme left is a throne-like settee with an ornate canopy, on which are seated a tall emaciated old man and a youngish woman with much-exposed breasts, who holds a melon to which she points with an imperious gesture. From the man's pocket hangs a paper entitled 'Mellon payable at Coutts'. In front of them, grinning and posturing, stands Skeffington, pointing at the lady, and displaying to Coutts a paper inscribed 'The Vertious Cortezan or generous Cut Throat MS'.[41]

Coutts continued to discourage Harriot from acting and on 30 June 1813 wrote to her, 'I am sure my opinion was strongly against your acting at the Lyceum – it appears to me that these gentlewomen, with or without name, who have these irregular Benefits – are never good for much'.[42] On 2 July he wrote again, 'I see you will act at The Close on Monday, 5th. The papers say the dispute in The Haymarket will keep it closed all the summer.'

The Theatrical Inquizitor, in its list of the new Drury Lane company, did not include Harriot Mellon, which is curious since she had a contract, but she was listed in 1814 among 'Ladies for Tragedy, Comedy, Farce, Opera and Melodrama'. However, the only actor who really interested managements at that time was Edmund Kean; Harriot was friendly with him and supported him and his family in the three months between his arrival in London and first appearance on the stage. She told him after his first performance in London, 'take the advice of one who understands theatrical management and do not be hasty in signing your articles'. He took her advice and eventually got £20 a week instead of the £8 first offered. Kean, who generally did not like the rich, always spoke of Harriot in terms of admiration.

As the end of 1814 drew near, it was generally understood that Harriot would not act much longer. The first Mrs Coutts died on 4 January 1815. Harriot's final appearance on the stage was as

---

[41] George, 1949, vol.IX, p.161.
[42] Coutts Bank Archives, 2390.

Audrey in *As You Like It*[43] on the 7 February. Mrs Baron-Wilson says Coutts was in his box at the theatre, and he disapproved of Harriot's costume – a black velvet hat, a yellow jacket laced with black velvet, a full and rather short striped petticoat, buckle shoes and yellow silk stockings. Thomas said he would have no more of her appearing thus for gloating admirers in the pit and boxes. So Harriot returned to the stage for the final curtain, curtsied to the audience, and left without anyone knowing her retirement was to be permanent – or that she had already gone through a wedding ceremony with Coutts.

To sum up Harriot Mellon as an actress, it must be admitted that although she was popular, she never reached the high level of her model, Dorothy Jordan, who was original, artistic and painstaking. Harriot's range was not extensive, though she was excellent in comedy characters where nothing was required beyond being her natural self. She was an excellent mimic and a good understudy, but when she took the parts usually played by Eliza Farren, for example, the artificial graces of a society lady of the period did not come naturally to her, so her imitations of the genteel were no more than respectable. Anne Mathews's opinion of Harriot was,

> Were we to require to name a model for Sheridan's heroine we should say that Miss Mellon at the time she married Mr Coutts was in all externals (and some essentials) the beau ideal of what Lady Teazle ought to appear – namely, a young glowing beauty, endued with great natural powers of mind, talents and vivacity, but with all these bearing about her an insuperable rusticity of air and manners.

When she left the theatre, Harriot did not forget her old friends and associates. Tom Dibdin praised her defence of actors,

> Nothing could more offend her than an illiberal remark, tending to bring actors, and more particularly actresses, into disrepute…a young man one evening gave publicly as his opinion that actresses had no moral principles (Harriot being an honourable exception).

---

[43]*As You Like It.*

Harriot... vowed never to see the young man again, and she carried out her vow.

Before their mother died, Thomas Coutts's daughters were friendly with Harriot. *The Essex Herald* of 19 December 1837 (after Harriot's death) recalled events of around 1807:

> Those whose play-going memories extend to 30 years back may remember Miss Mellon being frequently seen in the private box with Mr Coutts's family at Drury Lane, between the intervals of the play; and her professional contemporaries were often amused by telegraphic signals of his grandchildren during her acting. In Little Russell Street her humble neighbours used to reckon as a matter of curiosity the number of carriages at her door, and to watch the daughters of Mr Coutts (then Marchioness of Bute, Countess of Guilford and Lady Burdett) calling to see the young actress.

The enhanced personal fortunes of Coutts's daughters depended on the goodwill of their wealthy father (though they all had rich husbands), and as long as their mother lived they made the best of a delicate situation in regard to Harriot. The relationship was an open one. Thomas sent Harriot at least one letter by Lady Burdett;[44] in another he wrote, 'Lady G has whispered to me that she should go to the Strand today and meant if possible to call upon you'[45] and added in another, 'Lady G loves you extremely.' Judging by Lady Guilford's later behaviour this may be doubted, but her letters to Harriot in 1811 were very friendly: one dated 14 June[46] ends, 'Yours affectionately'; one dated 21 July[47] ends, 'God help you, my sweet friend, ever ever yours'; and one dated 30 November[48] shows her acting as a willing go-between,

> I am happy to confirm my report of this morning. [Papa] is charmingly well – what a blessing! and Oh, how thankful we all are! Dr Pearson has prevailed upon him to make assurance

---

[44]Coutts Bank Archives, 2381.
[45]Coutts Bank Archives, 2379.
[46]Coutts Bank Archives, 1116.
[47]Coutts Bank Archives, 1117.
[48]Coutts Bank Archives, 1119.

double sure, not to go out tomorrow. I have told him what we agreed; so you will write a line to-morrow as if you were going to Highgate and I think it would be very prudent to say 'I rather fear I shall be obliged to go again tomorrow' (meaning Wednesday), for if we can keep him at home another day I feel confident it will be safer. Take no notice of what I have said, only that I told you he had a little swelling in the face. Soon after three I shall hope to see a letter.

God bless you! I told him I was going to send something to you this evening... If he sends a note I shall enclose it in this.

Farewell!

Coutts's daughters and their husbands often visited Harriot. In June 1813 Thomas referred to a visit proposed by his daughter Fanny and her husband Lord Bute, whom Coutts clearly did not like, to Harriot's home in Highgate,

I hope nothing has occurred to prevent my dear Fanny's visit to Holly Lodge. If so I wish that I had been with you instead of Lord Bute, who, by a letter from dearest Fanny today, has insisted on going with her. I wish he had instead insisted on staying at home. You would both have been happier without him, or the honour of his presence.

The daughters probably hoped that their mother would outlive their father, or that his great age and devotion to them would preclude a second marriage. Thomas always gave his first wife the utmost care and consideration, and was clearly devoted to her. On 5 June 1811 he wrote to Harriot that he had taken his wife Susannah to Sidmouth, accompanied by a doctor, and added, 'It is wonderful the change for the better on her appearance and every way yesterday'. On 15 June he wrote, 'My sufferings have been great and I truly thought the awful moment [of her death] was near, but Dr R arrived at nine last night and what he prescribed really worked a miracle, restoring speech, and intelligence of mind, and producing not stupor but really sleep; and she has been better ever since'.[49] In 1813 Susannah was even more gravely ill, 'in a state of fever and irritation... her whole frame shaking, her

---

[49]Coutts Bank Archives, 2382.

lips quivering. If a tiger had come into the room she could not have shown greater signs of fear or agitation.' Thomas thought it was 'a most strange insanity'. He continued, 'I have quite given up all the world. My beard is grown long and I am sure I am a deplorable looking wretch... That Heaven may bless and preserve her is the constant prayer of my poor heart'.[50] These were unusual sentiments for a man to share with his mistress. While staying at Tunbridge Wells in July Thomas said Susannah was 'becoming daily more weak in mind, and more and more unquiet, though in bodily health very well and the appetite rather better'.[51] Soon afterwards he said his daughter, Lady Guilford and the doctor were pressing him to hand over the care of his wife to a nurse, their opinion being that she would be 'more easy and quiet' if she did not see her husband and daughters. About this proposal Thomas wrote in July,[52]

> Lord Bute has written a horrible letter to Lady Guilford which I detest; and I really think Lady G's life and health is quite as much in danger from her sufferings in this sad business as mine, or at least as Lady Bute's, though Lord Bute treats her coarsely, as if she had not the same feelings as we have, which is very untrue.

Writing in September from the home of Lord Bristol, Thomas said; 'It is plain Mrs C. is better without me, which is a sad reflection and makes my heart sink to despair'. An undated letter, probably written in December 1814, spoke of a consultation between physician and doctors with regard to Mrs Coutts's state of health, but there was no hint of crisis.

Susannah Coutts died in January 1815. According to Mrs Baron-Wilson, in early December 1814 Mrs Coutts accidentally overturned a quantity of boiling water over her shoulders, arms and chest, and 'after lingering three weeks in such pain that those who loved her most prayed for her release, she died at four o'clock in the morning of the fourth of January, 1815'. She was buried in the chancel of the parish church of All Saints, Wroxton,

---

[50]Coutts Bank Archives, 2402.
[51]Coutts Bank Archives, 2386.
[52]Coutts Bank Archives, 2395.

near Banbury, Oxfordshire, in the family vault of the Earl of Guilford, on 14th January, 1815. The funeral cortege would have taken several days to cover the seventy-five miles from London. There is, however, no contemporary record of the death and funeral of Susannah Coutts.

What is certain is that Thomas Coutts wished as soon as possible to marry Harriot. As Anne Mathews remarked, 'Mr Coutts's advanced age and precarious life rendered delay hazardous to his intention to provide for Miss Mellon as his widow.' Yet the marriage, between two people for whom there was no legal hindrance, was to cause endless scandal and recriminations.

Chapter VII
THE WEDDING DAY[1]

The Marriage Of Harriot Mellon And Thomas Coutts

On 18 January 1815, four days after his wife was buried, Thomas Coutts and Harriot Mellon were married at old St Pancras Church. On the day before, Harriot attended at the Archbishop's principal registry and obtained an ordinary marriage licence. On the same day, she and Thomas signed a pre-contract of marriage:

> Whereas a Marriage is in Contemplation… between Thomas Coutts of The Strand…and Harriot Mellon… of Holly Lodge Highgate. This agreement is to declare The terms on which the same is consented to by The partys thereto. First the said Harriot Mellon being now possess'd of her own right of certain real copyhold estates and personal property in The Countys of Essex and Middlesex and at Cheltenham in Gloucestershire, and of Stock in various Public Stocks or funds in her own name, Jewels Silver Plate and securities for money and money in the hands of her Bankers in London That she shall still continue to hold & enjoy the same and it is hereby agreed between The partys that all the property of the said Harriot Mellon aforesaid shall be always and entirely at her own sole disposal and command the same as if she was still unmarried….
>
> Finally The said Thomas Coutts binds and obliges himself & agrees to provide to the use of the said Harriot Mellon in case she should survive him one perfect and clear annuity of One Thousand pounds free from all Taxes or deductions … for all the Life of the said Harriot Mellon…

As we have seen, Coutts had already advised Harriot that when she married she should by her marriage contract secure her

---

[1] A play by Elizabeth Inchbald, in which Harriot appeared as Lady Contest in 1801.

fortune to be her own. This she did. Thomas was clearly a man who wanted his wife to be completely financially independent. On the other hand, at the time of their marriage he intended that if he died before Harriot, her only claim on his estate was to be an annuity of £1,000 a year. In view of her inheritance of his whole fortune as a widow only seven years later, it is important to bear this in mind. We shall see why he changed his mind.

Thomas and Harriot continued to live apart for some weeks after their secret marriage, and no official announcement was made, presumably to avoid gossip. From that time on, however, they regarded themselves as man and wife, and to the day of his death Coutts kept the 18th January as the anniversary of his second marriage. However, this proved to be mistaken, as we shall see. A note from Thomas to Harriot, written in February 1815,[2] spoke of 'our being made one for ever in the sight of Heaven' and one dated 11 February 1815 said, 'Good night, sweet Harriot, Lovely Coutts, Kind charming Wife, Friend, everything to me!'[3] Another dated 20 February 1815, was addressed to 'Harriot Coutts, wife of Thomas Coutts, private wife of Thomas Coutts Esq. Private' and said, 'The best and kindest and most affectionate wife in England, and if in England, in the world'. It was signed, 'Erisipelus' (sic).[4] Coutts was at the time confined to bed with an attack of erysipelas of the leg.

Why the marriage ceremony was contrived with such haste and secrecy, since there was no legal impediment to it, needs explanation. When it became known, many thought Thomas himself was to blame, since he was determined to make Harriot his wife indecently soon after the death of his first wife. Harriot, too, was anxious not to flout convention, knowing that an early marriage would create a bad impression with Coutts's family and London society. But Thomas was an old man, worried about how long he would live, and on these grounds she was persuaded to marry before the conventional period of mourning had elapsed. A factor which may have influenced her was that the Earl of Derby had married the actress Eliza Farren just six weeks after the death

---

[2]Coutts Bank Archives, 2504.
[3]Coutts Bank Archives, 2404.
[4]Coutts Bank Archives, 17077.

of his first wife in 1797, and gossip about that had soon died down. Doubtless she and Thomas hoped to avoid remonstrations from his daughters, whom he adored and whose tears he feared, and they hoped a fait accompli would eventually be accepted. In particular, Thomas was anxious to avoid arguments with his son-in-law, Sir Francis Burdett, ever a difficult person to deal with. He may have been afraid his children would question his sanity in making such a marriage, and indeed later Burdett threatened as much, but in fact Coutts was as shrewd in business in 1815 as he had ever been. He may have lacked moral courage in keeping his second marriage secret for a time (as he had also kept secret his first marriage), but he was not in his dotage.

Coutts devised a scheme for preparing his daughters for the news of his second marriage, by making over to them handsome money gifts and assurances of future support. Clearly Harriot knew all about the arrangements, since his letter to her dated simply 'February 1815' reads,

> I have given [Lady Guilford] my paper which you have seen (that lay with my will) but I rather think she has not yet read it. If I hear nothing from her by next Monday I will ask it from her again and send it to Lady Bute and acquaint Lady G. with 'The Happy Wednesday at St Pancras,' and a week after my paper goes I will acquaint Lady Bute of the same. Lady G. will probably tell Lady Burdett and I think I fully desire her to do so.[5]

Just what Thomas said to his daughters about Harriot at this time is not clear, but he did not yet tell them of the marriage. On 24 February 1815 Lady Guilford wrote to him as follows, obviously wanting to humour him,

> After all you have written what can I say to you respecting Miss Mellon? I should not speak the truth were I to say I considered that day as happy when you first met her at Cheltenham, or that if I could recall that day I would not. But no doubt all that IS permitted is to be considered as desirable in spite of all appearances and wishes – still there is something attached to this connexion which strikes at my heart. I cannot, cannot help it, and

---
[5]Coutts Bank Archives, 2405.

you must forgive me! – but I will certainly fulfil to the utmost your request [to be kind to Miss Mellon] as long as the Almighty in his infinite goodness is pleased to grant me life and capacity and with happiness too will I fulfil it in the full confidence that my dear Mama who is looking upon me must approve – as I do because it is YOUR wish…[6]

Lady Burdett wrote to her father in similar terms on 24 or 25 February.

> The instance in which I am so favour'd by heaven as to be able to satisfy you of my entire submission to your requests is in that which relates to Miss Mellon, and that kindness you ask of me to bestow upon her (supposing me to outlive your own dear self.)[7]

At this point, clearly neither daughter realised that the marriage had taken place. On 25 February Thomas wrote to Harriot:

> In the course of the week, perhaps before I see you, I shall communicate our happy marriage to both ladies here – on Tuesday sennight I shall inform Lady Bute… We shall then see how they receive it, or what they intend to do in consequence. Whatever it may be cannot make me unhappy… but I shall be much pleased to see them quiet and comfortable and I trust in Heaven and think surely the time will come when all will be pleased and content and see clearly the blessing you are to me and how happy you can make them all…[8]

Coutts was nervous about telling his daughters, and with good reason as it turned out, but before the end of February the daughters had discovered that their father had married again. On March 1815 *The Times* announced the event very briefly and somewhat evasively: 'On Wednesday at St Pancras Church, Middlesex, Thomas Coutts Esq., to Miss Harriot Mellon, of Holly Lodge, Highgate.' Now 2 March was a Thursday, so the casual reader would have supposed that the marriage had taken place the day before, rather than six weeks earlier. For the time

---

[6]E Coleridge, *The Life of Thomas Coutts, Banker*, 2 vols., 1920, p.323.
[7]E Coleridge, op. cit., p.326.
[8]Coutts Bank Archives, 2407.

being a March wedding was assumed, and congratulations appeared in *The Morning Post*. However, there was to be a scandal over the marriage. They did not know this, but the ceremony at St Pancras Church on the 18th January was technically an illegal marriage. Alongside the entry in the Marriage Register it states that it was illegally solemnised. It was later said there had been no second witness to the ceremony, but possibly it was performed before or after canonical hours, or the doors of the church were kept locked to ensure secrecy; any of these irregularities would have made the marriage illegal. The role of the curate who conducted the ceremony, Mr Champneys, was clearly devious; the most charitable view is that he was persuaded (and well paid) to conduct the marriage ceremony in the strictest possible secrecy, and that he got the signature of a second witness (who was in fact not there) and also entered two bogus marriages which filled up the page, hoping that the Vicar and the clerk would not notice the Coutts marriage. The Vicar noticed nothing amiss until his attention was called (probably by Coutts's daughters) to an important marriage ceremony having been performed without his consent and knowledge; he checked and (no doubt to the delight of the family) realised it did not comply with the terms of the Marriage Act. Since he was likely to be held responsible for any illegal act or mistakes made by the curate, he covered himself by putting a note against the entry in the register. The curate, Mr Champneys, was suspended from his post on 31 March, but was neither prosecuted, fined nor imprisoned for his 'offence'. Gossip said Coutts compensated Champneys for the loss of his job; if true it would not prove that he had asked the curate to commit an illegal act.

In late March Thomas and Harriot realised they must go through a second wedding ceremony. Once again, on 12 April 1815, a marriage by licence was performed at St Pancras Church by a new curate, the Rev W Fallofield. It is not known whether the old licence, which had not expired, was used again, or whether another licence was obtained from the Bishop of London's registry or the Faculty Office, but this time there was no irregularity. James Grant Raymond, Stage Manager at Drury Lane Theatre, an old friend of Harriot, who witnessed both the illegal and the legal marriages at St Pancras, 'gave Harriot away' at the ceremony.

Gossip regarding the Coutts marriage did not die down, although events of much greater national importance were taking place. In April 1815 Princess Charlotte, heir to the throne, married Prince Leopold of Saxe-Coburg-Saalfeld. From early March there had also been great world-wide excitement to report. Napoleon escaped from Elba and landed in France. His soldiers rallied in their thousands to their old leader and he advanced triumphantly upon Paris. At the beginning of June 1815, Napoleon defeated the Prussians at the battle of Ligny and the fate of Europe lay in the impending battle on the soil of Flanders between the Duke of Wellington's army of some 80,000 men and Bonaparte's with some 100,000. The losses on both sides were appalling, and it was not at first clear who had won the battle, but Napoleon knew he had lost and gave himself up to the British. On 22 June he abdicated for the second time and was exiled to St Helena.

Compared with all this, what happened in particular lives seemed small and insignificant events. But the public appetite for scandal seemed unquenchable, and perhaps money mattered more in Regency society than anything else. So the Coutts marriage was eagerly discussed throughout the year.

The year of Harriot's marriage was also the year her mother, Sarah Entwisle, died. She did not invite her mother and stepfather to her wedding, knowing they would have been unable to keep the secret. In any case, relations with her parents had not been cordial for some time.

During Harriot's ten-year relationship with Thomas Coutts before they married, Sarah lived in perpetual fear that her daughter might make an imprudent marriage with some young penniless admirer. The improvement in Harriot's fortunes had brought many gains to the Entwisles. Apart from other gifts, Harriot paid her mother an annuity of £200.[9] However, Sarah was always begging extra money from Harriot, and was not above

---

[9]Coutts Bank Archives, 2422.

playing mean tricks on her. Once she pretended she had sent a £50 note, in mistake for a £1 note, to some unfortunate actress who had asked for help, and she asked her daughter to make up to her the £49 she said she had lost. Harriot did not believe her, knowing her mother was far too keen on money to make such an error, and told her so. Her mother was resentful but did not pursue the matter further. But she was often angry about money that Harriot gave to people outside the family, and this Harriot found a very unpleasant side of her character, since she had not always been so uncharitable. Sarah was said to have spent a lot of time brewing fine ale (which was her passion) and to have been cheerful and full of jokes when she was in good humour.

Thomas Entwisle, Harriot's stepfather, became 'sedentary, epicurean in his tastes, and very corpulent' as he grew older. It was explained earlier that around 1805 Harriot obtained for him, through her connections with royalty, the job of postmaster at Cheltenham, which he nearly lost through incompetence. Entwisle wrote to Harriot soon after this, saying how annoyed he was about the attacks made upon him in *The Morning Herald* on the way he conducted the post office in Cheltenham, allegations he said were false. He threatened to prosecute the editor of the paper, but never did. He also acknowledged the curtains and pictures Harriot had sent to her mother, and gave a list of other things they wanted, asking for reimbursement of £60 for 'bell hangings'.[10] In October 1812, Harriot sent Coutts a letter she had received from her stepfather, responding to one in which she had refused an unreasonable demand for money,

> I received your kind letter. I have made myself a beggar, and your Mother a most unhappy wretch – never knowing my circumstances till now – and God forgive you for it! If you was as severe with the wretches about you as you are with me, you would not be so played upon... God almighty bless you with it! Your mother's heart is broken with your letter to me. You know it is not in my power to relieve her. I have made her a beggar to serve you. Ask your friend's advice about this, he has a family of

---

[10] Coutts Bank Archives, 2448.

his own. Your mother is now thrown upon a sick bed, in consequence, and if you wish to add to it return this letter.

Ungrateful Harriot Mellon!
T Entwisle
P.S. Be sure you let your friend see this.

Thomas said he suspected Entwisle was using her mother's illness 'to get back his lost power over her'. Coutts strongly believed in a child's duty to parents, but knew Harriot had always 'done more than her duty' to the Entwisles, though they were never satisfied by her generosity.[11] In a further letter he said Entwisle was 'a worthless, unfeeling brute, who knowing your feelings for your mother endeavours to work upon them and frighten you for his own immediate profit and to get at your money'.[12] The demands continued, and Thomas wrote, 'They have been accustomed to make you their instrument or Handle, and do not like to give up doing so – But they have no right to half what you do for them'.[13]

A letter of 29 December 1813 shows that Harriot paid for water damage repairs to the Entwisle house in Cheltenham, which had occurred as a result of 'the overflow of the Springs',[14] but there is no further correspondence in the archives until Good Friday, 1815 when Entwisle wrote from Cheltenham as follows (using the formal address 'My dear Mrs Coutts')

> Your mother was much better yesterday... I wish I could say she was so well today – she appears heartbroke that she shall never see you again – pray write to her. Dr Jenner has just been to her and speaks very favourable of her, but my fears and doubts are not removed. Pray heaven bless you! she has been two days disappointed in your not writing... I did get her to eat about half an ounce of boiled mutton to-day and take a glass of wine.
>
> I am, My dear Mrs Coutts,
> Yours most affectionately,
> T. Entwisle.[15]

---

[11] Coutts Bank Archives, 2484.
[12] Coutts Bank Archives, 2480.
[13] Coutts Bank Archives, 2460.
[14] Coutts Bank Archives, 2435.
[15] Coutts Bank Archives, 2445.

Harriot wrote to Sarah, and an undated reply from Entwisle said,

> Your letter today made your Mother a little comfortabler than she was – and where you expressed to embrace her once more I thought she would have fainted – and said she hoped in God you would – she wished much she could come to town but that is impossible in her present state and I am afraid she never will be better. She says she has lost (or somebody has stolen it) a pocket Handkerchief marked with her name in full – did you ever know she had such a thing – also I heard her tell Mrs Hunt that she should write to you or Miss Goddard to desire you would give her a diamond brooch that Morriset gave you... she knows nothing of my having sent the bills... she has had your letter read four times – she is in a most dreadful flood of Tears – she is sick every quarter of an hour...[16]

In fact, Thomas Entwisle was not exaggerating his wife's illness at this point, and Sarah died early in May, 1815, aged 63 years. Entwisle sent Harriot an account of the elaborate funeral expenses, which totalled £659.16s.7d., an amazing sum, which Harriot paid though she did not attend the funeral. She told Mrs Baron-Wilson that Sarah had 700 guineas (£735) in the house at the time of her death, despite telling Harriot that she was poverty-stricken.

Thomas Entwisle refused Harriot's offer 'to be settled in a cottage on the banks of the Thames with an annuity of £500', but he continued to pester her for money, which she supplied, as letters between Harriot and Thomas make clear. As long as he lived, Entwisle was made welcome at Harriot's London homes, despite his habits, such as heavy drinking, which were distasteful to Coutts. And some time after his death, when his brother and two sisters were on a visit to London, Harriot had them to stay with her for a month at Holly Lodge, despite the fact that the Countess of Guilford and her daughters were also in the house, and that the portly Misses Entwisle habitually smoked short clay pipes! Dr Thomas Christie notified Coutts on 5 June 1819 that Entwisle was having severe convulsions, and that his state was hopeless, though he had received every care from himself and 'Sir

---

[16]Coutts Bank Archives, 2446.

Arthur'.[17] Harriot had paid for the best possible medical treatment for her stepfather, as she had for her mother. A letter dated 5 June from Mr Cossens in Cheltenham thanks Harriot for entrusting the care of Entwisle's property to him; he said Mr Entwisle had given him instructions about his funeral, which he hoped would meet with Harriot's wishes. Trifles he wished to give to friends had been set out in his Will, and Cossens sent on a list of these to await Harriot's instructions.[18] Entwisle died soon afterwards, and was buried alongside his wife in St Mary's Churchyard at Cheltenham. In the south aisle of the church is a handsome white marble tablet in memory of them both, and in the west side of the churchyard is a gravestone, erected by Harriot in 1832, when she was Duchess of St Albans, for her mother alone.

On 20 August 1819 Sir Edward Antrobus, a partner in Coutts Bank, wrote to Harriot concerning Entwisle's affairs, saying her stepfather had died in debt, and since he hoped Harriot 'would not allow the creditors to suffer' he asked her to pay all the debts before taking possession of the land and cottage in Cheltenham. Harriot accepted his advice. A lawyer's bill dated January 1800 shows that Harriot had 'consented to enable [Entwisle] to complete the purchase on the property, being limited to Mrs Entwisle for her separate use during her life, then to Mr Entwisle for life, with the ultimate remainder to [Harriot]'. Though Harriot had paid for the land and cottage, Entwisle had wanted to appear to be the purchaser, for reasons of status and respectability, and Harriot had agreed to 'gratify him' as long as it did not prejudice her security. The real transaction was stated in a separate deed, but Harriot 'determined that the surrender should be made absolutely to Mrs Entwisle'.[19]

The Earl of Guilford, husband of Coutts's daughter Susan, had died in 1802, before Thomas met Harriot, and there is no indication in their correspondence about how Coutts felt towards him. Towards the Marquess of Bute, husband of his favourite daughter Fanny, Coutts was clearly hostile. On 7 July 1813 he wrote to Harriot, '[Lady G] happily cares little about what his

---

[17]Coutts Bank Archives, 2433.
[18]Coutts Bank Archives, 2434.
[19]Coutts Bank Archives, 2395.

Lordship says or does (and I am sure I care as little) but she refrains from telling him so, or giving him the answer he deserves, for fear of hurting her sister'. Lord Bute died in 1814.

Sir Francis Burdett, husband of Thomas's daughter Sophia, in 1796 became a member of parliament 'in the Newcastle interest' when Coutts bought for him one of the two seats returned by the rotten borough of Boroughbridge.[20] He became the leader of the Radical Parliamentary reformers. His enemy was the 'system' whereby, he believed, Whigs and Tories, both equally corrupt, were interested in nothing but fighting each other for the spoils of office. His enemies charged that his sole aim was to gain the applause of the mob, but Burdett's popularity arose from his efforts to expose the genuine grievances of the day – the increasing weight of taxation in consequence of the war, the continued restraints upon the expression of public opinion, and the abuse of power over those who were offensive to the government.

At the general election of 1802 Burdett stood for the county of Middlesex. He was elected by a considerable majority and sat for several years, during which legal proceedings went on with the object of nullifying the return. He won the Westminster election of 1807 and continued to sit as its member for the next thirty years. He spoke against the practice of corporal punishment in the army, supported inquiries into the selling of army commissions by the Duke of York's mistress, Mary Anne Clarke, alleged parliamentary corruption of ministers, and voted for Whitbread's motion on place-men and pensioners in parliament. He supported John Christian Curwen's Reform Bill. He was the chief thorn in the government's side.

An opportunity at length occurred which seemed to give the government an opportunity of silencing Burdett. A well-known radical orator, John Gale Jones, had been imprisoned by the House of Commons for raising a discussion on the practice of the House excluding strangers. Burdett, moving that Jones be discharged from custody, was supported on a division by only 14 against 153. He thereupon issued to the public a revised edition of

---

[20]Burnett, 1981, p.147.

his speech. It was first printed in Cobbett's *Register*, and subsequently reprinted as a shilling pamphlet, which had an immense sale. Mr Lethbridge was put forward to accuse Burdett of breach of privilege (in reporting debate in Parliament, a trumped up charge considering that Cobbett's Parliamentary Proceedings were currently in print), and a lengthy debate took place as to what to do to him. At length the Speaker of the House of Commons issued a warrant for his arrest, but Burdett refused to surrender except to superior force. On the fourth day of the warrant, a forcible entry was made into Burdett's house, where he was found reading Magna Carta to his small son, and he was conveyed to the Tower, with thousands of soldiers called out to guard the city.

Burdett remained in the Tower for several weeks, until Parliament was prorogued. He brought actions at law against the Speaker and the sergeant-at-arms, but did not succeed in obtaining redress. On the day he left the Tower, he quietly departed by boat along the River Thames. This caused him a temporary loss of popularity, as his constituents had prepared a triumphal procession and were obliged to content themselves with dragging an empty cart through the streets to Piccadilly.

This then was Coutts's flamboyant son-in-law, who lived next door to him as Coutts's non-paying tenant. When, on 9 April 1810, Burdett's house suffered siege and battery, and its tenant was taken prisoner and sent to the Tower of London, Coutts suffered a great deal in mind, if not in person, worried about the safety of his property and the feelings of his wife and his daughters. Whether he urged Sir Francis to hold out or to submit, we do not know. But whatever he felt, he knew it was useless to argue with the headstrong Sir Francis.

Lady Burdett wrote to her daughter Sophia in Wimbledon of these turbulent events:

> In greatest haste and flurry I write to tell you yr Papa was taken from his house this morning between eleven and twelve. A troop of Horse and Magistrates were set to force the doors which yr Papa had ordered to be shut – but thank God he is quite safe and secured tho' in the Tower.

In a later letter, Lady Burdett said:

> Your Papa has very comfortable apartments and is perfectly well –
> that last is the greatest comfort, so I hope all is well that ends well,
> or at least will be well…

Sir Francis was extremely comfortable in prison: a note from him to Thomas Creevey, the diarist on 10 May asked, 'When will [you] come again to dine? You shall have two bottles of claret next time, and as good fish [as before]'[21]

In a letter to Harriot dated 18 April 1810, Coutts merely said, 'Lady Burdett has been uncommonly well and merry these three days, and she is going up to town tomorrow to visit the Prisoner.'

That was the only reference he made to Harriot about what had happened. To others Coutts is said to have written, after Burdett's arrest, that he had not seen Sophia look so well for years![22]

The stage was set for the development of very frosty relations between Burdett, the high-born people's champion, and Harriot, the prudent daughter of the people.

---

[21]E Coleridge, op. cit. 1920, pp.270–272.
[22]Edna Healey, *Lady Unknown*, 1978, p.33.

Chapter VIII
THE DEVIL TO PAY[1]

Family Quarrels over the Marriage

For several months after their marriage, Thomas and Harriot Coutts lived either at Holly Lodge, Highgate, or at No. 17 Southampton Street, Covent Garden. This was because Thomas's daughter, Lady Guilford, who had lived with her parents after her husband's death in 1802, presiding over the household and helping to care for her invalid mother, stayed on in the Stratton Street house.

Through duty and affection to their father, and no doubt an unwillingness to forgo his generosity, Coutts's daughters visited their stepmother in the early months of the marriage. On 7 June 1815, *The Morning Post* reported that, 'The Countess of Guilford with the Ladies North [her daughters] have been rusticating during the last week with Mr and Mrs Coutts at Holly Lodge'. Harriot's position as Mrs Coutts was soon publicly recognised; a portrait of her appeared in *The European Magazine* on 28 April, and Thomas received warm letters of congratulation on his marriage from many friends. Harriot was also accepted into some exalted social circles. To Lord Buchan, on 3 May 1815, Thomas wrote, 'I have been honoured with the Princess's [Mary's] notice as well as of several others of the royal family, male and female'.[2]

The Times of 17 May 1815 reported, 'Yesterday the Prince Regent dined with Mr Coutts at his Highgate Cottage, where there was a select party of distinguished characters to meet His Royal Highness'. The Prince declared Harriot 'a well-bred

---

[1] A play by Charles Coffey in which Harriot played Nell in 1802.
[2] E Coleridge, op. cit., p.329.

woman' and others said, 'Her conversation is generally animated, her temper vivacious, her wit quick and sparkling, but untainted by malice'.[3] Yet with no sense of irony – considering that their own mother had been of lowly birth – Coutts's daughters refused to accept her as their equal, and the quick-tempered Harriot was ready to take offence.

Harriot was not at ease in a highly artificial society which had to accept her as Thomas's wife, but looked down on a former actress. At first sight it seems puzzling that she should entertain Royal Dukes and yet be cold-shouldered by so many aristocrats. But Harriot had yet to learn that royalty and blue-blooded aristocrats were accepted everywhere because of their birth, and bestowed their favours where they wished. So the Duke of Queensberry, one of the most disgusting old reprobates in the Kingdom, was socially acceptable everywhere. Yet polite society would not readily accept a woman of even doubtful virtue, as a former actress was assumed to be. Polite society in 1815 was largely composed of women who had been presented to Queen Charlotte at Court. George III had imposed a regime of propriety which the Queen formalized into a system of stiff etiquette. She refused to receive Lady Hamilton, who carried a Letter of Introduction from the Queen of Naples, because of her association with Lord Nelson. She ostracised Lady Holland, queen of Whig society, because of her previous divorce from Sir Godfrey Webster. As we shall see, Coutts's daughters made sure that Harriot was never presented to Queen Charlotte.

Thomas liked Harriot for what she was. He reminded her that the fashionable ladies of his younger days were not the mealy-mouthed creatures they had later become. He did not approve of loose sexual morals, but he liked women of spirit. He thought Harriot worried too much about saying and writing 'the done thing', telling her,

> If you did not study to express yourself particularly and could divest yourself of all fear or apprehension when you write to any person under whatever circumstances or of whatever rank, you

---

[3] A Person of the First Respectability, 1822, p.10.

can never fail to be approved... To me you always express yourself charmingly.[4]

To his daughter Lady Burdett, Thomas wrote in 1816:

> My wife... is of a most sensitive and feeling disposition, alive in a strong degree to every act of kindness shown her, but miserable at the smallest slight from those she loves and wishes to be in harmony with. While she feels herself cruelly treated, she is sensible she does not deserve it, but still cannot bear it, especially from any near connection of mine...

To Harriot, he wrote in April 1816

> Never regard nor be uneasy about what envious, malicious enemies can say against you; recall to your remembrance your kind, affectionate love and fidelity to me, the happiness and unbounded confidence in which we lived together, and the truly affectionate and devoted heart of your dear Husband... Thomas Coutts.

On the outside of this letter, Harriot wrote, 'God bless you, my kind, affectionate Tom, for this invaluable letter'.[5]

The Marquess of Bristol was a good friend to Coutts, and from his letters a man of balanced judgment and a peacemaker. A letter presumably written in early 1815, concerning Lady Guilford, reminded Thomas that his wife had only recently died, and his second marriage had followed quickly, so it was understandable that it would take time for Susan to accept the situation.[6]

Lord Erskine, the Lord Chancellor, another friend to Coutts, was deeply concerned about the family quarrel. His letter dated 25 September 1815, suggests there was then a truce: 'The manner in which you are now surrounded by your descendants must be peculiarly gratifying to Mrs Coutts, as it proves what the combination of good sense and good feeling can accomplish. I

---

[4]Coutts Bank Archives, 2393.
[5]Coutts Bank Archives, 2703.
[6]Coutts Bank Archives, 6241.

verily believe she has established a permanent union of confidence and kindness'. Erskine always praised Harriot, congratulating Thomas on his wisdom 'in selecting such a Hostess at your social board, so capable of dispensing pleasure to all around her, combining (which so rarely happens) the gaiest deportment with the most exemplary prudence and with so undivided an attention for yourself...'[7]

There were virtues and faults on both sides in the Coutts family quarrels: Lady Bute (Fanny) was Thomas's favourite child, and there was deep affection between them. She suffered ill health and after the death of her husband in 1814 she lived abroad in Italy. Her early relations with Harriot were cordial, and she did what she could to heal the breach between her father and her sisters. However, Lady Guilford and Lady Burdett were constantly reporting to Fanny grievances about Harriot, and the quarrel came to a head when Susan, Lady Guilford, refused to live in her father's house any longer if his new wife was to be its mistress. Not surprisingly, Thomas told her to accept his wife as lawful mistress or leave, but Susan then said her father had turned her out. In fact, she retreated to a house in Putney that her father had bought for her.

So Harriot took over as mistress of the great house in Stratton Street. But Thomas Coutts had surprising news for his family about this; in a letter to Fanny, dated 22 December 1815, answering her rebuke to him for 'turning Susan out', he said he and Harriot had wished to live at Stratton Street with Susan and her children, but this had become impossible because of Susan's behaviour. He felt Susan had turned him out of the house rather than the opposite. He then dropped a bombshell,

> I have sold the Houses to Mrs Coutts's Trustees. The houses in Stratton Street and Piccadilly are now belonging to the best of women who preserves my Life, my Health and my Comfort... it is obvious she will be more at her ease by the house being her own property... I sold her these houses for thirty thousand pounds and she sold out of the Stocks and paid me – which money will go into the mass of my fortune and you all three will

---

[7]E Coleridge, op. cit., p.363.

share it. Therefore I take nothing from Susan. She and her children may live with my wife and me until we die. [Coutts justified his decision to sell the houses by saying,] 'I have lent an enormous sum to the Duke of York, and indeed nearly the same to several old friends of my House in the Strand. I bought and paid for two country houses for Susan, and spend a good deal by having so many Establishments, so that I really wanted the money which Harriot had always been begging me to take of hers, which I felt to be injustice'.[8]

This letter of 22 December 1815 is interesting because it not only makes clear Thomas's belief in Harriot's goodness, but indicates that he still expected to leave most of his fortune to his daughters. His judgment was excellent in most ways, though he attributed to Harriot some attitudes that were more his than hers. For example, it proved true that she wanted above all to comfort Thomas and make the evening of his life happy; and she would gladly have given him her money if he had needed it. But to say 'she is a person quite regardless of Pomp and ostentation' who would 'prefer living in a small but clean and neat House rather than in any House in Grosvenor Square or such as are inhabited by The People of the first rank and fortune in England' shows that he perhaps underestimated her social ambitions. He also judged Harriot prematurely when he said, 'I am confident when I die she will never wish to live in [Stratton St]… and I am sure she will readily sell [the two houses] to any of my children if they wish it.'

Coutts had years earlier joined by an interconnecting door his house in Stratton Street to the one next door, where his daughter Sophia and Sir Francis Burdett lived. When Harriot bought their house, they were furious. A letter from Thomas to Sophia some months later said,

> (Sir Francis) wrote to me he considered himself degraded by remaining in the Piccadilly House, and proposed going immediately to an Hotel. Therefore I think he must be much more degraded by staying there for months. Most true is it that neither Mrs Coutts or myself could ever have even wished you to leave it. But indeed, my dearest Sophia, earnestly as I ever did and

---

[8]Coutts Bank Archives, 2414.

ever shall wish to promote your happiness, I feel as things are it is much better for yourself as well as for me that you should go to another house. I give my true feelings as they are, and I must add that Sir Francis must quit it, and it can be no hardship in him to escape degradation, and as I cannot separate man and wife, I can only grieve that he has put it out of my power to preserve you from this. Indeed, I earnestly wish he would leave it soon. My intention then is to offer it to Susan for all her own and her children's lives, or upon a lease, or in any other way she likes.[9]

Fanny wrote to her father on 25 May 1816, saying that as a result of Harriot owning the Piccadilly house, Sophia was 'under a pecuniary obligation to someone other than a Parent', and this would destroy Sophia's independence.[10] She said Thomas should repurchase both houses and give them to his daughters, but instead, he replied,

I wish to ask you what you should ask yourself, as you are in some degree in a position similar to what Mrs Coutts is now [Fanny was the second wife of Lord Bute] – what do you think Lord Bute would have said to any of his daughters or sons if they had treated Him as I have been treated. I am sure he would have said, 'I am master of my own actions and I am astonished how you should ever think of directing me on them.' I would also beg you...to ask yourself what you would have thought of your Son and Daughter in Law had they treated you with such coldness, refusing any approach made by you and showing you every sort of disregard.[11]

Relations between Fanny and Harriot improved after that.

To Lady Burdett, Thomas wrote in 1816 that, since her marriage, Harriot had received from his family 'coldness and neglect, hardly naming or looking at her, and to me passing her by as one not fit to be named'. On the other hand, he said his friends, and 'the world in general', had given her 'the kindest proofs of... regard and attention which even all you and Susan's neglect of her could not prevent'.

---

[9]E Coleridge, op. cit., p.337.
[10]Coutts Bank Archives, 2117.
[11]Coutts Bank Archives, 2504.

To Harriot of 22 April 1816, Thomas wrote,

> The shameful and despicable conduct of Sir Francis Burdett force me to measures more powerfully to protect you from their malice, *by showing you more and more kindness while I live and placing you in case you survive me, in such a situation as in my opinion may tend most effectually to your honour and happiness while you remain behind me…*[12]

The words in italics show how early in the marriage Thomas was provoked into thinking of leaving all his wealth to Harriot.

Meantime, however, Harriot was indeed mistress of her own house. Stratton Street became under her control a treasure house, magnificently furnished in flamboyant style. The bow windows of the downstairs drawing room were curtained in gold damask, the walls lined with blue fluted silk. There was a superb India-Japanned screen, display tables with scent bottles, and a grand piano. The great upstairs drawing room was even more splendid, with chairs of black and gold, swagged golden curtains, and cut glass chandeliers. Reflected in the mirrors, and dominating the room, was within a few years a huge marble statue of Thomas Coutts. The corridors were lined with books, the rooms hung with paintings and there were display cases full of priceless china as well as marble busts and gilded mirrors. When Angela Burdett took over the house in 1849, she found upstairs large wardrobes in the bedrooms filled with Harriot's clothes – shoes and muffs and bonnets and gloves; yards of fine Brussels lace, and twenty pairs of flannel drawers; seventeen Indian shawls, dresses in black velvet and white satin, and the white feathered headdress which the caricaturists had featured so cruelly, and which can still be seen in a display case in Coutts Bank.[13]

According to Clara Burdett Patterson, who stayed at Stratton Street in 1900, it was still 'a wonderful house to stay in. The great rooms contained many marvellous objects of art, costly and rare. In the upstairs ballroom was some lovely blue Sevres china, which

---

[12]Coutts Bank Archives, 2703.
[13]Edna Healey, op. cit., pp.49–50.

had once belonged to Marie Antoinette'.[14]

In the Spring of 1816 there occurred the first of the Royal Drawing Room fiascos suffered by Harriot. In terms of social recognition an invitation to Court was immensely important, and on the first visit it was necessary for a woman to be presented to the Queen by another lady of the Court. A letter from Harriot to her friend Mrs Trotter, dated 4 April 1816, tells what happened in connection with her proposed presentation that day,

> Today Lady Bessborough was to have presented me to the Queen and all my fine things were quite ready, when alas at twelve o'clock last night Mr Coutts and me were snug in Bed when Lady Bessborough came to us almost distracted to inform us of a most affecting calamity having happened in the family which made it impossible for her to go with me. She is in dreadful trouble… I fear it is now too late to find another Lady, so I must wait for another drawing room.[15]

Harriot's disappointment was acute. Lady Bessborough's 'inability' to present Harriot was a white lie, since Thomas heard that the Queen had said she would never receive Mrs Coutts. He asked the Duke of York to confirm or deny this, and on 13 May the Duke said he had asked his sisters about the report. He was told that 'though her Majesty had never declared that she would not receive Mrs Coutts, and though she was not at all addicted to pay attention to idle reports, yet she had mentioned the difficulty in which Mrs Coutts's presentation would place her'.[16] This was a clear reference to Harriot's previous profession of actress, but it seems likely that Coutts's daughters had blackened her name to the Queen. The Duke of Clarence wrote to Thomas regarding the presentation, that the circumstances were not known to him, but he would always be happy to show attention to Mrs Coutts.[17] Relations between Harriot and Lady Guilford got steadily worse, despite momentary recoveries, though Harriot tried to maintain the friendship. Her letter dated 21 August 1816, to Lady Guilford,

---

[14]M W Patterson, *Angela Burdett-Coutts and the Victorians*, 1953, p.3.
[15]Coutts Bank Archives, 195.
[16]Coutts Bank Archives, 3289,
[17]Coutts Bank Archives, 3518.

says,

> If you have unkind feelings about me believe me I do not deserve them, let us meet as friends and forever bury in oblivion on both sides all unpleasant reflections… I write this that you may join our parties if you please, but of this be assured at all times you and your children will ever find a most affectionate welcome and a warm heart towards you all from Harriot Coutts.[18]

Susan replied, 'I am very much obliged to you for your kind answer to the wishes. I have begged my Father to express that we should all meet again'.[19]

In December 1816 Harriot wrote to her friend Mrs Trotter that Lady Guilford and her daughters were living with them in kindness and harmony,[20] but the cordial relations did not last. Thomas wrote two letters to Harriot in late 1816 and early 1817, imploring her to disregard the unfriendly and suspicious attitude of his children[21] and he wrote to Susan on 25 June 1817,

> I have every day of my life done everything in my power so far as my poor ability enabled me for the good of you and all my children and I do believe the only offence I have given you and them is my second marriage with a woman of the most perfect character.

Worse was to come: in July 1817 Thomas heard that Susan had offered to present her stepmother at Court, well knowing that Queen Charlotte would refuse to receive her. He wrote to her on 5 July:

> Colonel M'Mahon has this evening told me that you told him that you knew very well the Queen was determined not to receive Mrs Coutts at the very time when you assured me, in the most solemn manner, you knew nothing of any such determination, or had ever heard her Majesty so resolved. So you was carrying my wife to the Queen when you well knew she was to be rejected

---

[18]Coutts Bank Archives, 2417.
[19]Coutts Bank Archives, 2418.
[20]Coutts Bank Archives, 2240.
[21]Coutts Bank Archives, 2408 & 2409.

and affronted: not to do her honor but to witness, and I must suppose, to enjoy her disgrace. What could be so wicked, so malicious, or so spiteful? I never [could] have believed you capable of it! How can I put up with or bear it; at the very moment too that all the world are admitting the settlements I am making are magnificent beyond example, and I am even told you yourself acknowledge they are so. But my horror of your treatment of me and my innocent, unoffending wife, who merits the greatest kindness from you in place of such malice, is such, that I must and will withdraw these settlements, and do determine to withhold them unless the matter can be cleared to my satisfaction.[22]

Thomas added that Susan had never done one kind act to his wife, and asked, 'Have you ever introduced her to anyone of your friends or connections, though you knew well this was the way to gratify me and to make an end of abuse from envious, illiberal people?'

The quarrels continued until Coutts eventually gave an ultimatum that 'all intercourse must be at an end,' and at the close of 1817 he said he was banishing Lady Guilford from his presence. On 23 January 1818 Susan asked Harriot to intercede with her father over his refusal to see her, saying, 'I have been considering most anxiously with myself what the cause may be as arising from my own conduct'. The Countess was clearly an insensitive person. Her father intercepted this letter and made a note on it never to show it to Harriot.[23]

In 1818, when Lady Guilford's stepdaughter, Lady Maria North, married the second Marquess of Bute, Thomas was invited to the wedding but Harriot was not. This was an insult Thomas could not forgive. He was asked to give away the bride, but refused. Then the Duke of York annoyed him by agreeing to give the bride away. Thomas tried to get the Duke to retract his promise, but the Duke would take no part in the family quarrel, so Susan scored a Pyrrhic victory which she would live to regret. The Duke and Thomas, however, remained friends [24]

---

[22]E Coleridge, op. cit., p.343.
[23]Coutts Bank Archives, 1124.
[24]E Coleridge, op. cit., p.182.

In 1818, Harriot wrote a statement of her feelings about the treatment she had received from Thomas's daughters and others. It is not known for whom this was intended, or to whom (if anyone) it was sent, but it survives in the Coutts archives:

> Some time ago I was most cruelly and contemptuously ill-treated and abused, held out as an abandoned and wicked woman; in consequence of which many friends who had always been kind and very civil to me turned their backs on me… I have proved by my conduct I never deserved such abominable treatment. A Respectable and amiable Gentleman happened to know me and was struck with the Honest sincerity of my character, and He has now been Three years my Husband, and a more Happy Couple does not and never did exist. And we hope it will please Heaven to keep us so for many years to come. Those who turned their backs on me – I never can see or receive. But if there are friends who have never behaved ill to me, I and my dear Mr Coutts are happy and always willing to receive them.[25]

As a result of Lady Guilford's appalling behaviour, Thomas wrote to Harriot in 1818 as follows,

> You too well know the misery I have suffered from my children not being easy and happy with you… [after my death] it is possible that they may not behave to you with the kindness and affection that you are so well entitled to from every connection of mine. I therefore write this as I know you have made your will, and left in succession to my grandchildren all your estates and property to say it is my wish and desire and request that you will alter that destination and leave the whole in any other line you please…[26]

This is the only indication that Harriot had made her first Will in favour of Coutts's grandchildren. Eventually, in 1820, there was a reconciliation, and a happy gathering when the daughters visited their father and he enjoyed their obvious devotion to him. But Thomas Coutts had determined as early as 1818 to leave all his wealth to his wife, as can be seen from the letter he sent to his

---

[25]Coutts Bank Archives, 2416.
[26]Coutts Bank Archives, 2408.

solicitor, John Parkinson, on 3 May 1820:

> I think it was about two years since I executed a final settlement of all my worldly concerns by giving all I might possess, or that hereafter I might acquire or be entitled to at my death, wholly and solely to my dear wife... but somehow I feel rather uneasy lest the deed I allude to should prove insufficient, and, therefore, my eager wish is... to execute a new deed giving in the most clear and full manner everything, real or personal or that I may in any way succeed to, or acquire from this day to the last of my life to my dearest wife, solely and entirely...[27]

The seven years of Thomas and Harriot's marriage were a period of great events abroad and misery at home. Unrest was general, summed up in a handbill, 'Present state of Great Britain: four million people on the point of starvation, four million with a bare subsistence, one and a half million in straitened circumstances, one half million in dazzling luxury'.[28]

Thomas Coutts believed that wealth had its duties as well as its privileges, and he practised what he called 'constant, but not promiscuous charity.' His contemporaries said he 'accorded unfettered permission to his wife to exercise the same divine gift', and Harriot appears to have run single-handedly her own system of charity for the poor. She never forgot that she had been brought up among the poorest and most despised people in England. She was a generous person, profoundly sorry for those less fortunate than herself, and she wanted to help them as much as she could. She began a lavish programme of almsgiving in 1817, when the end of the Napoleonic Wars let loose thousands of discharged soldiers and sailors who were more or less destitute. As 'A Person of Respectability' wrote in 1822:[29]

> What between the want of employment, and the incompetence of the wages paid to those labourers who have work, the great mass of the industrious exist in a state of constant starvation; seldom having the luxury of a hearty meal, even of the coarsest of food...

---

[27]E Coleridge, op. cit., p.368.
[28]Yvonne Ffrench, *News From the Past*, 1934.
[29]A Person of Respectability.

> The allowance recently bestowed by Mrs Coutts proved an efficient relief to many a poor family; and saved them from extreme suffering, perhaps from death itself.

But society at that time had on the whole a very callous view of poverty and the poor. Malthus had taught them that the poor, through early marriage and promiscuous breeding, were the cause of their own poverty, and Ricardo and the classical economists preached that there was work for all if only they would accept the market rate of wages. Social class position was taken to be fixed and almost immutable, and few voices questioned this in early nineteenth-century Britain. The traditional view was that 'a murmuring against the comforts of the rich and the privations of the poor is a murmuring against God's appointment. The rights of man have no authority either in God's word or God's providence'.[30]

Post-war England swarmed with beggars, and society's reaction was to form a Mendicity Society in 1818 and make begging an imposition that could be prosecuted. Constables and magistrates got busy, but there was no visible sign of a decrease in the number of beggars. Society justified its existence by collecting subscriptions to pay its officials. In 1817 a Commons Committee proposed to abolish the poor law, but a Lords Committee with the Government's backing, fearing revolution, ruled against it. Instead, Parliament passed the Select Vestry Act of 1819 which gave the larger ratepayers control over the supposedly wasteful distribution of poor relief. It tried repeatedly to tackle poverty by regulating the granting of poor relief and the punishment of vagrancy, with small success – witness the rapid succession of Acts, the groans of ratepayers, and the complaints of pamphleteers, which went on until the New Poor Law of 1834 which confined the able-bodied pauper (the unemployed) to the new 'bastille' of the union workhouse.

Yet in accepting that every destitute person had a right to maintenance from the Poor Law, the English differed not only from continental countries but also from Scotland and Ireland. The Act of Settlement (1660), under which relief was given only

---

[30]Elizabeth Rigby, *The Quarterly Review*, 1848.

in the parish where an individual was born or apprenticed, was complicated and its administration asinine, but as William Cobbett said, the poor man of England in distress made his claim on the parish officers not for alms but for his legal due. Some old-fashioned Tory paternalists, appalled by the new Ricardian economists, believed that relief not only helped the poor but stimulated the economy. The Duke of Kent, Queen Victoria's father, a tireless worker for charity and a friend of the industrial philanthropist Robert Owen, was far in advance of contemporary opinion in believing that charity was not enough to solve the prevailing distress. He told a public meeting that 'it was evident that no charitable provision or establishment could remedy the evil of a depressed working class', so that the poor law was a necessity.[31]

Meanwhile, Harriot Coutts was besieged at Holly Lodge by poor people, since she never sent anyone away empty handed. Crowds of tramps heard of this earthly paradise and clamoured for a share of the good things she offered. A tent constructed at the entrance to her pleasure grounds for the crowds of beggars to whom clothing, food, and money were almost indiscriminately distributed were ridiculed by her neighbours, and many of those she tried to help, wanting a bigger handout, were loudly ungrateful. The sights and sounds of ragged beggars, who had previously thanked her, uttering such ingratitude was such a shock to Harriot that she went to the other extreme and stopped almsgiving altogether for a time. She issued a circular saying: 'It is quite impossible for Mrs Coutts to examine a tenth part of the applications which are constantly pouring in upon her, nor has she the means of relieving the distresses of the multitude who apply'.[32] Harriot was so inundated with letters and petitions that she had to ask the General Post Office not to send on letters not franked (postage then was paid by the recipient) and those that were obviously begging epistles. The Holly Lodge porter was ordered not to take in begging letters or petitions. The friendly 'Person of the First Respectability' [1822] wrote of Harriot and

---

[31] Fulford, 1969, p.191.
[32] Coutts Bank Archives, 17061.

her neighbours,

> her charities were abused and misapplied by too many of the thankless wretches who had partaken of her bounty; and the envious squad of little gentry derided the conduct of Mrs Coutts, sending vagabonds of every description to her door, telling them the rich lady was so troubled with money she could not find beggars enough to receive her superfluous gold![33]

Harriot may not have set out to publish her acts of charity, but the newspapers found her wealth an all-absorbing subject, and the publicity they gave to her largesse simply increased the number of people who wanted a share of it. An unexpected and sad consequence of Harriot's bounty was that some parish officers deducted the relief money she gave the poor from the pittances they allowed these families, thus saving the pockets of those who paid poor rates and leaving the poor no better off. Harriot therefore changed her policy and from Christmas 1818 her bounty at Holly Lodge was limited to small gifts to the poor of the almshouses.

Apart from her benevolence to beggars, Harriot supported a number of individuals and charities, often by modest sums of money. Soon after her marriage, Bannister the actor left the stage, and she sent him a £10 note along with an unpretentious note:

Dear Bannister,
    Twenty years we have been fellow-servants together in Drury Lane Theatre. May your retirement from labour be as happy as I wish! I feel assured none rejoiced more sincerely than yourself at the happy and honourable exit I have made from my professional service.
    Yours truly,
    'Audrey' (the last part I acted with you),
    Harriot Coutts[34].

Among her papers is a receipt dated 1 June 1815 for £52.10s paid to the British Lying-In Hospital where poor women had their

---

[33] A Person of the First Respectability, 1822.
[34] Charles Pearce, op. cit., 1915, p.188.

babies delivered, and she became a Life Governor of that Hospital.[35] She paid a quarterly allowance of £4.6s.8d to Mrs Hogg, who had been her dresser at Drury Lane Theatre.[36] In March 1817 Miss N. Barker of Keswick reminded Harriot that she had earlier in life, when Harriot was playing in Stafford, sent her a dress; now her finances were low, she was sick and needed £100. She asked Harriot to buy five landscape paintings she had done for that amount. This Harriot did. In 1817 she paid a life subscription of £10.10s. to the Royal Society of Musicians, perhaps in memory of her violinist stepfather. In September 1817 Mary Keen wrote from Cheltenham to acknowledge Harriot's kindness to her and her daughter, in sending a dress, bonnet and handkerchief 'so costly and elegant' and she said, 'others have the means but not the will which led you from your cradle to acts of charity which are not forgotten by me and many others'.[37] The same month, actor-manager John Stanton, of the family which employed Harriot when she was a young actress in Stafford, asked for help to get out of Debtor's Prison in Lancaster. Stanton was there under the Insolvent Debtor's Act, and needed money to discharge 'the necessary law expenses' for getting free. Harriot sent the money, and he later wrote of her 'generous disposition from earliest life'.[38] Letters which acknowledged Harriot's acts of kindness must have comforted her when her public generosity was scorned.

When Princess Charlotte, daughter of the Prince Regent and heir to the throne, died in childbirth in November, 1817, her uncles, the Royal Dukes, had second thoughts on the subject of marriage. In 1818, the Dukes of Kent, Clarence and Cambridge married German princesses and began a frantic race to produce an heir to the throne. Lord Liverpool's Government, having proposed annuities of £6,000 a year each to the Royal Dukes, dissolved itself on the 10 June and there followed a General Election. The result was another Tory victory. The death of Queen Charlotte, the Prince Regent's mother, in 1818 and the

---

[35]Coutts Bank Archives, 2517.
[36]Coutts Bank Archives, 7907.
[37]Coutts Bank Archives, 16690.
[38]Coutts Bank Archives, 7239.

general poverty and unrest in the country, brought an end to a depressing year.

However, despite the gloomy national situation, their acrimonious family quarrels, and Harriot's disappointing experience of trying to help the poor, the married life of Thomas and Harriot Coutts, far above poverty, proceeded happily and in a constant whirl of social entertaining, as we shall see in the next chapter.

Harriot Coutts: By Sir William Beechey.
In possession of Coutts and Co.
Permission of Coutts and Co.

Statue of Thomas Coutts (1818): By Sir Francis Chantrey.
From Coutts Photographic Library.
Permission of Coutts and Co.

Harriot Coutts (1818): By Sir William Beechy.
In possession of the Natural Portrait Gallery.
Published in *The Connoisseur* 1921.
Permission of Coutts and Co.

Harriot, Duchess of St. Albans: Oil painting by Clint.
Owned By Coutts and Co.
Permission of Coutts and Co.

Angela Burdett Coutts.
Owned By Coutts and Co.
Permission of Coutts and Co.

Chapter IX
THE CONSTANT COUPLE[1]

Holly Lodge, Highgate, was a house that both Harriot and Thomas Coutts loved. The lease on the estate, as we have seen, was paid for by Harriot and taken in her name alone. It is difficult now to imagine what Highgate looked like almost two hundred years ago. William Howitt said Highgate Common was enclosed around 1812, and that, before the 'flying coaches':

> ...the people of Highgate made their visits to town in a stage coach which performed the journey in between two and three hours, fare half a crown, and such was the arduous undertaking that the passengers stopped to take tea on their return at the Assembly House, Kentish Town.[2]

However, Thomas and Harriot Coutts and their guests did the journeys between Highgate and central London much faster than this in their private carriages.

Soon after their marriage Thomas and Harriot altered Holly Lodge and enlarged the grounds. For an adjacent plot they wished to buy they were asked an extortionate price, and when they refused the owner tried to blackmail them. Though he had other means of access to his property, he brought carts of gravel, lime and sand over their grounds, using an ancient right of way through Holly Lodge to his land, and spilled some of the contents in untidy heaps. These activities increased when Harriot had grand visitors. The Duke of York commented one day on the slovenly appearance of bricks being laid down near the windows. When the matter was explained to him he couldn't help laughing,

---

[1] A play by George Farquhar in which Harriot appeared as Angelica in 1805.
[2] William Howitt, *Northern Heights of London*, 1869.

and decided the best thing was to build a high wall to shut off the view of the offending neighbour's plot. This was done, and their neighbour then agreed to sell the land on the terms originally offered, so the wall was demolished.

Because Harriot was superstitious, the highest step of a flight of white marble steps up to the front of Holly Lodge was disfigured by two rusty old broken horseshoes which she had found in the road and nailed on their threshold to avert evil and bring them good luck.

When Angela Burdett-Coutts acquired Holly Lodge, she noted the maps of the world hung in the hall, and in the dining room the long mahogany table and the looking glass with its carved eagle which reflected crystal chandeliers. In the drawing room was a grand piano, and in the conservatory exotic flowers bloomed. Upstairs, Harriot's bedroom was heavy with scent. Angela took away trinket boxes with watches and thirty mourning rings; she left seven cases of stuffed birds and a collection of sea shells. Harriot's red velvet curtains, and her bath and shower, remained unchanged until the Duke of St Albans' death in 1849, when Angela took over the house.

Harriot employed female companions both before and after her marriage. Sally Stephenson lived with her for some years, but was dismissed in 1812 after a quarrel. Sally had been entertaining a married lover in the Little Russell Street house, thinking to emulate her mistress, and Harriot would not allow this. Eleanor Goddard was Harriot's next companion, and she stayed for nineteen years from 1812. This period included the years of Harriot's first marriage, though Coutts did not like Eleanor because of her bad temper. He wrote to Harriot on 22 September 1816:

> I have always wondered how you could bear Miss Goddard's behaviour, but I wished not to disturb your kind heart or find fault with your goodness and indulgence towards her unfortunate situation and her distressing state of health; I was, however, always fearful she had not sense or temper to see the erroneous and ungrateful behaviour with which she breaks out from time to time – and instead of gratitude and attachment was full of

insolence such (especially of late) as became truly unbearable.[3]

Eleanor's aunt, Mrs Graham, intervened in letters to Harriot asking the Coutts to forgive her niece, and presumably Eleanor apologised profusely for her behaviour, for she stayed on for another thirteen years.[4]

Harriot had always liked having visitors, even when she was a poor young actress, and when she could afford greater hospitality it was very lavish, whether at Stratton Street or Holly Lodge. *The Morning Post* of 2 March 1819 reported, 'Mr and Mrs Coutts gave a splendid dinner to a large party of distinction. The dessert was the richest and most delicious seen in the west end of the town this season'. It was ironical that while the great mass of the people were half-starving, the luxurious life of the rich was never more conspicuous. During the Regency period, nothing was too extravagant in the way of eating and drinking for those who could afford it.

Despite their wealth and generosity, Harriot and Thomas did not like being overcharged by tradesmen or hotel keepers. Staying at an inn in Brighton in 1817, they gave a large dinner party each day, and once the Duke of Clarence sent them an immense haunch of venison. Harriot told the landlord of the inn the next day to serve venison to the other people staying there, and on the third day she asked for some hashed venison for Thomas. When the daily bill arrived, she found they had been charged a large extra amount for the hashed venison, and so incensed was she by this meanness that they left the inn immediately and moved to another.

Travelling was very popular in the early nineteenth century, because better roads, coaches and inns made it more pleasurable. 'Taking the waters' for medicinal purposes was one excuse for travel, and spas like Bath and Cheltenham were the first holiday resorts. Thomas and Harriot liked to have comfortable accommodation when they stayed in hotels, but they also liked good value for money. A letter dated 26 August 1820, from Charles Goodwin, their steward, gives a detailed account to

---

[3] Coutts Bank Archives, 2409.
[4] Coutts Bank Archives, 2442 & 2443.

Harriot of the rooms he had selected for them and their entourage for a forthcoming stay at York House, Bath, and the charges for food and drink.[5]

Thomas Coutts had a wide circle of artist friends, and had portraits painted of his friends and family. In 1816 he sat for a portrait of himself by Masquerier, whose work he had seen and admired, and arranged for Harriot too to have her portrait painted by the same artist.[6] Two years later Harriot was painted by William Beechey, and a receipt dated 23 April 1818 shows that she paid 200 guineas for the portrait.[7] Thomas and Harriot were enthusiastic patrons of the theatre; on 20 May 1819, at a dinner of the Drury Lane Theatrical Fund, a donation of £50 by Mrs Coutts was announced, and in the course of the evening the Duke of York 'proposed the health of Mrs Coutts, which was drunk with enthusiasm'. And they were friends of William, better known as 'Gentleman' Smith, who had been educated at Eton and Cambridge, but had to make his living on the stage when his father's business failed. He was distinguished in both tragedy and comedy, and made a substantial fortune. When he was old and in failing health, the Coutts sent him presents of fish, game, oysters, and bottles of rare and expensive cordials. In 1818–1819, when he was ninety years of age, he wrote some twenty letters to Thomas, mainly thanks and compliments in return for the delicacies he received, but also recollections of the fashionable world in which he had lived, and comparisons of his life then and formerly. He was greatly upset by the decline of Drury Lane: 'We have outlived the prosperity of Old Drury, and the fall is melancholy... That Old Drury should droop and die affects me much...'[8]

Coutts was a lover of Shakespeare, but seldom concerned himself with the lives or fortunes of contemporary poets or men of letters, other than playwrights. When young he had befriended the actor and dramatist, Arthur Murphy, who had fallen on bad times and was prepared to pledge his library in return for a draft of three hundred pounds. Murphy said Thomas told him 'he had

---

[5]Coutts Bank Archives, 15999.
[6]Coutts Bank Archives, 6180.
[7]Coutts Bank Archives, 3768.
[8]Coutts Bank Archives, 6135.

no time for books', but he nonetheless advanced the money and forewent the pledge. As some return the actor prefixed to his *Life of Garrick* (1801) a fulsome dedication to Coutts.

Coutts's remark was probably to save Murphy's self-respect and his books. He did indeed find time for books: he became a subscriber to such huge editions deluxe as *Macklin's Bible*, *Boydell's Shakespeare*, and Bowyer's edition of *Hume's History of England*. He wanted Harriot to appreciate books, too. In the first year of their marriage he gave her a complete set of the works of Hogarth, writing the following on the title page,

> 20th April: I am very happy to have obtained for you and given you the prints of the inimitable genius, William Hogarth, as there is no one more capable of understanding and appreciating talent than you are, by the nature and intuitive genius the Almighty has endowed you with, giving you 'an eye, an ear, a fancy to be charmed' and blessing you from nature (with merely a plain education) with the capacity of comprehending and enjoying, in a clear and supreme degree, every work of genius that comes your way... God bless you and preserve you, My dearest Harriot, (signed) Thomas Coutts.

Reading such letters, one cannot doubt the genuine love Thomas had for his wife, and their friends knew how much she cared for him. Lord Buchan wrote on 5 August 1818, 'it gives me great satisfaction to see my most dear and esteemed friend so happy, in the happiest state that can attach to old age with a faithful nursing Wife'. J T Smith, in *Joseph Nollekens and His Times*,[9] refers to Thomas having his bust executed in marble. He gave an amusing account of the sittings:

> The bust of the late Mr Coutts, the banker, was one of Nollekens' last productions and one in which he appeared to take much pleasure, but I must say that as to likeness it is certainly ridiculously severe... Mrs Nollekens assured me that during the numerous sittings which that wealthy man gave Mr Nollekens no one would be more attentive to him than Mrs Coutts, who never failed to bring with her in her carriage some of the most delicious

---

[9] J T Smith, *Joseph Nollekens and His Times*, 1828.

and comforting soups or refreshments that could possibly be made, which she herself warmed in her saucepan over the parlour fire... Mr Coutts was blowing his broth attended by Mrs Coutts, a lively woman most fashionably dressed: whilst Nollekens... nearly as deaf as a post was prosecuting his bust and at the same time repeating his loud interrogations as to the price of stocks to his sitter...

The bust was exhibited in the Royal Academy Exhibition in 1816.

Before he married Harriot Mellon, wealthy Thomas Coutts wore the costume of a decayed gentleman – very faded, worn-out clothes and a threadbare coat – to such a degree that strangers tried to give him handouts of money. But after his second marriage his wardrobe improved beyond recognition. A selection of his clothes is preserved at the Victoria and Albert Museum in London, and others are in museums around Britain and even in some foreign museums. He had six 'Brutus' wigs, which were of the finest make and the most expensive.

The most painful aspect of their marriage was the campaign of satire and vilification with which scurrilous journalists, no less prurient and malicious than today, pursued them. Between 1815 and 1825 a number of scandalous pamphlets, the so-called 'Lives' of Harriot Mellon and Thomas Coutts, were issued by the gutter press. They were published primarily to make money out of a gullible public eager for news of the rich and famous, the nastier the better. As now, they cleverly mixed truth with falsehood. The earliest, soon after their marriage, was *Fine Acting, or a Sketch of the Life of Miss H M of Drury Lane Theatre and of T C Esq., Banker.* [1815] Whoever wrote the story probably got garbled information from Sally Stephenson, Harriot's dismissed companion, who had lived with her in Little Russell Street and at Holly Lodge.

It is remarkable that Harriot Mellon, with all her good qualities, should have made so many enemies. But envy can distort perception. Even the apparently wise precaution of having a resident doctor to attend Thomas constantly, given his age and frailty, was turned into criticism against Harriot. Soon after their marriage, a Dr Hooper, married and not young, was engaged at the substantial salary of £500 a year to live in their house and provide constant medical attention. Anonymous enemies accused

Harriot in poison-pen letters of keeping a lover in her home, and it seems certain that the doctor's wife thought so too, was jealous of Harriot and, foolishly for her husband's career, fed the gossip. Harriot showed the letters to Thomas, who advised her to ignore them, but later when they were on holiday in Bath the doctor's wife followed them there and began to repeat the accusations, so the doctor's appointment was terminated.[10] The next doctor selected for the post, Dr John Andrews, was subject to bouts of depression and was a hypochondriac who took opium. He generally refused to be called to attend his patient during the night, and when wakened urgently one night he began to taunt Harriot with her origins, early poverty and profession, ridiculing Coutts for his infatuation with her.[11]

Why they did not get rid of this incompetent doctor is puzzling, but Thomas apparently liked him and his conduct was overlooked until it became more and more bizarre. He was furious when he was not invited to dine with the Royal Dukes of York, Clarence, Kent and Sussex, on their visit to Holly Lodge, apparently not understanding that the royals themselves decided the guest list, and did not dine with medical men, whom they considered mere servants. He also began to have fainting fits, which even occurred at table, and he was sent to recuperate at Ramsgate and then pensioned off with a good salary.[12] A few months later Dr Andrews committed suicide, and the press decided that Harriot was to blame, though the doctor's own son wrote to express gratitude to her for her kindness, and shock that she should have been so calumnied. Not to be bested, the press decided that the son had been paid to write such a testament, and the gossip continued.

Edward Antrobus, a young partner at the bank, did much to shield Harriot and Thomas from the danger of these accusations, and thus earned their undying gratitude. He suggested they should continue Dr Andrews' annuity to his dependent sister, and this Harriot agreed to do.[13] Percy Wyndham[14] revived the story of

---

[10]Margaret Cornwell Baron-Wilson, op. cit., p.113.
[11]*The Morning Post*, 6 April 1820.
[12]Coutts Bank Archives, 6104.
[13]Coutts Bank Archives, 7472/A.

the lottery ticket and detailed the supposed wrongs of the actor Ralph Wewitzer, whom Harriot was accused of neglecting in his later life when he was ill. Harriot was also accused of over-eating and drinking. William Oxberry, however, said Wewitzer was provided for by Harriot until he was 'victimized by an idle youth who lived at his expense'; Harriot stopped the annuity to prevent the money falling into this protégé's hands. Modern readers may feel it would have been kinder to allow her old friend to squander his money as he wished, but she did not like seeing her money wasted on a worthless hanger-on. Of Harriot's supposed gourmandising, Oxberry said Harriot was 'one of the most abstemious livers in existence – she gets up at seven in the morning even in the winter – and drunkards are never early risers', and that she had been known to lunch on 'a red herring roasted.' This Memoir was not a naive eulogy to Harriot, and is more believable than that of an avowed enemy like Wyndham.[15]

Other scurrilous attacks on Harriot and Thomas are described in Lowe's *Bibliographical Account of the English Theatre*.

In August 1819 it was reported in the press that 'Mr and Mrs Coutts have taken a large house at Brighton for the season and set off with their establishment to pass the next two months there.' One of the satirical engravings of the time depicting Harriot was by Williams, entitled 'Quid Est? – Why Brighton Dandies!' published in January 1819 by S W Fores of Piccadilly. The coloured impression shows Captain Augustus d'Este driving a high-stepping horse in a four-wheeled phaeton towards the Brighton cliffs. At his side sits Mrs Coutts, very plump, wearing a large bonnet and holding up a parasol. She turns to him saying, 'This is driving with Spirit indeed, to what I have been used to lately!' (a sexual innuendo on her elderly husband). He says, 'You do me honour I am sure, but there is no man of Sussex feels more pleasure than I do in driving the Ladies!'. Between his legs is a large band-box of full trimmed petticoats on which stands a large melon.

---

[14]Strictures, 1822.
[15]William Oxberry, *Oxberry's Dramatic Biography and Histrionic Anecdotes*, 1825–1827.

The more friendly 'Person of the First Respectability', who wrote the *Life of the late Thomas Coutts Esq.*, said however,

> The tongue of scandal was often very busy with the fame of Miss Mellon, and she was represented as a mercenary, intriguing and meretricious woman [but] he that writes these sketches has long admired and respected Mrs Coutts on account of her benevolence of heart…[16]

Royalty had no qualms about socializing with the Coutts. The earliest record of royals dining with Thomas Coutts at Stratton Street is in 1814, when his first wife was alive but old and confused. She mistook the Duke of Clarence for his father, George III, then insane and confined – a faux pas which fortunately only amused the Duke.

In the early days of their marriage Harriot and Thomas were often visited by Princess Charlotte of Wales and her husband, Prince Leopold, and after the Princess died in 1817 the Prince continued to dine with them. Thomas wrote by hand invitations for dinner parties, and only a few months before he died he wrote to Lord Darnley.

> Prince Leopold has written to me with an obliging proposal of dining with Mrs Coutts and me, and His Royal Highness the Duke of York has named the 16th of July as the first day he is at liberty. We hope it may also suit your Lordship and Lady Darnley, and any of her family to honour us at the same time. We think that Lady Guilford will be in England also, and our party probably be numerous.

Although Thomas was always businesslike in his dealings with the Royal Dukes, their correspondence suggests genuine friendship, and they often dined with him and Harriot. Coutts inspired the free-living, misbehaving princes with respect, and they won his sincere as well as loyal attachment.

The Royal Dukes wrote to Thomas in their own handwriting, whether on business or social matters. The Duke of York,

---

[16] A Person of the First Respectability, 1822, p.6.

attended by Mr Joseph Jekyll, dined with Thomas and Harriot in 1818. His letter of acceptance reads, 'I need not, I trust, assure you of the pleasure with which I shall avail myself of your and Mrs Coutts's obliging invitation to dine at Holly Lodge... I remain, ever Dear Sir, with kind regards to Mrs Coutts, Yours most sincerely, Frederick'.

On one occasion the Duke of Clarence accepted an invitation to dine at Stratton Street, but stipulated it should be for 7 P.M. 'Sooner,' he wrote, 'you cannot expect any visitors (or at least not sailor princes!)'. In 1821 the Duke ended another letter with the message, 'My best and warmest wishes attend Mrs Coutts; God bless and preserve you and ever believe me, Yrs unalterably, William.' In fact, the Duke was to undergo a considerable change of heart about Harriot when he became King William IV in 1830, as will be seen later.

Between 1816 and 1819 the Duke of Kent was a regular visitor at Stratton Street. He wrote regularly to Coutts on matters of business, especially the liquidation of his debts and the additional parliamentary grant he received when he married in 1818. On 24 May 1819, the Duchess of Kent gave birth to a daughter, the future Queen Victoria. In December the Duke tried to get Harriot to use her influence with Thomas about a large loan. A letter to Harriot dated 15 December 1819, from Andrew Dickie, Chief Clerk at the Bank, reads:

> I have looked over the Papers from H.R.H. the Duke of Kent, which you enclosed to me last night, and which are herewith returned, with a brief Abstract of their contents, as desired. Although Mr Coutts's admirable letter of the 5th inst. to H.R.H. did not hold out anything to invite a direct application to him for the loan, either in whole or in part, yet I did apprehend something of the kind would be made – and the Duke seems to have taken great pains to prove, in his usual able precise manner, that if it was acceded to the whole would be repaid in 1820, assuming for certain that Castle Hill will fetch £30,000 – I have heard, however, many Persons express their Doubts on this point – tho' it is possible they might be no judges of the value of such a place.

> Dear Madam, Your very obedient humble servant,
> Andrew Dickie.[17]

A letter to Harriot dated 15 December 1819 from Edward Antrobus, a partner in the Bank, concerns the same matter:

> Mr Dickie has shown me the extraordinary application made by the Duke of Kent, with the letter he wrote to you upon the subject... all these papers are now returned, and I will call at Stratton St on my way from the Strand, about five o'clock, which I suppose will be before Mr Coutts return, with an answer to it.
> I am, Dear Madam,
> Your Very Faithful Obedient Servant ...[18]

The loan was not made, and an undated letter to Harriot from Thomas shows that her intervention had much distressed him; he said the loan was not within his power otherwise he would have made it.[19] Coutts Bank must have been glad they had not made this loan, for a few weeks after this, on 23 January 1820, the Duke caught pneumonia and died.

The Prince Regent did not write personally to Thomas (custom or etiquette forbade direct communication between him and his bankers), but private secretaries, keepers of the privy purse, equerries and the like, wrote to him on matters of business and also doled out morsels of backstairs gossip. The Prince, accompanied by Sir William Gordon, dined at Holly Lodge on 1 August 1816. Gordon, in a letter dated 21 January 1819, suggested that Thomas should visit his friends in Brighton, including the Prince who was in perfect health. He also said 'Mrs Coutts's turkeys (a regular and most welcome Christmas present) were the wonder and delight of all present.' Other letters in 1819 suggest that Coutts was giving a lot more financial help to Prinny than the cost of turkeys.

On 30 January 1820 King George III died. Despite the long years of his illness and incapacity he was extolled in the newspapers to the detriment of his heir. Thomas was afraid the

---

[17] Coutts Bank Archives, 10661.
[18] Coutts Bank Archives, 10660.
[19] Coutts Bank Archives, 1339.

new king might decide to appoint a different banker, but that did not happen and Coutts remained the royal banker. However, George IV was exceedingly unpopular in 1820 and the situation with regard to his wife caused widespread public alarm. In 1795 he had married his cousin, Princess Caroline of Brunswick, only to please his father and to get his debts paid by Parliament. In the eyes of the Roman Catholic Church he was already married to Mrs Fitzherbert, but illegally by English law. He deserted Caroline three months after their only child, Princess Charlotte, was born. He had always hated her and treated her badly. Now, anxious to prevent her taking the title of Queen, he claimed she had committed adultery with her Italian secretary Bartolomeo Bergami with whom (along with his family) she had been travelling abroad. On 6 June 1820 he insisted the House of Lords should hold an enquiry into the Queen's conduct and establish a cause for divorce.

On 9 June Caroline arrived in England for her 'trial' and was received with great enthusiasm by the common people, who thought it obscene that a notorious rake and adulterer like George IV should point the finger at his Queen. The Queen's Trial became a cause célèbre and, coming so soon after the so-called Peterloo Massacre of August 1819 in which the Hussars had ridden down a crowd of parliamentary reformers and killed 11 including women and children in Manchester, threatened to provoke revolution.

Coutts was a friend to Queen Caroline, but he contrived not to offend her husband by keeping secret his help to her. In June of 1820, however, she put him in a fix by asking if she could stay for a few days at his Stratton Street house until she could find apartments, making clear she was short of money. Thomas was able to decline the honour of her visit, on the grounds of his ill-health, but he made sure, via the Prime Minister, Lord Liverpool, that the King provided her with money for her residence. Her allowance was paid through Coutts Bank, and Thomas referred to her in letters as 'The Queen', a title George denied, and acted as go-between for her with the King through the government.

Popular sympathy was behind Queen Caroline to an almost hysterical degree. Public feeling was whipped up by the Whigs, including Sir Frances Burdett, and Caroline became a pawn in the political game, but she was nonetheless a popular victim. In September 1820 the Trial of the Queen took place before the House of Lords. From all over the country loyal addresses to Caroline poured in from sources as varied as 'the Females of Bath' and the weavers of Spitalfields. Not even at the funeral of Lord Nelson, said *The Times*, was such a prodigious concourse ever witnessed on the Thames as on the day Lord Brougham made a speech in the House of Lords in defence of the Queen. From Southwark to Hammersmith, 'every creek and landing place sent out fresh numbers to swell the augmenting procession.' With flags flying and bands playing aboard steam yachts and civic barges, the Company of Lightermen and Watermen and the loyal parishioners of St Saviour's, Southwark, sailed up river to Brandenburgh House. Here they presented loyal addresses to Queen Caroline, expressing 'detestation of the vile persecution your Majesty has suffered.'

In November 1820, the government bowed to public opinion and the King's case was abandoned. Despite the utmost efforts by the King's friends to prove adultery, no evidence was ever found that Caroline had been other than indiscreet. Parliament voted her £50,000 a year and allowed her to assume her title.

On 13 November 1820, having dined with Thomas and Harriot, the Duke of York went up with them to a room at the top of Holly Lodge and watched the 'splendid Illumination' of London that evening, in consequence of the Bill of Pains and Penalties against Queen Caroline having been given up. But the King was still determined that she should not be crowned Queen, and indeed when news of Napoleon's death reached London in 1821, and the King was told his greatest enemy was dead, he exclaimed, 'No, by God! Is she?'

However, the public was fickle in its regard for Caroline. People became bored by the whole affair. At George IV's Coronation in July, 1821, Queen Caroline tried to attend the ceremony but was refused entry to Westminster Abbey. Her action, which was felt to have spoiled a splendid spectacle, alienated many people, so she left England, and died in August of that year. The King promptly demolished her home at

Brandenburgh House.

Harriot's happiest memento of the Coronation of George IV was a splendid present. The Duke of York had worn for the ceremony a magnificent diamond cross borrowed from his jeweller; the next day the jeweller called at Stratton Street as Harriot and her husband were eating dinner, and Thomas bought the cross for her, paying with a cheque for £15,000.

There are scanty records of the closing years of Thomas and Harriot's married life, but the few letters between them portray a pleasing and agreeable relationship. Not only do they suggest kindness and faithfulness: the partners also depict themselves as married lovers. On 18 September 1819, Thomas wrote to his wife (who was in the next room):

> I write this on my birthday... entering on my 85th year; and on 1820, the 18th of January next, we shall enter into the seventh[20] year of our marriage, during which time I can truly say I have every day been more and more convinced of your goodness, purity and unbounded kindness to me, and to all belonging to me or connected with me, and of your truth, fidelity, and honourable and virtuous attention and love to me.[21]

Long journeys and visits to great country houses came to an end, but there were excursions for health or pleasure to Brighton in 1819, to Salt Hill in 1820, to Tunbridge Wells in 1821. In September 1820 it was reported that,

> Mr Coutts' birthday was celebrated on Monday at York House in Bath by an elegant dinner given to a large party of friends, amongst whom were Lord Erskine, the Hon. Mr Pretty, M.P., Mr Fuseli, R.A. and Col. Ray. On this occasion twenty poor deserving families were liberally regaled and made happy by Mrs Coutts presenting them with a seasonable supply of bedding, clothing, and money.

Almost the last time Thomas played host to royalty was at the dinner to celebrate his and Harriot's seventh wedding anniversary

---

[20] In fact, they were entering the sixth year of their marriage.
[21] Coutts Bank Archives, 3754.

in January 1822. Thirty people sat down to dinner, including the Dukes of York, Clarence and Sussex. Creevey reported at second-hand in his diary that 'old Coutts and his bride [were] sitting side by side at the top of the table', that musicians and songsters were placed at side tables, and that one of the latter had been paid £100 for his trip.[22]

Though frail in body, Thomas kept a firm hold on life to the end. In the months before his death he was apparently still transacting business, arranging the time and terms of a loan to one of his 'titled constituents'. But neither care, attention, love nor money could stave off the inevitable, and eventually Thomas Coutts died on 24 February 1822 at the age of 86. He had been failing in health for some months. Among the Burdett papers were found later three copies of an anonymous epigram.

> An apple we know was old Adam's disgrace.
> Who from Paradise quickly was driven;
> But yours, my dear Tom, is a happier case,
> For a Mellon transports you to Heaven![23]

The bond of affection between Thomas and Harriot was mutual. On the flyleaf of her Book of Common Prayer Harriot wrote, after Thomas's death,

> 'I never lose my spirits.' My blessed Tom said these words to me in a dream. After he had kissed me and laid his dear head on my bosom, I felt his tears on my cheek – I was so happy, but so melancholy happy. He looked so well, tranquil and divine. He anxiously desired me to change my shoes, for fear of taking cold, as I had walked through water to him... I see him at this moment, upright, beautiful and composed, as in his long and immaculate life. He looks just as I first saw his dear, blessed face upwards of twenty years ago. This dream has made a strong impression on my mind. The constant repetition to me of 'pray remember, be happy; look at me, I never lose my spirits; for my

---

[22] J Gore, ed, *Creevey's Life and Times*, 1934, vol.ii, p.3.
[23] M W Patterson, op. cit., 1953, p.15.

sake do the same'.[24]

For the rest of her life, Harriot was devoted to Thomas's memory. His statue continued to be the principal ornament of her great drawing room, and she always had his picture in her boudoir. The pillow on which he lay when he died was always placed in her carriage when she travelled, and she would never sleep on any other. She frequently went and read in what had been his sitting room in the Strand, and on the anniversary of their wedding day she used to kiss the desk at which he used to write. Such behaviour seems morbid by modern standards, but was not uncommon then, and in Harriot's case it was a genuine case of mourning.

Letters of condolence sent to Harriot show that many of Thomas's friends appreciated how happy she had made her husband. Lord Erskine, for example, wrote on 27 February 1822 to thank her for 'her most exemplary conduct' towards Thomas and for 'giving him a new and happy existence when most men cease to exist, and without which he must long ago have left us'.[25]

According to the report in *The Morning Post* Thomas was given a funeral full of pomp and circumstance, in the style of the day: ten horsemen, two and two, mutes, plumes of feathers, bearers, the hearse drawn by six black horses, bearing on the palls the armorial escutcheons of the family. There were supporters with scarves, three mourning coaches with six horses, the carriage of the deceased drawn by four black horses, followed by more than forty noblemen and gentlemen's carriages, among which were those of Their Royal Highnesses the Dukes of York, Clarence and Sussex, Lords Coventry, Cawdor etc. Supported by his grandson Lord Dudley Stuart and Sir Coutts Trotter – in the last year of his life Thomas Coutts had asked the new King to award a baronetcy to his friend and partner – Harriot Coutts was the chief mourner.

The funeral procession left Stratton Street on Monday, 4 March, on its way to the Parish Church of Wroxton, near Banbury, Oxfordshire. The journey took five days, the cavalcade proceeding with no great haste, but at a comfortable rate of

---

[24]E Coleridge, op. cit., 1920, p.366.
[25]Coutts Bank Archives, 3779.

eighteen miles a day, presumably due to the state of the roads. The procession had to put up each night at a posting inn, to make sure the horses were in good order for the funeral proper. One halt was at the George Inn, Windsor, where a room hung with black and decorated with escutcheons had been prepared to receive the coffin. On the fifth day, the procession reached its destination, and the coffin was laid in the family vault of the Earl of Guilford, alongside the remains of Thomas Coutts's first wife, Susannah, and his little grandson, Frederick Augustus, Lord North. Then or soon afterwards, a plain marble tablet was fixed to the wall of the Chancel in memory of Thomas Coutts; it was not until a century after her death that Lord Latymer erected a second tablet to record the birth and death of his great-grandmother, Susannah Coutts.

All kinds of rumours were afloat in 1822 as to the amount of Thomas Coutts's fortune and its disposal. Who was to benefit, and to what degree? This was soon to become known to an astonished public.

Chapter X
THE AGREEABLE SURPRISE[1]

The Richest Widow in Great Britain

Thomas Coutts's Will startled everyone, especially his daughters. Apart from certain trust property in which he had no personal interest, passed on to his partners as trustees, Thomas left everything to his wife. No one else, even his daughters, received a penny. Harriot had full control of all his property, stocks and shares, and his controlling partnership in the bank. He left it to her discretion whether and to what extent to share her fortune with her in-laws. Whether or not Harriot had foreknowledge of her inheritance is not known, but her husband expressed his total confidence in her good sense and business capacity.

Coutts's fortune was valued for probate at £900,000, which was an understatement since probate until 1898 excluded real property, i.e. freehold houses and lands, which meant large landowners were very much undervalued.

Coutts was not a great landowner, but his London property was very valuable, and he was one of the richest men to die in England in the first half of the nineteenth century. Only 74 persons left £500,000 or more in 'unsettled personalty' between 1809, when precise figures begin, and 1858, when probate was transferred from the Archiepiscopal courts of Canterbury and York to the national government. These included both Thomas and Harriot of course, and only a handful of women, so Harriot was doubly exceptional.[2]

Immediately after the reading of the Will, Harriot left her

---

[1] A play by John O'Keefe in which Harriot appeared as Cowslip in April 1798.
[2] W D Rubinstein, 'The Structure of Wealth-holding in Britain, 1809–1839', *Historical Research*, 1992.

Stratton Street house and went to the home of Sir Coutts Trotter, another partner in the Bank and an executor of the Will. She said she needed peace and quiet not only to grieve but to accustom herself to the news of her immense inheritance, but she doubtless also found it difficult to face Thomas's daughters. Lady Guilford remained at Stratton Street, and the following morning Lady Burdett went to Bath to join her family.

People were amazed at the 'singular disposition' of Coutts's property, and some said he had made the exclusive bequest to his wife to avoid legacy duty, which was charged on each bequest, but for so careful a man this was unlikely. According to the 'Friendly Person',[3] a few days after Coutts's death a famous law-lord met a friend who said, 'What a foolish Will old Coutts has made!' His Lordship replied, 'Mr Coutts never acted so wisely before; his wife knows his intentions, and I am sure she will perform them conscientiously, to the letter'. Baron Rivers wrote to Sir Edmund Antrobus, a director of the bank, on 8 March 1822, 'He could not have taken a more effectual method of proving her worth, of justifying his choice of her…'[4]

Coutts thus demonstrated complete trust in his wife's ability to handle business affairs. His Will was concerned not only with a family fortune but with the future of one of the great banks of Europe. Harriot as chief partner immediately began to take an active part in its management. The Duke of York wrote to her on 3 July 1822:

> Having learned from Mr [sic] Coutts Trotter the very handsome manner in which you have been so kind as to come forward to my assistance in consequence of my application for an advance of five thousand pounds from the Treasury I should not do justice to my feelings if I were to delay expressing to you myself my sincere thanks for this further mark of that attention that I have ever received from Your Self and Your late lamented husband.
> With kind regards, I remain, Dear Madam,
> Your very obedient Servant, Frederick.[5]

---

[3] A Friendly Person of the First Respectability, 1822, p.9.
[4] Coutts Bank Archives, 3921.
[5] Coutts Bank Archives, 6601B

Harriot had pressed the Bank to make the loan when the Treasury declined to do so.

Harriot intervened again when the Duke of Sussex asked the bank in August 1824 for a loan, and was told that the partners said its terms were 'contrary to the regulations of the House'. She wrote to the Duke offering the loan herself, and sent Andrew Dickie, the Chief Clerk, to deliver the letter personally. The Duke's reply, dated 14 August, thanked her for her offer, but said he had already had to 'seek relief elsewhere since it was urgent'. He felt no ill will to the partners, but 'had put his affairs into other hands and withdrawn his account from the Strand'. However, this 'made no difference to his personal feelings to Harriot, or towards the other partners'. He recalled the 'affectionate regard which he had entertained for Mr Coutts'.[6]

Andrew Dickie was a faithful man of business both to Harriot and to the other partners, but like Harriot he was treated with hauteur by Coutts's daughters. It was therefore with great amusement that Harriot received the following letter dated 12 January 1824 from Nell Goddard, her paid companion who was in Brighton. Nell reported that Andrew Dickie had been in Brighton on business, and went on:

> Mr Dickie called to take leave – I never really saw any man look so happy – it was delightful to see him. He told me he had been to pay his respects to Lady Guilford. She received him most kindly but regretted she could not ask him to dine, since she was already engaged out to dinner. With a low bow he thanked her Ladyship for the honour intended him, but said anyway he was engaged to dine at the Pavilion [with the King]. How I wish you had seen him, and heard him tell the different receptions he had met with… his Carriage – the Royal Carriage – was waiting at the door to take him to pay some more visits before he returned to the Pavilion to dinner.[7]

In 1826 Harriot ordered the bank to make gifts to Andrew Dickie of '£100 a year now and in future' (£50 at Christmas and £50 at

---

[6]Coutts Bank Archives, 3595.
[7]Coutts Bank Archives, 2878.

Midsummer).[8] In 1827, she insisted that her 'dear Andrew Dickie' should be made a partner in the Bank.[9] In this, as in so many other ways, her judgment was excellent, though the latter action would probably not have been approved by her late husband, who chose partners only from men of substance. In 1777, the bank had been so successful that Thomas needed an additional partner. Charles Taylor, his chief clerk who had worked in the House for nearly twenty years, demanded to be made a partner 'or he would leave that hour'. His claim seemed so absurd to Coutts that he agreed to let Taylor go at once, saying to the other partners, 'I hardly know any person I think more improper in every respect to be a Partner in a Banker's Shop than Mr Taylor'. Andrew Dickie became a remarkable partner, and was trusted by Harriot in all her affairs.

Harriot was also helpful to clients of the bank less exalted than royal dukes. She intervened when, in 1823, a gentleman who had amassed an immense fortune in India, on his death bequeathed £150,000 to Coutts Bank, leaving his widow only £500 per annum, which severely depleted her standard of living. Harriot got the bank to agree to allow the widow the interest on the money for her lifetime (she was aged 45 at the time her husband died); she then got an income of £7,500 for the rest of her life. In 1826 Robert James Potter, who had worked for the bank for ten years, threw himself on Harriot's mercy, asking for help with his debts. She had the Bank pay them, and also make him a gift of £150.[10] Harriot also intervened on behalf of Richard Johnson of Portsmouth, who confessed to forging a letter of credit for £250 in Harriot's name, but was caught, tried and sentenced to death. He threw himself on Harriot's mercy, writing to her on 2 February 1824 and telling her he had a wife and eight children.[11] She got his punishment transmuted to transportation for life, and she paid for his whole family to emigrate with him to Australia.[12]

In 1822, soon after Thomas's death, she divided a sum of

---

[8]Coutts Bank Archives, 4539.
[9]Healey, *Lady Unknown*, 1978, p.41.
[10]Coutts Bank Archives, 6689/8.
[11]Coutts Bank Archives, 15775.
[12]Margaret Cornwell Baron-Wilson, op. cit., Chapter XI.

thirty thousand pounds in equal portions between her three stepdaughters. A tenth of the total came from investments which had been promised or bestowed on his daughters in their father's lifetime, but the remaining £27,000 was an entirely voluntary gift from Harriot. Nonetheless, the daughters' relations with Harriot were strained. Always a valetudinarian, Lady Burdett wrote a few months after her father's death, saying she wished she could comfort her stepmother 'but alas! my own too generally suffering state renders me almost at all times a useless person where such exertion is required.'

On 10 August 1822 Harriot wrote to Edward Antrobus increasing the quarterly allowance paid by her to Coutts's daughters but guessing, correctly, that they would not feel grateful. She said wistfully, but with a little humour:

> I sincerely trust and hope you do not think I shall act wrong by altering the present paper-bond quarterlies signed by me – I own I am very foolish and weak God knows but I feel that some time or other these ladys will be obliged to acknowledge even to themselves that I am and ever have been their friend, and what I freely do for them is from my self alone and not by any wish or desire of my lost beloved Tom [but] I don't think Lady G ever will be affectionate or cordially friendly to me, which hurts me much, but as my saint used to say to me, 'I cannot help it, I have done my best' – there it must rest, but still my good kind friend, if you think I had better let what is now done remain it shall be so. The kind interest you have taken for me and my efforts is the only comfort I have left. God keep you for it and as you say it is possible to live on my small fortune. I will endeavour to make two ends meet and buy a lace veil or scarf if I like it.[13]

It is not clear how long these annual payments were made, but in 1824, two years after her husband's death, out of Harriot's gross income of £52,946 13s. 2d, a sum of £29,394 16s. 10d was disbursed to 'the Ladies'; whilst out of a net income of £23,551 16s she spent £21,685 on herself, thereby saving (according to Harriot) 'only a paltry residue of £1866'. The archive papers suggest that the allowances to Coutts's daughters continued on a

---

[13]Coutts Bank Archives, 16754/1.

generous scale down to 1831, when they were greatly reduced because Harriot's annual profits dropped by over £15,000.

Another letter from Harriot to Antrobus in July 1823, written from a hotel in Worthing, asked for a wedding present to be sent on her behalf to Lady Frances Stuart (Coutts's granddaughter) and Lord Sandon. She continued, 'The first wish of my heart is in all things to act wherein I may be concerned conformable to the advice and good judgment of you and all my kind friends in the Strand, as I am quite sure for the sake of beloved Mr Coutts… you will all ever continue friendly and affectionate to me'.[14] She retained the respect and goodwill of the partners and clerks at the Bank, though she was never to be treated well by Coutts's daughters, or by the popular press.

It was after Harriot was widowed that she was most severely lampooned and mocked. Her critics may have feared the wrath of Thomas Coutts and held their fire whilst he was alive, but anything that concerned 'the richest widow in Britain' (whether or not that description was strictly accurate) was of prurient interest to newspaper readers. Sir Francis Burdett encouraged his journalist friends to attack Harriot, because he was furious that his wife, and of course himself, had, in his opinion, been done out of her rightful inheritance.

One of the earliest and most bitter enemies of Harriot was Percy Wyndham, one of whose books bore the shamelessly libellous title *Mr Percy Wyndham's Strictures on an Imposter and Old Actress, formerly Bet the Pot Girl, alias the Banker's sham Widow, with Particulars of her Appearance at the Bar of Bow Street, of the Child Manufactury at Highgate, and Madam's Sleeping at the Horns at Kennington.*[15] He wrote of 'The indecent effrontery of this Vile, Wicked, Lying, Boasting, Puffing, She Pharisee, who would fain make you believe that instead of being the most vindictive Mercenary wretch upon Earth, is the most kind, unostentatious Charitable being in existence.' Hysterical, badly written, scurrilous and unbelievable, the book nonetheless sold well.

Before her marriage to Coutts, Harriot was not considered a

---

[14]Coutts Bank Archives, 16754/2.
[15]Percy Wyndham, 1822.

major target for caricaturists, so for many years she was spared the indignities her fellow actress, Dorothy Jordan, suffered at the hands of Gilray, but as a rich and famous widow she was fair game. She was pursued by avaricious suitors, who made excellent objects of satire. An engraving by Heath, dated 21 April, 1822, is entitled 'A Bold Stroke for a Wife no Chicken Hazard!' It showed Harriot standing between two kneeling suitors. She wears evening dress, ringlets, a tiara and her signature white ostrich feathers. On the right the obese Duke of York in tight uniform with sword and boots kneels, his hand on his breast, saying, 'Oh the delicious Fruit, could I but once obtain a Taste I should be my self again I'll put it to the Hazard.'

On the left a dandified Marquess of Worcester says, 'I never met with Flower or Fruit possessed of half the Charms I have and see in you.' Both add, 'So meet for our Necessities.' Harriot answers: 'Believe me, Sirs, I'll never Hazard all my happiness on dangerous Rocks where others have been wrecked. *The Gentleman's Magazine* reported that the Duke of York proposed marriage to Harriot, but there is no actual proof, and since the Duke was a great gambler, it is unlikely that Harriot would have accepted him, or that the King would have allowed his brother to marry a commoner.

For the first eighteen months of her widowhood Harriot lived a fairly quiet life, visiting friends, including the Duke of Devonshire at Chatsworth House in Derbyshire. When her mourning period was over, she resumed a full social life. It was not much noticed by the press until she gave a fête at Holly Lodge in July 1824. This took the world of fashion by storm and became the talk of London. *The Morning Post* wrote: 'Notwithstanding the unfavourable state of the weather, it was attended by about seven hundred Ladies and Gentlemen of the first rank and fashion in the country'. The guests included four Princes, three Dukes, two Duchesses, six Marquesses, four Marchionesses, ten Earls, ten Countesses, and numerous gentry. *The Morning Post* also reported that the guests' servants 'received two shillings each from Mrs Coutts's treasurer to purchase refreshments in the houses of victuallers in the neighbourhood. More than £200 was thus circulated on this occasion alone, in extending the sphere of the

Lady's hospitality'.

On this calculation the coachmen and footmen numbered over 2,000, representing in those days of 'vails' (gratuities) a large tax on hospitality. It was usual to tip the hostess's servants when visiting, but Harriot was reversing the custom, though the guests were expected to tip hers too. She knew that the servants' hall, though not as great as in the eighteenth century, was still a powerful ally in social advancement.

Five years later, when Harriot had become a Duchess, *The Court Journal* reported that her entertainments had become legendary:

> It was in 1824 that Mrs Coutts first shone forth a resplendent luminary in our fashionable hemisphere. In consequence of Lord Sandon's marriage [to Harriot's step-granddaughter], Lady Harrowby had taken her by the hand, in conjunction with Lady Stafford and the more influential members of Mrs Coutts's family who had profited by her Grace's liberality, and she was pronounced *bon ton* by a fiat not to be gainsaid. Exuberant as was the first fête at Holly Lodge... nothing was known of it till a few days beforehand, but when proclaimed all were dying to be of the élite... Fétes of equal magnificence have since taken place, but I question if a similar constellation of the supreme *bon ton* has shone with such lustre on any subsequent occasion.

Pace *The Court Journal*, Harriot was never fully accepted into the *bon ton*. Aristocratic women attended the first fête to satisfy their curiosity. At her subsequent fêtes noblemen in plenty were to be found, but their wives did not always accompany them, which made the event less socially respectable. This was a measure of the power wielded by those upper-class women who made the rules for society. A royal duke or two could always be counted on at Harriot's parties, but they could come without obligation since they were not bound to return her, or anyone else's, hospitality.

Like their successors today, some social diarists gave Harriot's social occasions more space than they really deserved, and she became the butt of malicious humour in the magazine *John Bull*, of which Lady Cowper wrote shrewdly to her brother in January 1821:

> There is a new paper published in England, called the *John Bull* which makes everybody angry. The editor is Theodore Hook. I am told it is clever but very abusive, and some times blackguard. It is aimed at the Whig Radicals, and I think it is abusing women very infamous...[16]

Such a licensed jester as Hook could not resist making fun of fatuous paragraphs on the trivia in Harriot's life that appeared in papers such as Brighton's *Morning Post*, which recorded her stay there in the winter of 1824–5. Worried that she might withdraw her patronage, it editorialized: 'It is much feared that Mrs Coutts, for whose presence and charities the indigent poor have come to pray, has changed her intention and will not return to Byham House this spring if much before the autumn of the year'. *John Bull* understandably poked fun at such reports. At length *The British Lion* rose to her defence and, in a long article on 17 April said indignantly:

> We assert that the unceasing worrying which Mrs Coutts experiences at the hands of *John Bull* is as uncalled for as it is unmanly, brutal and disgusting. About twice a month latterly this lady has figured in the columns of the newspaper we have just mentioned, either connected with some ribald jest on her possible re-marrying or some unwarrantable allusion to the supposed indiscretions of her early life. Does the *John Bull*, which is always affecting (for it gives not a tittle of proof, but what makes against the pretence) that its intercourse is with the noble and the great – does it dream that systematic and wanton personal attacks on such an individual as Mrs Coutts can be acceptable, nay, can be construed as anything short of a direct insult to the royal and illustrious personages who are not ashamed (and very rightly so) of the society of that lady? They, however, who are thus insulted will deserve it all if they continue to patronize the print which insults them.

This prompted *The Age*, in its first number on 15 May 1825, to go one better than *John Bull*,

---

[16]Lady Mabell Airlie, *Lady Palmerston and Her Times*, 1922, vol. I, pg.82.

> If people will thrust themselves forward and create public enquiry, they must expect public controversy. Why will the poor foolish woman make herself so notorious, and why will her friends do it for her? When the papers talk of her boundless charity and we know she never gave away a shilling but for the sake of ostentation, and has often paid as much for puffing as the sum puffed, we laugh – but when they will tell us of any really good action she ever did in her life we may manage to shed a tear. From the length of a purse she is introduced into the highest circles of the land... and as a great catch by way of winding up, sets her cap at my Lord Burford!

Lord Burford, heir to the dukedom of St Albans, and Harriot first met at a large dinner party. The guests were kept waiting so long that Harriot enquired the reason and was told they were waiting for the Duke of St Albans and his son, by his courtesy title Earl of Burford. The party was held to allow the son to get better acquainted with a great heiress of his own age with whom he contemplated marriage. After the dinner, Lord Burford, 'a retired, gentlemanly young man', instead of devoting attention to the heiress, took his place beside Mrs Coutts and remained there for the rest of the evening. They discovered a sympathetic bond in their mutual admiration of Shakespeare. After that evening Lord Burford, aged 23, paid court to Harriot, encouraged by his father, the Duke, who visited her at Holly Lodge with his daughters, Lady Charlotte and Lady Maria Beauclerk (the family surname).

Harriot's friendship with Burford was reported favourably by most journalists. However, *John Bull* published on 6 March 1825 an 'Advertisement – Wanted, by a widow, at the head of a long-established Banking-house in the metropolis, a Beau Clerk... should he be approved upon trial, he will probably be admitted as a sleeping partner...' Cruikshank fastened on the same pun in an engraving in March 1825 entitled, 'A Beau – Clerk – for a Banking – Concern', showing Harriot, fat, swarthy, and moustached, sitting at a table, holding out a cheque for £100,000 to Lord Burford. Harriot, décolleté and bejewelled, wearing a turban trimmed with a bird of paradise plume, is saying: 'I shall expect you will employ your time day and night for the benefit of the Concern, you must also be humble and submissive, should this be realized on Trial I will make you a Sleeping Partner'. The gold-bordered tablecloth is weighted with balls inscribed £20,000 and £9,000.

On 5 June 1825 *John Bull*, teasing the Society of Arts about their prizes for inventions, again took the opportunity to pillory Harriot: 'Mrs Coutts received the great golden cornucopia for her invention of transporting of atmospheres by means of large bags. The plan has been successfully acted upon, and the Sun and Air of St Albans, may be found at this moment in a process of adaptation to some extensive Melon beds at Highgate.'

On 8 June 1825 Harriot attended the Royal Drawing Room, presented by Lord Graves. According to Mrs Baron-Wilson, 'George IV received Mrs Coutts with the most marked kindness, and his amiable sister... addressed some phrases of courteous encouragement to Mrs Coutts, who, already agitated by her novel position, was nearly affected to tears by the considerate kindness of the princess.'

A similar Drawing Room in 1831, under William IV, was described in a letter from the historian, Thomas Babington Macaulay, to his sister:

> At half past one we reached St James's Palace... I have seen finer houses... Beef-eaters with their red coats and gold lace stood here and there; and now and then we met a magnificent looking person in a blue suit loaded with dazzling embroidery. A large anti-room [sic] had a few good pictures... I caught a glimpse of one of Vandyke's Henrietta-Marias as we passed through... we passed into a reception room, and squeezed ourselves into the presence-chamber. The room is handsome, the walls and ceiling covered with gilding and scarlet hangings... Fronting us was the throne under a gorgeous canopy... His Majesty was seated in all his glory... I could see little of the attendants of the King, by reason of the crowd.[17]

After Harriot's attendance at Court, *John Bull* on 12 June reported with heavy irony,

> While this Lady was merely received at the houses of those who,

---

[17] Haight, 1985, pp.3–6.

pleased with novelty and gaiety, gave her entertainments in return for those which she had given them, we saw no reason to question the evidence we possessed, or the facts which we had accumulated touching her conduct and character: but the case is now different, the Lady has been presented and received at the Court of St James, therefore we are certain that we must have been misled, and we should consider ourselves as committing not only a shameful violence towards her, but an act of the greatest disrespect in the highest quarters if we presumed to set our humble knowledge in array against the unequivocal result of an examination into the Lady's pretension which must have taken place before she could have appeared as the associate of all that is great and good in the Palace of the King of England.

George IV was certainly great but hardly good. The King was an egotist and a libertine. Before he was 21 his mistresses had included the Duchess of Devonshire, Lady Augusta Campbell, Harriet Vernon, Lady Melbourne, and the actress Mrs Robinson. Later he had affairs with the actresses Mrs Armistead, Mrs Billington and Mrs Crouch. He then married Mrs Fitzherbert, illegally under the 1702 Act of Settlement since she was a Roman Catholic, and doubly so under the 1772 Royal Marriages Act since they did not have the King's consent. There followed his legal marriage to Princess Caroline of Brunswick in 1795, during which Lady Jersey was his mistress, though he returned to Mrs Fitzherbert for a time. Lady Hertford succeeded Lady Jersey, and she in turn was supplanted by Lady Conyngham, known as the Vice-Queen when he became George IV, who remained his mistress until his death.

The caricaturists had not finished with Harriot. In an engraving in June 1825, Cruikshank satirised the social elevation of two theatrical celebrities, entitled, 'A visit to Court – or – All the World's a stage/ And all the men and women, merely players'. Mrs Coutts advances, her train held up by the (future) Duke of St Albans (a paper so inscribed hanging from his pocket). She is swarthy and moustached, jewelled and befeathered; her dress is bordered with cornucopias showering coins; a cross hangs from her neck. She carries a melon-shaped reticule.

These attacks did not deter her admirers; *The Morning Post* described 'a breakfast of one of the most sumptuous and luxurious description', of which it took several issues to give a full account, including a list of the 'titled personages present at the fete, including a couple of dukes and Prince Leopold.' The Duke of Gordon proposed the toast: 'I have by the blessing of God just attained my ninetieth year and I feel highly honoured in proposing the health of Mrs Coutts with three times three [cheers]'.

Two cartoons featured Harriot at the theatre. In one published by John Fairburn, dated July 1825, and entitled 'Some-thing! Peeping at No-thing', she is portrayed as a stout woman in full evening dress, with feathered tiara, in an opera box, staring at Giovanni-Battista Velluti, the last of the great Italian male castrati, who visited England for the first time in 1825. Harriot is looking at him through a large opera glass and saying, 'Really I can see nothing to admire about the Creature, He will never prove a loadstone of Attraction, for he is not perfect in his parts!' In another cartoon by Cruikshank, dated September 1825 and entitled 'The Living Skeleton', Harriot, among others, is staring at Seurat, who says, 'I am de Anatomie Vivante dat is come to Londres to please all de pretty Lady, and give dem all de much satisfaction'. Harriot is saying, 'Poor creature, he seems very little calculated in my opinion to please the ladies, tho' really he is as stout as the Old Banker was.'

The 8th Duke of St Albans died on 17 July 1825 and his eldest son succeeded to the title. Harriot wrote to him the following day:

> Dear Lord Burford: I received this morning the melancholy information of your Father's Death – with sincere sorrow I address you. You are now placed in a most important situation. You must exert all your faculties – be noble and honourable, just and kind to all dependent on you – and above all remember to humble yourself to God, implore his blessing on all you undertake… remember me affectionately to your sisters, for they will need all your kindness at this most desolate time. Sincerely yours, Harriot Coutts.[18]

A new and still more brilliant phase of Harriot Coutts's life was

---

[18] Coutts Bank Archives, 1340.

about to begin. Lady Cowper commented in a letter to her brother dated 17 July, 'The Duke of St Albans is dead and so now Mrs Coutts may be a Duchess, if she thinks it worth while'.[19] Lady Cowper plainly did not think Harriot was the one who would gain most advantage from the match. But what do we know about the very young and innocent Duke who now courted Harriot?

---

[19]Lady Mabell Airlie, op. cit., 1922, p.121.

Chapter XI
SHE WOULD AND SHE WOULD NOT[1]

Courtship by a Duke

The Dukedom of St Albans was created by King Charles II, to ennoble his son by his mistress, the Drury Lane actress Nell Gwyn. When William Aubrey De Vere Beauclerk was born, on the 24 March 1801, the principal family seat was Redbourne Hall in Lincolnshire. He was styled Earl of Burford from 1816 to 1825, when he succeeded his father to the dukedom. The irony of the ninth Duke courting a former Drury Lane actress was not lost on early nineteenth-century cartoonists.

The Dukes of St Albans had not been either illustrious or accomplished. Lord Hervey said of the 2nd Duke that he was 'one of the weakest men either of the legitimate or spurious brood of the Stuarts'.[2] Horace Walpole called his son 'the simple Duke of St Albans', but he managed to pack his life with 'a glittering crescendo of feats of incompetence quite unparalleled in the lives of any other dukes in the eighteenth century'.[3] By the time he died in 1786, the St Albans finances were in chaos.

The 4th Duke, second cousin to the 3rd, was a close friend of George III, but he was only duke for a year before he died, unmarried, at the age of twenty-eight. The 5th Duke was a cousin once removed to the 4th, and his son, the 6th Duke, according to Lady Harriet Cavendish, was 'the most hideous, disagreeable little animal that I ever met'.[4]

---

[1] A play by Colley Cibber in which Harriot appeared as Vilette in October 1811.
[2] Cockayne.
[3] D Adamson and P Dewar, *The House of Nell Gwyn*, 1974, p.49.
[4] Letters, p.36.

Compared with these ancestors the 9th Duke, who courted Harriot Coutts, was a paragon of simple virtue. A few years earlier, he had been engaged to Elizabeth Conyngham, daughter of the reigning mistress of George IV. Lady Conyngham told everyone that Elizabeth would be mistress of the home because he was 'odd'. Lady Cowper commented, 'They should know that sometimes fools are the most difficult to manage.' Thomas Creevey wrote in his diary that the young man 'became so unmannerly and cross that the lady sent him a letter of dismissal', and others thought she had been lucky to avoid the marriage. Mrs Arbuthnot wrote in her journal that Lord Burford was 'all but an idiot and had been confined', but Lady Cowper, who was nearer the truth, said, 'The fact is, he is not an innocent or an idiot, but a very raw, uncultivated strange Cub, and I believe not a bad kind of person'. According to *Cockayne's Complete Peerage*,[5] Burford was 'admitted nobleman at Christ's College, Cambridge, on 30 June 1828; created LL.D. (Cambridge) the same year; and bore the Sceptre with the Cross at the Coronation of William IV on 8 September 1831. A Whig in politics, he voted in favour of the Reform Bill in 1832.' Above all, as dukes go he was poor and in need of a rich wife, so why not court the richest woman in Britain?

In September 1825, Harriot set out on a tour of England and Scotland, accompanied by the new Duke of St Albans and his sister Lady Charlotte Beauclerk. Some newspapers reported her journey in sycophantic terms, but hostile journals treated her as an upstart of dubious character. *John Bull* said:

> We have not any... animosity towards Mrs Coutts, but we would ask her minions and myrmidons if they suppose the world will bear to hear of Mrs Coutts and suite accompanied by the Duke of St Albans doing this and doing that? We say No... let Mrs Coutts stand fairly in society as the widow of a banker... and... enjoy her wealth... but do not let her imagine that money can alter her real character and attributes...

A week later *John Bull* attacked a trivial piece from The *Morning*

---

[5]Cockayne's Complete Peerage.

Post on Harriot's visit to the Earl of Lauderdale and the Earl of Breadalbane, saying: 'This mummery must be put down; it is as disgusting as it is disgraceful'.

Harriot was generous with gifts during her tour, and was everywhere well received. At Edinburgh she presented the Lord Provost with a silver vase, and gave £150 to different charities. *John Bull* sneered at her modest donation of £20 to the poor of Edinburgh, to be shared, it guessed, between 38,000 persons. Yet she was held in high respect for her charities by poor and working people in Scotland. Constable the publisher told C R Leslie that Meg Dodds – mistress of an inn halfway between Edinburgh and Abbotsford – said Sir Walter Scott 'had ill-obliged her by not giving her notice that so great a lady as Mrs Coutts was coming, in order that she might be prepared to receive her properly.' Meg thought that 'the greatest woman in all England was on her way to visit the greatest man in all Scotland'.[6]

Sir Walter Scott invited Harriot and her friends, the Duke and his sister, to stay at his home, Abbotsford, with 'old fashioned Scotch folk who give our friends the best reception they can and never trouble them with apologies if the accommodations are not what they are used to'.[7]

This was not Harriot's first visit to Abbotsford, since Scott had a family connection with Thomas Coutts. Sir Coutts Trotter, her partner at the Bank, wondered whether Harriot was seriously considering marrying the Duke, and wrote to Scott: 'There is no one from whom she would be so willing to receive advice… as from you who are her cousin and who, I hope, will also be her counsellor'.

No person of consequence visited Scotland without being invited by the novelist to his home. By the 1820s Scott was no longer the 'Great Unknown' writer of the Waverley novels; his publisher Constable thought he was the most extraordinary man living. Lord Byron dedicated his poem 'Cain' to him, and when George IV visited Edinburgh in 1822 he said Scott was the man he most wanted to see. French by birth, Lady Scott was kind and

---

[6]C R Leslie, *Autobiographical Recollections*, 1860.
[7]Coutts Bank Archives, 3781.

witty, despite her 'rouge and roses and strange jabber' which gave some the impression she was a brainless oddity. Sir Walter excited envy by his rise in prosperity and style of living, so he sympathised with Harriot about her treatment as *nouveau riche*.

Guests whom Scott called 'birds of passage' descended on him in droves, but the house was large enough to accommodate ten of them at a time, as well as their servants. Harriot was enchanted by the magnificence of Abbotsford. Scott had whimsical inspirations and often changed his mind during the construction of the house, which was lit by oil gas, with a generating apparatus on the site of the old stable. The chimney piece of the entrance hall was carved out of local dark-red freestone, in a design modelled on a cloister-arch at nearby Melrose Abbey, and in the hall were countless animal horns, enough, Sir Walter said, 'to furnish a whole world of cuckoldom.' He had grained Jamaica cedarwood, of the colour of gingerbread, for the woodwork of both the drawing room and the library, including the bookshelves.

Lockhart reported that when Harriot first visited Abbotsford in 1824 several ladies of high birth and rank were there, who behaved rudely to her. Sir Walter was upset, and appealed to 'the youngest and gayest and cleverest, who was also the highest in rank, a lovely Marchioness', saying he knew that the fine ladies in London accepted invitations to Mrs Coutts's grand balls and fêtes, and then in private circles 'tipped her the cold shoulder', but he could not believe the Marchioness would behave so. He said all his guests had known beforehand that Mrs Coutts would be joining them, so they could have left before she arrived, and he asked those who had stayed to behave decently towards her. According to Lockhart, the Marchioness promised to make amends, and soon Harriot was relaxed and happy, telling anecdotes of her early theatrical years and joining in the singing.[8]

C R Leslie gave a different version of events. He said he had no doubt Sir Walter did have a word with Lady Compton, for he remembered that she was very polite to Mrs Coutts in the evening and sat down to the piano to accompany her in a song. But Harriot was not mollified, and did not stay as long as

---

[8] J G Lockhart, Memoirs of the Life of Sir Walter Scott, 10 vols., 1891.

expected.[9]

Leslie said the other women were offended because of what had occurred before Harriot came. On the day she was expected she was late, and dinner was postponed for two hours, until Harriot sent word that she was delayed until the next day for want of horses. Sir Walter may not have intended discourtesy to his other guests by keeping them waiting for dinner, but he was more impressed by wealth than by rank. As his son-in-law, John Lockhart wrote, 'I dare not deny that he set more of his affections during the great part of his life upon worldly things, wealth among others, than might have become such an intellect'.

Stewart Newton was also at Abbotsford at the time. Later, at one of her fêtes at Holly Lodge, he reminded Harriot that he had 'had the honour of meeting her at Sir Walter Scott's'. She replied, 'Oh, I remember, it was when those horrible women were there. Sir Walter was kind and did all in his power, but I could not stay in the house with them'.

Scott took Harriot to visit Melrose Abbey.[10] Concerned about the ancient ruins owned by the Duke of Buccleugh, he had offered to oversee the repair work to the Abbey himself. He copied for Harriot an inscription on one of the tombstones there:

> The Earth goeth on the earth glistering like gold
> The Earth goeth to the earth sooner than it wolde
> The Earth builds on the earth castles and towers
> The Earth says to the earth all shall be ours.

Harriot kept the paper, and wrote under the inscription: 'Abbotsford Sept. 11th 1824 / Written with Sir Walter Scott's own pen / sitting in his own Chair/ How I shall be envyd. Harriot Coutts'.[11]

Harriot was considerate enough not to arrive at Abbotsford in 1825 with all her retinue (she left behind in Edinburgh four of her seven carriages), but the appearance of three coaches was 'trying to poor Lady Scott'. Harriot had two doctors with her, 'for

---

[9]C R Leslie, *Autobiographical Recollections*, 1860.
[10]Coutts Archives, 79.
[11]Coutts Archive, 79A.

it had been considered that one doctor might himself be disabled in the course of an expedition so adventurous', and 'besides other menials of every grade, there were two bedchamber women for Mrs Coutts's own person... because in her widowed condition she was fearful of ghosts, and there must be one Abigail for the service of the toilette, and a second to keep watch by night'.[12]

On relations between Harriot and the Duke, Scott wrote, 'Mrs Coutts told me she had declined his addresses... I think however she may change her mind'.[13] He showed conditional approval of the possible match in his journal:

> Mrs Coutts, with the Duke of St Albans and Lady Charlotte Beauclerk, called to take leave of us. When at Abbotsford his suit throve but coldly. She made me, I believe, her confidant in sincerity; she had refused him twice, and decidedly; he was merely on the footing of friendship; I urged it was akin to love; she allowed she might marry the duke, only she had at present not the least inclination that way. Is this frank admission more favourable for the duke than an absolute protestation against the possibility of such a marriage? I think not... If the duke marries her, he ensures an immense fortune; if she marries him, she has the first rank. If he marries a woman older than himself by twenty years, she marries a man younger in wit by twenty degrees. I do not think he will dilapidate her fortune; he seems good and gentle. I do not think she will abuse his softness of disposition – shall I say, or of – head. The disparity of ages concerns no one but themselves; so they have my consent to marry if they can get each other's. Just as this is written, enter my Lord of St Albans and Lady Charlotte, to beg I would recommend a book of sermons to Mrs Coutts... recommended Logan's... The mission, I suppose, was a little display on the part of good Mrs Coutts of authority over her high aristocratic suitor. I did not suspect her of turning devote; and retract my consent as given above, unless she remains 'burly, brisk and jolly'![14]

Besides noting the mental deficiencies of the Duke, Scott also gave his opinion of Harriot, whom he had always found 'a kind,

---

[12]Margaret Cornwell Baron-Wilson, op. cit., p.188.
[13]Correspondence, ix, 1935, pg.267f.
[14]J G Lockhart, op cit., 1839, vol. viii, pp.72–6.

friendly woman, without either affectation or insolence in the display of her wealth... She is a very good natured person and has been very liberal of her wealth and not injudiciously where she could relieve distress.' Sir Walter also commented that 'so much wealth can hardly be enjoyed without the appearance of ostentation'.

A footnote to Harriot's friendship with Scott was that at the end of his life, when Sir Walter was desperately in debt, an anonymous donor offered him a large sum of money, but he refused it. The offer came from Harriot, though she did not wish to publicise it. After her death, Lockhart, wishing to record the offer in his memoirs of Scott, asked permission of Angela Burdett-Coutts. She refused, saying the Duchess had not wished it to be known and so it should remain.[15]

The tour of Scotland over, Harriot returned south, and the English newspapers were again able to write about her dinner parties and her musical assemblies, many of which were held in Brighton. *The Brighton Morning Post* said that after some hesitation Harriot had rented a mansion on Marine Parade and held a ball for her fashionable friends, where 'the supper table embellishments were as fanciful as rich'.

In 1825 a journalist called Mitford published a fictitious biography entitled, *A Tale of the Last Century: the Secret Memoirs of Harriott Pumpkin, a celebrated actress; from her infancy to her seduction of, and subsequent marriage with A BANKER.*[16] Harriot was deeply upset by its false allegations, and she bought up and had destroyed as many copies of the book as she could get hold of (there is one in the British Library), but its contents became widely known and caused great amusement. She never sued for libel, since for members of Society such calumnies were supposed to be beneath contempt.

In England in 1825 the economic boom suddenly turned to black depression. In December the great banking house of Sir Peter Pole closed its doors, and seven other banks broke in quick

---

[15]Edna Healy, *Coutts & Co: The Portrait of a Private Bank*, 1992, p.271.
[16]Mitford, *A Tale of the Last Century: the Secret Memoirs of Harriott Pumpkin, a celebrated actress; from her infancy to her seduction of, and subsequent marriage with A BANKER*

succession. The financial situation was serious, and industrial production reacted to it. There was general poverty, and in the North and Midlands some rioting and destruction of the machinery blamed for causing over-production and unemployment. A cartoon by Marks was entitled 'Stout as Ever: Didicated [sic] to those Gentlemen loanist [sic] who brought the City to this Momentary Confusion'. In a bank vault with chests, moneybags, and coins, Sir William Curtis, of Curtis, Robarts and Curtis, and Harriot Coutts face each other, both seated on chests. A comic figure, wearing an alderman's chain, holds out a bag of Cash, saying, 'How d'ye do madam wish you a happy Christmas glad to see ye look so Stout, hard blowing weather this Houses firm, no fear of tumbling – happy to have it in my power to serve you in any way madam...' Mrs Coutts, who is good-looking but very fat, answers, 'Tight as a melon Sir William, glad to see you so well weather rather squally – but I think we are both Stout enough to bear it'.[17] The implication was that Coutts Bank was sound enough to survive the crisis, which it did.

Unlike Jane Austen, who said in *Mansfield Park*[18] 'Let other pens dwell on guilt and misery. I quit such odious subjects as soon as I can', Harriot was constantly moved by the distress she saw around her. She still gave a lot money to charity, despite the bank crisis and the critical reception of her earlier philanthropy. She supported liberally the famine-stricken Irish peasantry, to which her maternal grandparents had belonged, but she had learned to be more careful than she had been in the early days of her marriage. Horace Smith wrote of her later philanthropy:

> She never trusted to the representations, however sad and plausible, which were addressed to her every day in scores of letters, but subjected them, in the first instance, to the investigation of her secretary or treasurer, who made enquiries among such of the permanent residents as were best acquainted with individual cases of distress, as well as with the wants of public charities and institutions. Rarely, indeed, was bounty

---

[17]M Dorothy George, *Catalogue of Prints and Drawings in the British Museum: Division 1, Political and Personal Satires*, vols. 5–11, 1949, p14809.
[18]Jane Austen, *Mansfield Park*.

withheld where the claims proved to be just.

The Brighton Morning Post was in a state of excitement regarding Harriot's movements during her stay there in January and February 1826: its report that 'Mrs Coutts and Lady Dudley Stuart arrived on Monday last to dinner at the Albion Hotel, where they occupy fifteen rooms', provoked *The Age* to write facetiously: 'With the dimensions of Lady Dudley Stuart we are not particularly acquainted, and although we always knew Mrs Coutts to be what is styled vulgo, a whapper, we could not have imagined such circumstances would ever have compelled her to occupy fifteen rooms!'

Rumours of marriage between Harriot and the Duke of St Albans provoked in February 1826 Cruikshank's cartoon 'Paul Pry at Widow C----'s'.[19] The actor, Liston, playing the part of Paul Pry, was then the talk of the town. The cartoon shows Harriot, with moustache and feathered hat, standing in her bank, her back to a counter covered with moneybags, and huge stacks of sovereigns on the floor, when Paul Pry enters hat in hand. He says, 'Good morning, my dear Madam, I hope I don't intrude, Just dropp'd in, in passing, to enquire after your welfare, sad times these for Bankers!... I beg pardon, I had nearly forgot to ask how the Duke is, he's very often at your house they say, you have not made a Match of it yet have you?'. She answers: 'Indeed Mr Pry you are a most impertinent fellow, and I desire that you will quit my House immediately'.

The Morning Post reported: 'Mrs Coutts gave her first ball for the season at her house in Stratton Street on Monday. Nothing could exceed the grandeur and magnificence of the entertainment, which was honoured by the presence of their Royal Highnesses the Dukes of Sussex and Gloucester, and Prince Leopold, and about 700 distinguished fashionables'. In June 1826 there was a General Election. Lady Cowper wrote, 'People think this new Parliament will be a curious one, such strange things have turned out. There are three stockbrokers in it, which was never the case before'. The (upper) middle class was

---

[19] M Dorothy George, op. cit., 1949, p15159.

infiltrating the citadel of political power.

Yet public attention seemed as much focused on the possibility of Harriot Coutts becoming a Duchess as on politics. A cartoon by Heath appeared, entitled 'Life of an Actress. Auspicium Meliores Aevi' [a sign of better times], in which Harriot's life was shown in an ascending series of prints, each resting on the rung of a ladder which broadens as it goes up. (1) At the base, where mushrooms are growing, is a print of a Cinderella figure kneeling to scour pots. (2) She acts on a makeshift stage in a barn. (3) Harriot acts behind the footlights, while an elderly admirer (Coutts) watches from a stage box. (4) Coutts and Harriot sit together; he points to a large bag of gold. (5) In widow's weeds she stands among countless moneybags. (6) In evening dress, Harriot is tête-à-tête with George IV. Behind is the motto: 'Honi Soit...Pence [altered to] Pense'. (7) A tiny duke stands beside the massive lady, pointing to a signpost 'To St Albans'; behind Harriot is her banking-house inscribed 'Strand'. She holds a cord, the end of which extends above the print to a large coronet which rests on the top rung of the ladder and is flanked by empty purses.[20]

The caricaturists and newspaper hacks were not the only people to make fun of Harriot, as Creevey's diaries show. Thomas Creevey, born in 1768 of a Liverpool merchant's wife, but allegedly the illegitimate son of the 1st Earl of Sefton, became a barrister and M.P. for Thetford, a pocket borough jointly in the gift of the Duke of Norfolk and Lord Petre. He was a notoriously malicious gossip. Apropos of Harriot Coutts he wrote, at Cantley on 16 September 1826

> As for [the Countess of Tankerville]... I have made her tell her stories over and over again. I think she shines most about Mrs Coutts, with whom she has lately become acquainted at Worthing. It is impossible by letter to do justice to her acting, and her broken English: 'A play being acted at Worthing... Mrs Coutts... left her own box, and came to ours, and sat herself upon an empty bench, just behind us, and almost directly she began, 'I am sure, Lady Tankerville, you must find this a very wicked and

---

[20]M Dorothy George, op. cit. 1949, p.15085.

ill-natured world, I know I find it so myself. I dare say you have heard all the stories they tell of me going to be married to Lord Burford. Good God, how can you think I would marry a boy. He is quite a child as compared with me, and when I think of my dear Coutts, how is it possible? To be sure Lord Burford is quite charming; then his sisters are so charming. It is so delightful to me after spending a morning with those vulgar people at my Bank to enjoy the society of these enlightened girls… I have not a friend in the world, every body cheats me; I pay three times as much as any body else for every thing; then I can't manage my accounts, and tho' dear Mr Coutts left me so much, I am very often short of money. Ill-natured people say I married Mr Coutts for money, how could that be when I give his Daughters £35,000 a year …?' So I said, 'My dear Mrs Coutts, surely you might get somebody who is poor to take care of your concerns for £200 or £300 a year?'[21]

This could only be fiction. It was never Harriot's way to speak disrespectfully of her partners and employees at the Bank, nor would she have said she could not manage her own business affairs, since she was so astute, but Creevey was happy to pass on and embroider malicious gossip.

Sir Walter Scott wrote in his journal for October 1826: 'Dined with Mrs Coutts. Tragi-comic distress of my good friend on the marriage of her presumptive Heir with a daughter of Lucien Bonaparte'. Lord Dudley Coutts Stuart, grandson of Thomas Coutts and also Harriot's godson, had married Christina, a niece of Napoleon Bonaparte, in 1824 in Florence. Lady Bute, his mother, wrote to Harriot immediately from Italy, saying the scandal could 'only be obviated by the immediate sanction of my family and friends'. She asked Harriot to see how essential it was to her happiness 'to efface the humiliation'. She begged her to receive Dudley and his wife kindly, and give him the position in the Bank planned for him. She (Lady Bute) had received Dudley's wife 'as if her consent had previously been given'.[22] The newly-weds returned to England, and Harriot gave Lord Dudley the bank position and an annual income of £2,000, though she

---

[21]J Gore, ed, op. cit., 1934, pp.216–217.
[22]Coutts Bank Archives, 2060.

considered Christina a spendthrift. The marriage was not officially recognised until 1828, because the Count of Fosse claimed to be already married to Christina, and it took four years to sort this out and get the Stuart marriage recognised in Rome. If Harriot had ever intended to make Lord Dudley Stuart her heir, which is doubtful, she changed her mind when he married a French woman. She was prejudiced against all foreigners, and the French most of all.

The Duke of St Albans regularly stayed with Harriot at Brighton, accompanying her wherever she went during 1826; with Sir John and Lady Dashwood King he attended her on a visit to Essex, where the faithful *Morning Post* reported that she put up 'at the Black Boy, Chelmsford, to pay her respects to her tenantry'. He is said to have made his first proposal of marriage in the spring of 1826. Harriot was flattered but feared that a young man of 25 could scarcely know his own mind and might soon regret proposing to a woman of almost 50. She told him to return in a year's time, and if he then repeated the proposal she would accept him. During that year he was much in her company and she later told Mrs Baron-Wilson: 'I became exceedingly attached to my handsome young duke, and quite vexed when people talked of his marrying with any other person.' A year later, in 1827, the duke proposed again, having sent her in February a beautiful Valentine card with two golden hearts at the top, scrolls bearing romantic couplets, a pink rose in the centre which could be opened by pulling a string, to reveal and a pair of turtle doves beneath. Harriot still vacillated because a woman friend had ridiculed the match and prophesied disaster as the outcome, but eventually she accepted the proposal and gave instructions to her lawyers to prepare the marriage settlement.

On the 13th June, 1827, Harriot wrote to inform King George IV, as a loyal courtier, of her impending marriage:

> Sire, The condescending notice with which Your Majesty has always been pleased to honour me induces me to hope that I may venture to intrude on Your Majesty with a communication of deep interest to myself.
>
> Permit me, Sire, humbly and dutifully to acquaint Your Majesty that arrangements have been finally made for my

marriage with the Duke of St Albans on Saturday next. But as these arrangements were not completed until yesterday, I did not think it would be respectful to trouble Your Majesty with the occurrence before.

I have the honour to remain, Sire, with every sentiment of duty and grateful acknowledgment of Your Majesty's untired kindness,

Your Majesty's Most dutiful and loyal subject and servant,
Harriot Coutts.[23]

The King replied from Royal Lodge on the 14th June,

Dear Madam,
Anything that can contribute to your happiness will always give me sincere pleasure, and I beg to offer my congratulations to you and the Duke upon the occasion.
Your very sincere friend,
George Rex.[24]

The royal message was read out at the ducal wedding breakfast.

---

[23] Coutts Bank Archives, 1341.
[24] Coutts Bank Archives, 80.

Chapter XII
A BOLD STROKE FOR A HUSBAND[1]

Duchess of St Albans

When she married the 9th Duke of St Albans in 1827, Harriot Mellon was the sixth actress to marry an English peer.[2] He was then 26 years old, and she was almost 50. Harriot's stepson-in-law, Sir Francis Burdett, sat up with her until four in the morning on the night before the wedding, trying to persuade her not to go through with it.[3] But the ceremony took place, by special licence, on Saturday, 16 June 1827 in her home in Stratton Street. They were married in the great drawing room, which had been magnificently decorated for the event. An altar was erected, covered with crimson velvet richly ornamented with gold lace and fringes, and the chairs and cushions were all in a similar red velvet. Harriot wore a gown of Brussels lace that had cost 300 guineas, and had a diamond comb in her hair, which was still raven black. The ceremony was performed by the Rev. Lord Frederick Beauclerk, the duke's uncle, better known as a cricketer than as a divine – he was one of the founders of the Marylebone Cricket Club (the M.C.C.).

Immediately afterwards, the Duke received from his bride a wedding present of £30,000, plus an estate in Essex valued at £25,000, from Harriot's own separate property. The Duke gave the bride some jewels, along with his hand, heart and title. On the wedding day, Harriot gave a lavish entertainment at the Freemason's Tavern for all the clerks in Coutts's banking house.

Mary Wollstonecraft wrote that marriage was 'the only way for

---

[1] A play by Hannah Cowley in which Harriot appeared as Olivia in 1803.
[2] J M Bulloch, Notes and Queries, 10 August 1935, vol.169, pp.92–94.
[3] P Dewar & D Adamson, op. cit., 1974, pp.97–9.

a woman to rise in the world'.[4] Harriot Mellon and many other actresses improved their living standards by their talents and earnings on the stage, but marriage to someone from a higher stratum in society was the most likely way for a woman to achieve upward social mobility. The aristocracy frequently exchanged titles for wealth, in a so-called marriage market, and the marriage of a wealthy widow such as Harriot to an impecunious nobleman like the Duke was not unusual; it was uncommon only in that she was old enough to be his mother.

If the Duke married for money, he did not secure long-term advantage. Harriot had no intention of handing control of her fortune to her new husband. Only a modest portion of her immense fortune came to him on her death, and even then as a life annuity. Yet the Duke recognised Harriot's innate kindness and generosity, and with ups and downs they were to live comfortably together until Harriot's death ten years later, though he endured much mockery both before and after the marriage. A caricature published in November 1825, entitled 'The New Banking Company's Scales of Equity' shows a pair of scales, one scale filled by a large melon from which a slice has been cut, and by a paper: One Million Sterling! The scale is inscribed 'The times are Rank Hamlet', and it slightly outweighs the other which is filled by a ducal coronet and deeds.[5]

Cruikshank made a series of scabrous prints about the marriage. One dated June 1827 is entitled, 'The Morning after Marriage – or the New Maid Dutchess Delighted: a Scene in the new Farce of the Honey Moon, now performing with unbounded applause at Highgate Places taken at ye Horns'.[6]

Another is entitled 'A New Farce in High Life'. In the centre a handsome well-dressed barber and the Duke of St Albans face each other in profile. The Duke says: 'Frisby, here's £250 to furnish the house in a better style. Mum, don't say a word about it to my old Dutchess. Take the Gift and drive off immediately, tell my dear Girl I'll fly into her Arms as soon as possible – away my Barbatum! away!' The Duchess enters and, says, 'Poor Boy! I will

---

[4]Mary Wollstonecraft, *A Vindication of the Rights of Women*, 1792.
[5]M Dorothy George, op. cit.,1949, p. 15453.
[6]M Dorothy George, op. cit., 1949, p. 15456.

allow him to indulge his Fancy the Title is all I wanted, indeed it is all he could do for me, however he must mind his P.'s and Q.'s – or I'll Cut him off with a shilling'.[7] A third engraving, of July 1827, was 'The Ripe Melon! – and Musty Pumpkin! Dedicated to the New Maid Dutchess!' There are two designs side by side: one shows Harriot Mellon with Tom Coutts who is kissing her and saying: 'take all my bags of Gold, my love! but let me enjoy the Melon ripe and plump!' In the second design Harriot, now fat, elderly, and dressed like a child's nurse, sits on a low chair holding the Duke of St Albans on her knee. She holds up a bag of Gold, saying, with a coaxing smile, 'Here's a Gold Plumb for you my dear Boy, only put that Coronet on my head, my darling beauty!'[8]

There was much unkind comment on Harriot's appearance. She became more hirsute in later life so she was often caricatured with a moustache. A cartoon by Cruikshank, entitled 'A Sketch at St Albans – or – Shaving the New Maid Dutchess!' showed the Duke of St Albans standing over his wife, holding her chin, a razor in his hand. He was wearing a coronet, and dressed like a barber, with short striped jacket, knee-breeches, and apron with comb, curling-tongs etc. in the pocket.[9]

Despite these vicious representations, Harriot stayed calm. She wrote to Sir Walter Scott from Stratton Street on 16 July 1827 a letter which shows her true feelings:

My dear Sir Walter Scott,
Your most welcome letter has 'wandered many a weary mile after me'. Thanks, many thanks, for all your kind congratulations. I am a Duchess at last, that is certain, but whether I am the better for it remains to be proved. The Duke is very amiable, gentle, and well disposed, and I am sure he has taken pains enough to accomplish what he says has been the first wish of his heart for the last three years. All this is very flattering to an old lady, and we lived so long in friendship with each other that I was afraid I should be unhappy if I did not say I will – yet (whisper it, dear Sir Walter), the name of Coutts – and a right good one it is, and ever will be,

---
[7] M Dorothy George, op. cit., 1949, p.15457.
[8] M Dorothy George, op. cit., 1949, p.15458.
[9] M Dorothy George, op. cit., 1949, p.15455.

dear to my heart.

And she perceptively and poignantly summed up for him her fairy tale life:

> What a strange, eventful life has mine been, from a poor little player child with just food and clothes to cover me, dependent on a very precarious profession, without talent or a friend in the world! 'to have seen what I have seen, seeing what I see'. Is it not wonderful? Is it true? Can I believe it? – first the wife of the best, the most perfect being that ever breathed, his love and unbounded confidence in me, his immense fortune so honourably acquired by his own industry, all at my command… and now the wife of a Duke. You must write my life; the History of Tom Thumb, Jack the Giant-Killer, and Goody Two Shoes will sink compared with my true history written by the Author of 'Waverley'; and that you may do it well I have sent you an inkstand. Pray give it a place on your table in kind remembrance of your affectionate friend,
> Harriot St Albans[10]

Unfortunately, Sir Walter Scott did not follow up her suggestion, which would have been stranger than many of his fictions.

Harriot guessed that the aristocracy to which she now belonged by marriage would not rush to accept her, so she and the Duke lived quietly for some months, hoping the coarse satires would abate, However, a lithograph dated 1 October 1827, by H.B, entitled 'This is no Caricature' showed the new Duchess possessively taking the arm of a dejected Duke of St Albans; and an engraving by Heath renewed criticism of the marriage.[11]

Rumours began to circulate that Harriot and the Duke were having difficulties in their personal relations. On one occasion, not long after marriage, it was said the Duke ran away when they were staying at a hotel in Portsmouth with three of his brothers. One morning the Lords Frederick, Henry and Charles Beauclerk, all in their teens, breakfasted early to go sailing with the Duke. Harriot was always worried about his health and safety; she did

---

[10]Charles Pearce, op. cit., 1915, p.264.
[11]M Dorothy George, op. cit., 1949, 15461, 15462.

not wish her husband to go sailing, and burst into a terrific fit of rage. The Duke would not stand for this, and went off to London. Harriot followed him, and a reconciliation took place. She did not like the Duke to hunt, and tried without success to dissuade him, yet in a letter to her in October 1826, before the marriage, the Duke had said he was 'buying two horses to hunt at Brighton', and asked whether she would pay for their keep, saying 'I own you are very liberal in paying for the hire of a horse for my use, and think the keep of two horses would come as cheap'.[12] This is the only indication in the archives that before their marriage Harriot was already paying some of the Duke's expenses.

A more serious problem was alleged in a newspaper cutting (without date or attribution) in the bank's archives:[13] it said that the Duke and Duchess of St Albans had left Brighton 'a short time since', because a bill for £30,000 had been presented at the Strand banking house bearing the signature of the Duke, but was said to be a forgery. The report continued:

> We have reason to believe the signature was genuine, and that the bill was paid. The circumstances arose out of a transaction between the Duke and a certain Marquess of gambling celebrity, who, it is said, won of his Grace a very large sum of money (report says, upwards of one hundred thousand pounds) at écarté; £40,000 of which has been discharged by the Duchess, under an idea that the loss did not exceed that sum. The bills given, we are informed, amount in the aggregate to £130,000. If this report be really true, we hope and trust this will be the last error of the kind into which his Grace will fall. His imprudence in opposing his inexperience against the practised skill of such a dexterous veteran as the Marquess, is highly reprehensible; and is such an incontestable proof of the wisdom and sagacity of the Duchess in keeping the purse strings in her own hands.

Document 15745 shows that by 24 February 1829 the Duke had received £30,000 from 'the late Mr Coutts's property', and it is possible this covered the gambling debt mentioned in the newspaper. Since there is no later evidence of the Duke having

---

[12]Coutts Bank Archives, 1316.
[13]Coutts Bank Archives, 17062.

any gambling debts, Harriot clearly reined him in.

The Duke was fond of amateur theatricals, but Harriot did not enjoy watching his performances. One day he was reading the part of Brutus in 'Julius Caesar', while his friend Mr Seymour read the part of Cassius; and he was just saying 'I'd rather be a dog' etc. when Harriot entered the room and said, 'I wish you were. Mr Seymour, I am vexed that you should encourage the Duke to make a fool of himself; he knows no more of acting than a goose! No repetition, I beg!'[14] If true, not perhaps the most tactful way to deal with a new husband, but they soon learned to live together amicably, and appeared to enjoy each other's company.

They went to Brighton in the autumn of 1827, taking a house with enormous stabling which they rechristened St Albans House, but life outside London was not what Harriot had in mind. As Mrs Coutts she had got used to the glamour of the fashionable world, and now hoped to be even more acceptable as a Duchess. In the spring of 1828 she and the Duke returned to London, and after spending £21,000 on decorations and sculptures for Stratton Street they plunged into a succession of revelries. She knew that the 'Fashionables' did not care for her, but her hospitality was fabulous and they could not accept it without inviting her back.

Regency society worshipped the stomach. Wealthy people were much fatter than the rest and did not mind how much they spent on dinners given in their private houses, as long as they were talked about as *bon viveurs*. They then had to dose themselves or 'take the waters' regularly. Apart from over-eating, people played cards or danced at parties. By 1828 the waltz had taken firm root in England, though there had been a long struggle to suppress it because it was the first dance to involve close bodily contact. Only when the Emperor Alexander of Russia was seen waltzing round the room at Almack's did the opposition surrender. Duchess Harriot was never admitted to Almack's, which was regarded as the holy of holies. The *grandes dames* had blackballed her.

---

[14] Charles Pearce, op. cit., 1915, p.256.

Harriot and the Duke were invited to the (Royal) Drawing Room of 23rd April, 1828. *The Times* reported that the Duchess of St Albans was resplendent in 'an elegant blond lace dress with a rich white satin slip, with flounces looped up with diamonds, also a superb diamond stomacher; train of rich white satin trimmed with broad blond lace looped up with diamonds to correspond with dress. Head dress a profusion of diamonds and feathers. The Duke wore his uniform as Grand Falconer.' A Paul Pry caricature by Heath, 'Making Decent or Preparing for St Georges Day', showed them dressing for Court.[15] Heath guyed their Drawing Room attendance in 'The Presentation of Dollalolla accompanied by the mighty Thumb'. (Dollalolla is the Queen in Henry Fielding's *Tom Thumb*.) Harriot is caricatured as stout, bejewelled, over-dressed and overpowering. She sails towards the throne, leading her small husband, who hurries beside her, in quasi-Elizabethan dress with two falcons on his arm. The King stands in front of the throne, welcoming them with hand extended.[16]

The snobbish Mrs Arbuthnot, intimate of the Duke of Wellington, who objected more to married upstarts than to royal mistresses, wrote in her journal in September 1829,

> It is all the King's fault, he has let down the royal dignity, has received at his Court the Duchess of St Albans and Mrs Manners Sutton, both *des femmes entretenues*, and now one is almost laughed at if one objects to receiving any woman, however atrocious her conduct.[17]

Most people who were invited came to Harriot's sumptuous parties at Holly Lodge, some of which cost £2,400 apiece. Prince Pückler-Müskau wrote that it was a real blessing to dine in the country, and he was delighted to sit at table next to a lineal descendant of Charles the Second.[18] But Harriot was shocked to discover that her husband's two unmarried sisters, Louisa and Mary, were shunned from some houses where they had formerly

---

[15]M Dorothy George, op. cit., 1949, p.15597.
[16]M Dorothy George, op. cit., 1949, p.15597.
[17]Arbuthnot, 1950.
[18]E M Butler, ed., *A Regency Visitor*, 1957, p.312.

been visitors, merely because they were living under her roof.

On their first wedding anniversary, 16 June 1828, Harriot and the Duke gave a Grand Fête Champêtre at Holly Lodge. The Royal Dukes of Cumberland and Sussex, Prince Leopold (soon to be King of the Belgians) and Prince Pückler-Müskau were among the hundreds of guests. The Duke of Sussex proposed the health of the St Albans and the Duke replied 'he would if he could have revived the old custom of claiming a flitch of bacon at Dunmow' (the Dunmow flitch was the annual prize for the most happily married couple in the Essex village). Instead, he begged the Duchess as a mark of his affection and regard to accept a silver fruit basket on which was engraved a flitch of bacon, and to the amusement of everyone he recited these lines:

> In love connubial, formed to live and last,
> This gift records a blissful twelvemonth past;
> We claim then, boldly claim, thy flitch, Dunmow,
> First of the blest, who kept the marriage vow.

The Duchess then announced her gift to her husband, a six-oared cutter called 'The Falcon'; the boatmen, in the Duke's livery, carried their oars into the conservatory. *The Age* ridiculed the display in verses entitled, 'The Bacon Flitch, or the Loves of Queen Dollalolla and Lord Noodle'. Heath's engraving, entitled 'A scene in the Honey Moon or Conjugal Felicity', shows the little Duke staggering under an ornamental basket which supports a side of bacon, inscribed 'Best Wiltshire', while the Duchess holds on her shoulder a cutter with six oarsmen with oars erect, and a helmsman.[19]

Creevey wrote maliciously in his diary about the party:

> When old Dow Coutts made her rounds… I was presented, and a more disgusting, frowsy, hairy old B. could not have been found in the Seven Dials… I think of poor people actually starving for want of victual, and this prodigal fool and devil to be alive and

---

[19] M Dorothy George, op. cit., 1949, p.15600.

merry.[20]

Creevey himself never gave money to the starving poor, but was happy to sponge on the hospitality of the rich he gratuitously abused. Lady Holland, doyenne of the Whigs, noted how spitefully Harriot was treated: 'The ladies did not behave prettily or at all like *grandes dames* to the Duchess of St Albans. They really shouldered her on their bench. How can women behave so to one another!'[21]

Harriot felt her isolation, saying, 'All is coldness, reserve, and universal ennui'.[22] *The Age* commented in July 1828:

> Considerable offence, it seems, has been given to a certain Duchess… the Marchioness of Londonderry did not invite her Grace on the evening of her magnificent fancy ball. The Duchess has been talking a great deal about 'ingratitude' and has sent round to all her employees announcing discontinuing her fêtes and parties. The scandalous newspapers, she says, have used her so abominably that she curses her country and retires to the Continent.

It was true. The repeated shafts of satire had proved too much for Harriot. The snobbish treatment she had endured as Mrs Coutts was even more intolerable to the Duchess of St Albans. She had thought higher rank would protect her from malice, but it made her even more vulnerable to spiteful enemies. Retirement from the scene – for the time being at least – was the only thing to be done. *The Globe* reported on 2 August 1828: 'The Duke and Duchess of St Albans are gone to reside (it is said, but we hope untruly) permanently in France'. They added: 'We trust this statement will prove unfounded… various trades people, among whom she expended great sums of money, would suffer materially by her permanent absence'. When Harriot arrived in France, the stories of her vast wealth had preceded her and she was received with great enthusiasm. But soon *The Brighton Gazette* reported that the Parisians saw the Duchess 'as a fit subject for the

---

[20]J Gore, ed, op. cit., 1934, p.265–267.
[21]Ilchester, 1946, p.116.
[22]Margaret Cornwell Baron-Wilson, op. cit., p.184.

exercise of their rapacity', which did not please her.

Harriot was publicly defended in the autumn of 1828 in an *Epistle to Harriet [sic], Duchess of St Albans, or, The First Lash of Nemesis*. It was a castigation of those who lampooned and libelled the Duchess, and ended:

> In modern English minds there lurks a vein
> Of cherish'd rancour, envy, and disdain –
> A cold, saturnine phlegm, whose bliss is still
> In hearing and disseminating ill…
>
> They best can occupy a ducal chair
> Who seat themselves by their own genius there…
> Thy friends are all the generous and good
> Incens'd to see a woman thus pursu'd!

It finished with the best answer to her detractors:

> They may not pluck the jewel from thy brow
> Thou art the Duchess of St Albans now!

As for Harriot's relations with the Coutts family, they were never more than cordial at the best of times. Lady Bute was the least hostile of Thomas's daughters, but she lived abroad most of the time for her health. She wrote in July 1827 that she heard of Harriot's proposed marriage to the Duke of St Albans from her daughter Fan, though she had expected Harriot to write herself.[23] As we have seen, Fan, Lady Frances Bute, had married Lord Sandon, later Earl of Harrowby, in 1823, and Harriot had given the bride a dowry of £20,000. Far from being grateful, Fan made no effort to conceal her disdain and disapproval of Harriot, and discouraged her visits. At her mother's request, in 1827 she 'did the odious duty… of composing letters of congratulation to Mrs Coutts on her approaching marriage'. She also wrote that she considered Harriot's fête on her wedding anniversary in 1828 'vulgar and disagreeable' and wrote scornfully to her mother of

---

[23] Coutts Bank Archives, 2061.

'haymakers in costume'. She accepted Harriot's invitation to take the place of honour at her side, but 'only gave myself as much trouble as civility required'.[24]

She wrote to Andrew Dickie in July 1828 that Harriot had called to tell her she was leaving for Paris, 'which if she had not herself apprised me I should hardly have credited it... I hope their Graces find their wishes in this expedition answered'.[25]

Harriot was too shrewd not to notice and be hurt by Fan's behaviour, and Fan got her come-uppance when Harriot died, for she did not receive a penny in the Will. Her brother, Lord Dudley Coutts Stuart, remained on good terms with Harriot, since he worked at the Bank, but he too was excluded from Harriot's Will.

There is little correspondence between Harriot and Lady Guilford during the years 1827–37, though Lady Guilford attended dinners and parties at Stratton Street and Holly Lodge, as did her stepson the Earl of Guilford and his wife. In October 1835 Harriot was invited to the wedding of Lady Guilford's daughter, Susan, to Colonel John Doyle. Harriot replied that the marriage was 'a sad affliction', but since it could not be prevented she would say no more about it. A curious footnote to this story is that in 1838 Lady Susan Doyle wrote to Mr Marjoribanks, who was an Executor of Harriot's Will, requesting a clock which stood in her grandfather's room at the Strand which she said belonged to her mother. Lady Guilford had asked for the clock several times, she said, but Harriot had always said she wanted everything to remain the same as Thomas Coutts left it. Whether or not Lady Susan got the clock is not known.

Sir Francis Burdett sent friendly letters to Harriot in November 1827, acknowledging money orders, mentioning hunting with the Duke in Leicestershire, and saying his daughter Sophia had the measles. Another in January 1829 said his steward would send the Duchess an order of the best toasting cheese.[26] Other letters show that Burdett frequently dined with the Duke and Duchess, and in July 1829 he wrote:

---

[24]Harrowby MSS, 1xi, f.391.
[25]Coutts Bank Archives, 16919.
[26]Coutts Bank Archives, 412.

My dear Duchess,

I am glad in having it in my power to evince by a trifle the deep sense I entertain of your kind, considerate, & judicious conduct, by which I am satisfied you have saved me, & my dear from great misery, & perhaps irretrievable disgrace. I write this as a record which may be produced in evidence against me, in case I should ever so far forget myself as to fall into that odious but common vice of ingratitude. Do therefore, my dear Duchess, accept from me the figure you so much liked, of the Hebe & I trust it will be in your eyes not only an emblem of perpetual youth, but of perpetual gratitude.

I remain dear Duchess,
Yours sincerely, F Burdett[27]

Exactly how Harriot rescued the Burdetts and from what 'irretrievable disgrace' – presumably by giving them money – is not known, but Sir Francis's perpetual gratitude lasted only two years, when Harriot was forced to reduce her annual payments to Coutts's daughters, including Burdett's wife. As explained earlier, Harriot paid a sum of £30,000 a year to the daughters, divided equally, from 1822 to 1831. Then, Harriot's share of profits from Coutts Bank dropped by over fifteen thousand pounds. Lady Guilford[28] and Lady Bute[29] accepted the cut in income, though grudgingly. Sir Francis, however, despite having written to her on 6 July 'Sorry to hear so bad an account of the Strand House', assailed Harriot in a letter dated 12 July 1831:

So then Duchess, you really grudge Mr Coutts's daughters the crumbs that fall from their Father's Table! and... you have the face to talk to them of the sums received by them, and their poor Relations. But you feel no compunction at squandering, with unexampled profusion, their property, naturally and equitably theirs, which you yourself declared was left you as a Trustee, and in confidence, by their Father. I am aware of the writing and paper you possess, but they will prove nothing against the claims of the virtuous, Dutiful and ever affectionate daughters of Mr Coutts, nor anything but his sad, and cruel, infatuation. The Will is too iniquitous to stand...,

---

[27] Coutts Bank Archives, 419.
[28] Coutts Bank Archives, 3745.
[29] Coutts Bank Archives, 3744.

He went on to say that Coutts was of unsound mind when he made his Will, which he would challenge in Court and, if that failed, he would raise it in Parliament. Finally, he said, 'I have written to Sir C. Trotter to transfer all my affairs from the Strand to the House of Drummond.[30]

Sir Francis Burdett's radical ideas about liberty, expressed so frequently in Parliament, did not extend to the right of a man to leave his property to whom he pleased, or Harriot's right to dispense her legal property as she chose. In reply to this attempt to bully and threaten her, she forbore to remind him of his pledge never to be ungrateful to her, but wrote on 19 July,

> I have not deserved the unkind letter you have sent me, Sir Francis Burdett. It gives me deep concern that one of Mr Coutts' family, to whom I felt nothing but kindness, should have expressed himself in such terms. I have delayed answering your letter in the hope that by this time you would have felt how cruelly unjust your accusation was, and that you would now, as you have done before, have acknowledged your error and unkindness, but as this is not the case, I write to you with a light and happy heart to assure you that if you really doubt the legality of Mr Coutts's will, as you say you do, nothing can be more joyful to me or so great a blessing as your putting into execution the threat of having it investigated; also I trust that my connection before and after my marriage with Mr Coutts, and my conduct to him and his Family, will appear as clear and honourable in the eyes of man as I know and feel it does in the knowledge of God.[31]

Sir Francis replied on the 21st July, saying he realised he was mistaken about Harriot's behaviour, and apologised for his previous letter, which had been written in haste and which he hoped would now be passed over and forgotten. He said Sir Coutts Trotter had already half convinced him of his mistake, and 'you have moreover done me kindness which I have not been slow or reluctant to acknowledge... nothing could be more distressing to me than to be instrumental in breaking those bonds in which Mr Coutts has bound us so strongly together and which

---

[30]Coutts Bank Archives, 414.
[31]Coutts Bank Archives, 415.

could not be severed without incalculable mischief to us all'.[32]

Harriot was not satisfied with Burdett's letter, and asked that he apologise further. He did so, and added, 'I should be miserable to wrong either Mr Coutts's memory or yourself, from whom I will never say otherwise than that I have received kindness from and am under obligation to you'.[33] Burdett was never averse to asking for help from Harriot, either for himself or his friends, but Harriot decided that the money she would leave to Lady Burdett in her Will would be for her use only, so that none of it could be touched by Sir Francis.

The daughters of Thomas Coutts, and his son-in-law Sir Francis Burdett, were constant thorns in Harriot's side, but she generally overlooked their unkindnesses and continued to support them with lavish incomes. She also determined to enjoy life in the exuberant manner so characteristic of her, as will be seen.

---

[32]Coutts Bank Archives, 416.
[33]Coutts Bank Archives, 417.

Chapter XIII
THE ROMP[1]

The End Of An Era

If Harriot and her husband ever intended to settle in France, they soon changed their minds. In September 1828 they were back in Lincolnshire at the Duke's country seat. A Lincoln newspaper reported:

> It seems to be the intention of the Duke and Duchess of St Albans to resume the spirit of the ancient and manly sports of our forefathers at their seat at Redbourne near this city. Lord Frederick Beauclerk and Lord Emilius [sic] Beauclerk, the uncles of the Duke, passed through this city on their route to Redbourne Hall, where is it understood a series of amusements for the autumn will be kept up, relieving and supplying the usual sports of the chase, shooting, coursing etc.

According to their own idealised view of themselves, the English upper classes, unlike their continental counterpoints, were firmly rooted in their estates. They knew the land, and enjoyed its ways and its sports. They were expected to look after their tenantry and their servants, and have an easy and natural relationship with the lower orders. They boasted a sense of duty, which led them to devote much of their lives to public service. Their lives were supposedly a happy mean between country sports and pastimes, public service, and the cultivation of the mind. Their houses were filled with beautiful pictures and fine furniture. Their libraries were well stocked with books bound in vellum or tooled leather; temples and classical monuments dotted their parks. They shared

---

[1] A play by T A Lloyd in which Harriot appeared as Miss Le Blonde in December 1795.

their lives with their friends, in a liberal hospitality in one of the most enviable ways of life ever devised.

Such a picture was largely a myth, which comparatively few lived up to. Though it could be matched in individual houses or in the lives of individual owners, the reality was generally different. There were many dull or ugly country houses, and many grasping landlords. In the days of 'Old Corruption' before the nineteenth-century reforms, the aristocracy took anything they could get out of the public purse. Their servants and dependants often had a less admiring view of their employers than their 'betters' liked to think, since much of the prosperity and beauty of country houses rested on cheap labour, high rents, government sinecures, and on massive enclosures of agricultural land which, along with population growth, had reduced many farm labourers to a life of misery and starvation.

The landowners were often very boring people. They had enough money to do nothing, and did it well; it did not produce interesting people. Like Jane Austen's ladies they might do needlework, play the harp or pianoforte, read novels, paint watercolours, drive into the country, visit friends and relatives nearby, or call on the poor. Evening amusements included cards, music and singing, or reading and conversation. Staying in a country house could be highly enjoyable for the guests, but it could also, as numerous letters and descriptions testify, be dull and disillusioning. When roads were unpaved, distances great, and horse or foot the only means of transport, anyone who came to a big house on business or for a meal almost automatically stayed the night. Prince Pückler-Müskau said of an evening at Cobham Hall in 1827:

> Our suffering host lay on the sofa, dozing a little, five ladies and gentlemen were attentively reading in various sorts of books... another had been playing for a quarter of an hour with a long-suffering dog; two old Members of Parliament were disputing vehemently about the 'Corn Bill'; and the rest of the company were in a dimly-lighted room adjoining, where a pretty girl was playing on the piano-forte, and another with a most perforating voice, singing ballads... A light supper of cold meats and fruits is brought, at which everyone helps himself, and shortly after

midnight all retire.[2]

All foreign visitors commented on the cold of English houses, even though huge quantities of coal were used to heat the barn-like rooms. In the late eighteenth century Joseph Brahmah's newly-invented water closets were installed in some great houses, and only in the late nineteenth century did fixed baths and radiators appear, along with piped hot and cold water. Before that, hip baths filled by servants carrying water cans were the rule. The baths were warm for the ladies, but cold for the gentlemen.

Landownership dominated the lives of country-house families. It made the greatest of them semi-feudal overlords of hundreds or even thousands of people. Land was the basis of their wealth, the most frequent reason for marriage, and looking after it could occupy a lot of time. They led an 'amphibious' life, and their position as members of the ruling class constantly drew them to London – to attend court, or parliament, or the London Season, to fill government offices, to travel, or just to have a good time. Those who could afford lived part of the time in London, Bath or Brighton, or travelled on the Continent. Many gentry families, like Jane Austen's characters, seldom went to London, because they could not afford it, and some families vanished for years to Europe because it was cheaper to live abroad.

The Duke of St Albans was a Lincolnshire magnate, owning 5,255 acres in the county. He and Harriot spent little time there, being more interested in life in Society, but the Duke had to manage his run-down estates. Now he could call on Harriot's aid, and he wrote to her in February 1832:

> In the last interview with my Steward, Mr Smith from Lincolnshire... he stated that the Bills to the amount of £750 remaining unpaid in Lincolnshire should be discharged as soon as possible; as the tradesmen and workmen to whom they are owing are not men with any ready money at their command. Mr Smith also stated that he would require the sum of £500 to pay workmen and purchase foreign timber to carry out necessary repairs... on which conditions the Tenants cancelled their old

---

[2]Prince Pückler-Müskau, *Tour of Germany, Holland and England*, 1832, vol.III,p.14.

> Agreements, which were objectionable to me but favourable to them, and have engaged to sign fresh agreements… I leave you to judge if what is about to be done is for my interest. As I have no ready money I reluctantly apply to you to use your influence at the Strand to lend me £1,250…
> I remain, your affectionate husband, William.[3]

Harriot helped him out, as she always did, and he continued to rely on her generosity and keen business instincts.

The Duke was the Hereditary Grand Falconer of England, for which sinecure the public purse paid him £1,372 a year. Soon after he married Harriot, a letter arrived for him at Cheltenham, sealed with the Royal arms; it said his immediate attendance was required at Windsor, together with his hawks. At that time he had neither hawks nor falconers. His aunt, Lady Frederick Beauclerk, urged him not to go until hawks and falconers had been obtained. 'It may be', she cautioned, 'a snare laid to discover if you really keep the hawks and if not, to make it a pretence to bring the inutility of your office before Parliament and to deprive you of it.' The letter turned out to be a hoax, but it gave the Duke the incentive to set up a hawking establishment, thus combining the current taste for medieval chivalry with Harriot's pride in her husband's dignities and privileges. The vogue for falconry was short-lived; just coming alive in 1827, by 1837 it was all but dead. The same romanticism produced the Young England movement, the Eglinton Tournament, and the medieval novels of Sir Walter Scott, and left its legacy in the Pre-Raphaelite Brotherhood of Dante Gabriel Rossetti and William Morris.

The Duke laid on a huge falconry display at Redbourne Hall, his ancestral seat in Lincolnshire, in September 1828, and invited all the local notables. Falconers were imported from Germany, where falconry was far from a dying art. In mock Gothic fashion, they wore green and orange velvet trousers, with long white gauntlets and steeple-crowned hats with bands of gold and adorned with black plumes. *The Lincoln Herald* of 27 October 1828 reported that he gave 'a Falcons Hunt on the Race Course of this city in front of the Grand Stand', attended by 20,000 people. The

---

[3]Coutts Bank Archives, 1316.

Duke was dressed in his ceremonial costume of Grand Falconer, and escorted by a page in Lincoln green. The paper said, 'Partridges were let loose, pursued at a short interval by hawks, but it was not ordinary pursuit, as the beauty of the hawk's flight came when it soared aloft and then swooped after its quarry. Equally remarkable was the hawks' obedience to their trainers' skilful control'. In appreciation the freedom of the city of Lincoln was conferred on the Duke, and Harriot was invited to become patroness of the Dispensary Hall, though she was asked to limit her monetary support because it might be difficult to find a patroness to succeed her! It was the rich patron most people wanted to see, and at his inauguration dinner the mayor proposed her health. The Duke responded: 'I am proud of my wife and I love her – the Duchess and myself despise the miscreants who assail her,' which *The Lincoln Herald* said was received with applause.

When the Duke and Duchess visited Louth in Lincolnshire they were mobbed. *The Stamford News* reported:

> On the arrival of the retinue at Louth the inhabitants to the amount of some thousands thronged the streets in such a manner that the carriages could only proceed at a foot pace to the inn. This assemblage did not consist of the mob alone, but chiefly of the inhabitants misnamed 'gentry' and the assemblage was not for the purpose of welcoming his Grace, but for indulging in the vulgar stare to perfection. On the arrival at the King's Head it became necessary to employ constables to keep the mob out of the house, and though this plan succeeded in preventing the ingress of the ragamuffinly part of the assemblage still the well-dressed rabble male and female thronged the passage of the house gracelessly eager to peep at her Grace as she passed from one room to another. Such as could not get into the inn thronged the upper windows of a grocer's house opposite in the hope of there gratifying their curiosity. The rabble in the streets lifted each other up to look in at the windows.

The only people who called on the Duke and Duchess at the inn were supplicants for public charities, to which Harriot contributed liberally, including the bellringers who asked ten guineas for their steeple music. The Duchess sent them four guineas by Lord Emelius Beauclerk, whom they mistook for an old valet and on whom they showered abuse, saying the Duchess had sent them five guineas but he had pocketed one of them!

When Harriot visited a few shops in Louth local women followed her everywhere, staring through the windows when she made her purchases, so she said she would never go there again. The *London Globe* reported the incident differently, and lectured the Duchess on her behaviour:

> Whatever may have been the rudeness of the Louth people… we cannot help thinking that the reception her Grace experienced there will teach her a lesson in prudence. She has often been reproached for a fondness for public exhibitions, and an ostentation in her munificence… She may now learn that privacy will be more congenial…

Harriot was the butt of everyone's humour. One newspaper wrote:

> Her sudden elevation has made her name familiar to every class of our readers, and the public are more amused with a matter affixed to *her* name than to one of which they have never heard. Some papers began by attacking her perhaps from mercenary motives, with the hope of being 'bought up', and we continue it for the fun of the thing'.[4]

Of the newspaper attacks on her at this time, Harriot later said:

> At my time of life I have outlived all sense of annoyance from external causes, and indeed, I defy them now to invent anything worse against me than they have already done; but when I was young, and the attached wife of the venerable man to whom I owe everything, these unjust accusations used to destroy my peace and health more than the most malicious writer could have intended.[5]

Harriot stopped visiting Cheltenham after an artist there

---

[4]Margaret Cornwell Baron-Wilson, op. cit., p.249.
[5]Margaret Cornwell Baron-Wilson, op. cit., p.247.

caricatured her, though he said he had meant her no disrespect. But she took in all the newspapers that attacked her, and had them placed in the library of her house for the benefit of her guests. She was afraid that if the stories were no longer published, people would think she had bought off the writers, and this she said she would never do.

The Duke and Duchess had a happier time attending a musical festival in Liverpool, where she had triumphed as an actress. Crowds gathered to see her enter her hotel, and constables dispersed them, but Harriot said, 'Pray do not use force to prevent the approach of any Liverpool person, for most probably some of their family were kind enough to pay for seeing me at the theatre in my younger days.'

They also enjoyed visiting Nottingham, another town where she had been a favourite. A local lawyer suggested that perhaps he might be of service to Harriot when he was next in London, and he asked where he might call on her. She replied, with a ripple of laughter, 'The Old Shop in the Strand will find me.'

When Harriot was depressed she often went to Brighton, which William Wilberforce called 'Piccadilly by the seaside', where she was freer of censure. She went there in December 1828, where according to the local paper the Duke 'made a trial of his celebrated hawks with pigeons instead of partridges on the Race Down, but the former, as if indignant at the change, refused to act. The usual incentives and decoys were had recourse to, but all ineffectually.' The hawks' perversity was annoying since the Duke was 'habited as the Grand Falconer', so it was fortunate that 'but few spectators appeared on the ground'. At the second attempt a few days later, the falcons' favourite quarry having been provided, 'a partridge was struck in good style and killed.' But the Duke's favourite falcon 'winged its flight to Rottingdean and was there shot by a wandering fowler.' The bird was valued at 100 guineas, and the Duke gave orders that it should be stuffed. The Duke's grief evoked a song entitled 'The Falconer's Lament'. For the Brighton hawking parties Harriot was dressed in 'green velvet, with a black hat and feathers, and a superb diamond hawk suspended from her girdle.' She rode in her carriage, the Duke on horseback by her side. He had a hawk on his wrist and was attended by falconers and servants in green livery. Afterwards the guests were invited for music, dancing and a banquet.

Although the Prince of Wales was Regent from 1810 to 1820, the Regency period conventionally covers the period 1800 to 1830. By 1829 there were signs that its boundless prodigality was coming to an end. The decay of the monarchy was reflected in the air of exhaustion which seemed to pervade society. The aristocratic appetite for continual routs, balls, déjeuners and dinner parties began to pall, and the glory of Almack's was fading. The 1820s, when Harriot was a merry widow and then a Duchess, saw the last efforts of the 'Fashionables' to maintain their incessant round of gaiety. Cock-fighting and bare-knuckle fighting were still popular, but the newspapers of 1829 suggest that reckless pleasure was no longer flaunted. Middle-class morality and respectability (at least in its outward forms) were becoming fashionable among the upper classes; the young were much less bawdy in speech and less tolerant of hedonism than their parents and grandparents. Yet the prudish members of the upper class were no more sympathetic to the poor than their libertine parents.

The rich were not ignorant of the terrible living conditions of the 'lower orders' at this time, since it was everywhere too plain, whether in town or country. The Parliamentary Committee on child labour in the mills and factories sat in 1828, and its proceedings, published verbatim in *The Times* day after day, cannot now be read without a shudder. But most members of fashionable society were undisturbed. Harriot St Albans gave much more money to the poor than did most of the rich, and for this her peers only despised her.

The Duke and Duchess were not much seen in public in the early months of 1829. By 5 April *The Age* commented,

> To the numerous enquiries of correspondents after her Grace the Duchess of St Albans we beg leave to say that the noble lady is not dead, but sleepeth – that is, she now for the first time since she became a Duchess is living quiet, easy, and retired, as becometh a demi-respectable of her class, and while she continues to do so neither the taunt of Inquizitor [their columnist] or any other motive hunter shall induce us to interfere.

Harriot kept up appearances, never failing to attend Court in the Season; in a cartoon in April 1829, entitled 'Lady Day at Court', she figures among the corpulent society dames of the period, and a coloured print dated 29 May, entitled 'Run, Neighbours, Run', shows her dancing a quadrille. After this the cartoonists left Harriot alone, having found more satisfying satire in the indiscretions of George IV and his mistress, Lady Conyngham, but *The Age* started to attack her again on 7 June:

> We thought the Duchess of St Albans had given up the practice of publishing her parties, but we find by *The Morning Post* that her Grace has resumed it. But it is rather fortunate that she should publish her company also, for really a more raff set never invaded a tea garden. There is the Duke of Sussex to be sure, but his Royal Highness goes everywhere from Houndsditch to Holland House, where there is anything to eat – and Colonel D'Este follows his papa.

The one Royal Duke not seen at Holly Lodge in 1829 was the Duke of Clarence. He probably wanted to forget his long association with the actress Dorothy Jordan, and meeting Harriot, her Drury Lane associate, was embarrassing at a time when the king's declining health was bringing him nearer the crown.

The Royal Drawing Room was always followed by one of Harriot's fêtes at Holly Lodge. In 1829 it was described by *The Court Journal* as 'without exception the most attractive and complete thing of the kind that the fashionable season has hitherto produced'. Its account of the Duchess's fête champêtre rhapsodised thus:

> by four o'clock the scene... was alive and sparkling... with a more choice collection of female beauty in face and form and... splendour in out-of-door attire than any similar re-union of the season has presented. [The guests] were received by the Duchess in the open air, from whence to the house a footway of green cloth was placed, and immediately on paying their respects to their hostess they dispersed themselves through the grounds.

At the concert there were songs from Madame Stockhausen and Madame Vigo, and six figurantes of the King's Theatre danced national dances from the ballet in 'Masaniello'. The *pièce de résistance* was 'the pretty little pastoral' arranged on the lawn, with two Alderney cows dressed in flowers *à la Suisse*; while Mme. Stockhausen sang the 'Ranz des Vaches' a syllabub was prepared with milk straight from the cow, and distributed by the Duchess to the visitors. *The Age* burlesqued,

> the admiring and expectant company gathered round the milk-white animal... but unfortunately, as the precaution of infusing into the mind of the cow a preparatory taste for Swiss melody had been neglected, she no sooner heard the sound of the harp than up went her head and her tail, away went the flowers and the ribands, away ran the vocalist, down fell the harp, and off ran the company.

According to *The Court Journal*, Harriot greeted her friend and partner Andrew Dickie at the fête with the words, 'I've found an honest man'. About this *The Age* commented, with inaccurate malevolence:

> When we consider the set who haunt the Duchess we do not wonder that she was tempted to make an exclamation of wonder at seeing an honest man among them. But we doubt the story, for we are assured that neither Dickie nor Coutts Trotter, nor Marjoribanks, nor any other clerks of the shop in the Strand are ever allowed to enter their mistress's house (except on business), except once a year when she gives a dance to her steward Toady, Lord Freddy, and the other household attendants.

Harriot's neighbours in Stratton Street were prone to malice, too. According to *The Court Journal*:

> *on dit* that the inhabitants of Stratton Street have requested Colonel Rowan to allow two of his Blue Devils to be constantly stationed in front of the Duke of St Albans' house in order that the street may be kept clear and not blocked up (as it is at present) by the crowds of persons who loiter there to see the Duchess step into her carriage. At least two hundred of the lowest order were collected on Wednesday morning, attracted by the not very unusual spectacle of three of the St Albans' carriages prepared to convey their Graces and suite from the *rus in urbe* [sic] of London

in the autumn to the *urbs in rure* [sic] of Brighton in the winter.

The 'Blue Devils' were Sir Robert Peel's new police force, established in 1829.

Harriot continued to entertain on a grand scale. She celebrated May Day 1830 with a festival at Holly Lodge. *The Court Journal* said, 'the cow and syllabub which were made last season the source of so much ungracious comment by the public press, were again brought forward, and we cannot but congratulate her Grace of St Albans upon her resolute superiority to such attacks and her staunch defiance of such assailants'.

In June 1830 came the long-expected death of George IV. *The Annual Register* published a candid obituary:

> There have been more popular monarchs – there have been many who held out to their subjects a far better model of moral excellence, and George IV was subject to the disadvantage of standing in immediate contrast to the long life of his revered father.

The King died at the end of the London Season, so few fashionable functions had to be cancelled.

The new King, William IV, had ten illegitimate children by Mrs Jordan; they took the telling surname of Fitzclarence. When he married Princess Adelaide, daughter of the Duke of Saxe-Meiningen, he made clear he would continue seeing his children. Adelaide's own four babies died in infancy, but she was always kind to the Fitzclarence brood, and received them at Court. Lady Louisa Percy wrote, 'It sounds immoral, but the quantity of natural children the King has certainly makes *la cour* pleasanter. They are all, you know, pretty and lively, and make society in a way that real princesses could not'.[6] The young Princess Victoria, heir apparent to the throne, was forbidden by her mother to associate with the King's illegitimate children or to attend the Coronation of her uncle in 1831.[7]

Towards the end of 1830 the Duke and Duchess of St Albans

---

[6]Percy, Vol.2, p.99.
[7]Elizabeth Longford, *Queen Victoria: Born to Succeed*, 1964, p.38–40.

went to Brighton for the winter, and in the following Spring the King and Queen spent several weeks at the Pavilion there. Mary Frampton reported in February 1831,

> The magnificence of the parties given by the King and Queen at the Pavilion at Brighton are spoken of as realising the ideas of the entertainments described in the *Arabian Nights*, the diners consisting daily of about forty persons. The King very temperate. The Queen too, drawing some degree of line as to character of those she invites, has not even sent a card to the Duchess of St Albans, the famous Mrs Coutts, formerly an actress, Miss Mellon.[8]

According to Creevey, 830 persons were present at one of the royal balls, and hardly anyone of substance in Brighton was excluded.[9] By such pointed omission of Harriot, the highest in rank after herself of the women in Brighton at the time, the Queen, following no doubt her husband's guilty memory of Mrs Jordan, humiliated the Duchess. Worse was to follow: for the Queen's Ball a few months later, the Duke of St Albans was invited, together with his sisters Louisa and Mary, but not the Duchess. The Duke was unwilling to go without her, and after establishing that the snub was deliberate his sisters also refused to attend, much to the satisfaction of their uncle, Lord Emelius Beauclerk. Shortly afterwards, however, Emelius quarrelled with the Duke over the dismissal of a farm bailiff, and then spitefully took Louisa and Mary to the Queen's Ball. Emelius, never tactful, aggravated matters by asking Harriot soon afterwards to finance a naval cadetship for one of his protégés; she refused, so then Emelius asked his parson brother not to have any further dealings with the Duke and Duchess.

Harriot retaliated by asking the Beauclerk sisters to leave her house. *The Court Journal* reported on 7 May, 1831, 'it is understood that the circle of the Duchess of St Albans will in future be deprived of the attraction of his Grace's beautiful sisters, who are henceforth to reside with their married sister, Lady

---

[8]Mary Frampton, *Journal*, 1885.
[9]J Gore, ed., op. cit., 1934, Vol.2, p.217.

Carton Capel.' Just how angered Harriot was became clear after her death: in her Will not a single memento was left to the Ladies Beauclerk.

Harriot was invited to the Royal Drawing Room of 1831, since exclusion would have cancelled the favour previously shown her by George IV. Etiquette demanded that she should be presented to the new Queen by a member of her own family, but Lady Guilford pleaded ill-health and Lady Caroline Dundas, the Duke's aunt, refused point blank, so Lady Salisbury stepped in. On this occasion Queen Adelaide did speak to Harriot, commenting on her splendid dress.

At William IV's Coronation on 8 September 1831, Harriot's high rank could not be ignored. In his capacity as Hereditary Grand Falconer, the Duke of St Albans was to carry the Royal Sceptre with the Cross, the last of the regalia to be conferred on the newly consecrated king. At the Coronation service Harriot was dressed with great splendour, and stood third from the Queen, only the two Duchesses of Richmond standing before her as senior in rank. As she stood behind the daughters of a Duke and a Marquess in the line of Duchesses near the throne, it must have seemed the pinnacle of her life, a grander moment than any in the make-believe of the theatre. For the Coronation, London was brilliantly illuminated, the theatres and Vauxhall Gardens were thrown open free, and there was a display of fireworks in Hyde Park.

Five days later Harriot was received at Court again, and also attended a dinner in honour of Talleyrand, then French ambassador. The other ladies at the dinner gave Harriot the cold shoulder; the Queen, though Harriot had the place of honour next to her, could hardly bring herself to speak to her, since she 'well knew what the Duchess's former life had been.' Perhaps she was punishing Harriot as a proxy for Mrs Jordan.

William IV was not a distinguished monarch. Known as 'Sailor Bill' since his naval days, he was a bluff and genial man with little political common sense, but as conscientious and well-meaning as he was irresolute. His manners were not always good. One day he spat out of the windows of the Royal Coach, and the angry Cockney crowd cried out, 'George IV wouldn't have done that!'

Yet Harriot told Mrs Baron-Wilson:

> People are constantly saying that King William is deficient in the courtesy, the elegance, the grace, of George the Fourth, but the true gentleman is known by the benevolence of his heart, rather than by his dress or address, and, measured by this standard, I maintain his present majesty to be the finest gentleman that ever lived'.[10]

The King must have shown Harriot more kindness than his wife did.

In the Spring of 1832 St Albans attended the House of Lords regularly, and Harriot made him promise to write her a note each time about the proceedings. On 22 March he apologised for not being able to join Harriot that evening at Lord Dudley and Ward's, 'but the Dukes of Sussex and Norfolk said it was essential for me to stay for the Division'.[11] On 11 April he said many peers were speaking in the debate on the second reading of the Catholic Emancipation Bill; the Bishop of Exeter had declared it would crush the Protestant church, though the Bishop of London said state affairs made the bill necessary.[12] On 13 April he reported debates on education in Ireland, the Reform Bill and the Poor Laws – 'those laws which gave the poor not the degradation of supplicating but the right of demanding'.[13]

In 1832 the London Season opened, but an outbreak of cholera caused everybody who could to flee from London. Raikes reported that at a dinner at Lord Hertford's the conversation turned chiefly on the cholera, and 'Champagne, ices and fruits were neglected in favour of plain meats, port and sherry, for fear of the dreadful malady'.[14] Harriot and the Duke sought safety in Cheltenham and Tunbridge Wells. They passed the winter as usual in Brighton, where the King and Queen began to include them in their parties, for the King had become seriously interested in falconry and establishing heronry, which brought

---

[10]Margaret Cornwell Baron-Wilson, op cit., p.216.
[11]Coutts Bank Archives, 1318.
[12]Coutts Bank Archives, 1319.
[13]Coutts Bank Archives, 1320.
[14]T Raikes, *Journal*, 1856.

him closer to the Duke. Yet Harriot, on bad terms both with the Duke's family and with the daughters of Thomas Coutts, was less pleased with her high social station than she had expected to be, which put her in the doldrums, as we shall see.

Chapter XIV
THE DOLDRUMS[1]

The Dog Days of Autumn

Harriot's relations with her partners at the Bank were good, and she relied on them for advice, though she was also capable of deciding for them, as well as for herself. That she continued to be involved in the bank's business on a regular basis, and that the other partners had to take account of her power, can be judged by a letter from Coutts Trotter to another partner, Edward Antrobus. Trotter had visited Chatsworth, home of the Duke of Devonshire, and on 12 August 1827 he reported 'the sad consequences of Mr White's misconduct' which would involve a loss of about £25,000. The full nature of the misconduct was not spelled out, but he wrote:

> You mentioned that the Stock withdrawn must be replaced. I hope this refers to Stock which was in their own names or under their own management and not in any that ought to have been in our name or in the names of any of the House's friends… the idea of Stock being withdrawn had not occurred to me. The communication will be a very unpleasant one to make to the Duchess of St Albans, but it must be done, and you will I am sure do it in the best possible way.[2]

The Court Journal of 1829 bore witness to Harriot's willingness to step in personally when the Bank felt unable to help someone financially. It referred to the painter Sir Thomas Lawrence, who was heavily in debt, and explained:

---

[1] A play in which Harriot played Emmeline in January 1798.
[2] Coutts Bank Archives, 15812.

> Sir Thomas Lawrence was informed a few days previous to his death that Messrs Coutts would demand immediate payment for a bond of five thousand pounds. Sir Thomas went in a great state of agitation to the banking house and was shown into the private room, where to his surprise he found the Duchess of St Albans. Her Grace, perceiving his agitation, inquired the cause, and having ascertained it, shook him kindly by the hand and said, 'Lay aside all anxiety on this subject: I will be personally responsible for the amount, which you can repay at your own convenience'.

Presumably repayment never took place.

Another matter in which Harriot overbore her partners concerned the Alexander Trotters. Her antipathy reflected Thomas Coutts's dislike of them. It had begun when Coutts's friend and customer, Henry Dundas, Lord Melville, was impeached for 'High Crimes and Misdemeanours' during the years 1786–1800 when he was Treasurer of the Navy. With him was charged his Paymaster, Alexander Trotter, also a Coutts customer. Melville had allowed his Paymaster to transfer navy funds from the Bank of England to Trotter's account in Coutts, where Trotter invested them on his own behalf. Ironically, Melville had introduced in 1785 an Act intended to prevent corruption in the payment of government funds. Trotter's defence was that he regarded himself 'as banker rather than accountant to the state' and as such he was justified in using its money wisely. He claimed the nation had lost nothing and that he had paid all bills regularly. But there is no doubt that Melville and Trotter enriched themselves from the interest on the immense sums involved.

Both men were finally acquitted in 1806, though it was clear Melville had been negligent and Trotter incompetent. Although Coutts had spoken in defence of Alexander Trotter, who was brother to his partner Coutts Trotter, he strongly disapproved of Trotter's actions and thought he had brought disgrace to the Bank. Alexander Trotter and his descendants were to feel the chill wind of both Thomas's and Harriot's disapproval.

A letter of 21 January 1831 from Alexander Trotter, Jr. to his father tells of the new Banking House being established by Lafitte's nephew in Paris, and of his optimism of joining the Staff.

He 'feels it would be a chance of being well free of her Grace of St Albans'.[3] A letter from Coutts Trotter to his brother, Alexander Trotter Sr. a week later suggests he was right: Coutts Trotter was afraid Alexander Jr. would endanger his career if he remained in Paris 'where everything is in a state of revolution' (during the 1830 French Revolution) and went on:

> I have weighed well... the degree to which it would be useful to enter into any discussion with the Duchess of Alexander's claims – upon the whole I think it would be at least useless – you will remember that when I called on her on the occasion of Mr David Marjoribanks and Sir John [Marjoribanks, his father] making an attempt to get the former admitted into the Strand and thus opening a better share for Alexander in the City – she closed the conversation at once by saying she would not speak on the subject till a new partner became necessary which was not the case at present. If it needed any confirmation I am sorry to say I think it will be found in her not having taken any notice of a letter I wrote to her on Tuesday the 25th, mentioning the opening and Alexander's having gone to Paris with the approbation of Mr Marjoribanks and the other Partners to look about him.[4]

Harriot's antipathy towards the Alexander Trotters was to blackball them long after her death because of provisions she laid down in her Will.

As senior partner Harriot kept a firm hold on the Bank. She wrote to Edward Marjoribanks on 2 July 1831:

> Your kind good wishes affected me deeply, and I do flatter myself that all my kind dear friends in the old Shop are well pleased with me and convinced how dear to my heart is the prosperity of our splendid House conducted by such excellent men and that their happiness and comfort will always requite your affectionate friend,
> Harriot St Albans.[5]

She continued to help the disadvantaged. The famous Quaker

---

[3] Coutts Bank Archives, 15827.
[4] Coutts Bank Archives, 15843.
[5] Coutts Bank Archives, 1343.

prison reformer, Elizabeth Fry, wrote to her in 1836 requesting an interview when Harriot passed through Dover, 'to represent something of importance to her kind friend the Duchess, who formerly so kindly and liberally aided her in the Prison cause'.[6] Dr Thomas Chalmers of the Infirmaries Dispensaries, the pioneer of charity organization, wrote on 13 November 1835 that he 'cannot refrain from expressing his admiration and gratitude for a munificence so noble – a feeling he shares in common with the managers of the various Institutions which have so benefited from her Grace's generosity'. Harriot had given £230. 'It is his earnest prayer that the Giver of all things... may shower its richest blessings on her who devises so liberally in behalf of the poorest of its members'.[7] Hearing of a woman who was living in poverty in Brighton, she disguised herself to visit her, and left behind an envelope containing £300.[8] After Coutts's death she increased the amount paid annually to a niece of Thomas Coutts's first wife.[9] In 1836, at a time of distress among the Spitalfields weavers, Harriot subscribed the same amount as the Queen, and gave an upholsterer a private order for a suite of satin damask curtains for Stratton Street, taking 500 yards of material at a guinea a yard.

In November 1835 she gave money to the National Benevolent Institution, and to Elizabeth Gough, wife of an actor who had previously played in the same company as Harriot. Gough had died at Cheltenham, leaving his wife with four young children and no means to live.[10] When she was staying in Southampton an actress, Mrs Felton, she had known and loved as a child in Lancashire, appealed for help. Harriot gave her food, clothes, and a weekly income for life, saying the woman had been more talented than she had ever been but had made an unfortunate marriage and then failed in her profession.[11]

She received scores of begging letters each day, and these were first sifted by her secretary or treasurer. If the claim seemed just,

---

[6]Coutts Bank Archives, 83.
[7]Coutts Bank Archives, 82.
[8]P Dewar and D Adamson, op., cit., p.144.
[9]Coutts Bank Archives, 10608.
[10]Coutts Bank Archives, 4399.
[11]Margaret Cornwell Baron-Wilson, op. cit., p.205.

she gave help. She usually gave money to the town authority when she was staying in a particular place, so that they could distribute fuel, food or clothes to the poor. *The Gentleman's Magazine* obituary, in October 1837, said:

> The charities of the Duchess of St Albans might fill a column... Her liberality to the two Theatrical Funds is well known... Miss Stephens, Miss Foote, Miss Smithson, young Kean, and many others, have experienced the benefit of her fostering kindness; and whatever may have been the faults of the late Duchess, it is certain that we may look far and wide ere we find one who has ensured to others so much happiness or effected so much good.

But Tom Dibdin said some actors who accepted Harriot's help were ungrateful:

> We have heard Miss Mellon much blamed for her fondness for publicity respecting her good deeds, in a conversation in Drury Lane green-room, in which the person who acted as censor did it very ungratefully, as he had been more indebted to that lady's pecuniary kindness than any other member of the theatre.

Dibdin also said few other actresses who married wealth had helped their professional associates.[12]

Lord Broughton wrote in his diary for 22 May 1830, after a visit to Holly Lodge, that he 'saw many ways by which the good-natured hostess tries to make all the world forget that such a person as Miss Mellon ever lived'.[13] This does not square with the evidence: Harriot often recalled her days at the theatre; never forgot the people who had been kind to her in her early years; often helped players who fell on hard times, and was a constant patron of the theatres. She was, for example, kind in 1836 to Charles, son of Edmund Kean the famous actor, getting him introductions to the principal families in neighbourhoods where he had provincial engagements.[14]

The Duchess of St Albans was part of a small, aristocratic,

---

[12] Thomas Dibdin, op. cit., 1836.
[13] Lord Broughton, *Recollections of a Long Life*, 1909, vol. iv. P.22.
[14] Margaret Cornwell Baron-Wilson, op. cit., vol. II, p.46.

profligate and extremely expensive world centred upon Mayfair and Brighton. She had so much wanted to be part of this charmed circle, but found the life less full of *joie de vivre* than her life at Drury Lane Theatre:

> Ah, those were pleasant days! Few persons have seen so much of the various aspects – I may say of the two extremes of life – as myself, and few persons, therefore, can be better judges of the difference between great poverty and great wealth; but after all, this does not, by any means, constitute the chief and most important distinction between the high and the low states. No, the striking contrast is not in the external circumstances, but in the totally opposite minds of the two classes as to their respective enjoyment of existence. The society in which I formerly moved was all cheerfulness – all high spirits – all fun, frolic, and vivacity; they cared for nothing, thought of nothing, beyond the pleasures of the present hour, and to those they gave themselves up with the keenest relish. Look at the circles in which I now move; can anything be more 'weary, stale, flat, and unprofitable' than their whole course of life? Why, one might as well be in the treadmill, as toiling in the stupid, monotonous round of what they call pleasure, but which is, in fact, very cheerless and heavy work. Pleasure indeed! When all merriment, all hilarity, all indulgence of our natural emotions, if they be of a joyous nature, is declared to be vulgar. I hate that horrid word – it is a perfect scarecrow to the fashionable world, but it never frightens me, for I had rather be deemed 'unfashionable' occasionally, than moping and melancholy at all times. There is no cordiality where there is so much exclusiveness and primness – no, all is coolness, reserve, and universal *ennui*, even where the starchness of manner is unaccompanied by any very strict rigour in matters of conduct. I look out for cheerful people when I can find them – I do everything in my power to make them happy – and yet, were it not for the merry and frequent laugh of dear old General Phipps, could you not swear that my dinner parties were funeral feasts? Look now, at those quadrille dancers in the other room; they have been supping – they have been drinking as much champagne as they liked – the band is capital – the men are young, and the girls are pretty – and yet did you ever see such crawling movements – such solemn looks – as if they were all dragging themselves through the most irksome task in the world! Oh, what a different

thing was a country dance in my younger days![15]

She said there was no such thing in high life as youth – people were old when they first 'came out', the men 'all grave and revered signors', and the girls 'too fine and fastidious to enjoy anything'. They behaved as if the world was not good enough for them.

In the 1830s, as mentioned earlier, middle-class morality and respectability were becoming fashionable among the upper classes, and older people found it confusing that manners, speech and behaviour had changed so much since their youth. Harriot continued to spend prodigiously on entertaining the rich and famous at her mansion in Stratton Street, at Holly Lodge in Highgate, and at St Albans House in Brighton. According to *Old and New London*,[16] for one party at Highgate she hired all the birds from all the bird-dealers in London, and put them in the grounds. A band played in the garden, Chinese tumblers and jugglers exhibited on the slopes, groups of theatrical gypsies camped under the trees, and an Adelphi *corps de ballet* danced. On the lower lawns were targets, butts and equipment for archery. There were two more bands for dancing, one in a tent and one in the conservatory, and mountains of food to be devoured by the guests.

Social events were brighter in 1833 than during the Reform crisis of the previous two years, the Royal Drawing Room being well attended, Harriot among them. For an appearance at Court she wore between £1,000 and £2,000 worth of diamonds. Her entire jewel-case consisted of diamonds, except for three large sapphires. About one of her annual festivities on 19 May *The Age* wrote, 'We have received several letters about our Duchess's fête at Holly Lodge on Thursday last, but as she has had the good taste not to publish anything in the newspapers we shall not intrude upon her private affairs. It was the ostentation not the woman that we disliked.'

Harriot was not fond of the way high society stayed up half the night and often turned up late for her parties, going to two or

---

[15] Margaret Cornwell Baron-Wilson, op. cit., p.210–12.
[16] *Old and New London*, vol. V, p.398.

three others before they got to hers. She not only specified the hour at which people were expected, but underlined it on her invitation cards. On one occasion, annoyed at the emptiness of her rooms two hours after the appointed time, and knowing from past experience there would be a great crowd of late-comers, Harriot gave orders for the street door to be shut, and no more visitors admitted that night. Presently a party of cavalry officers arrived, and receiving no answer to repeated knocks at the door, they began to batter it with the hilts of their swords. Carriage after carriage drove up, without being able to set down its occupants, and before long the whole street was full. Harriot would have stood the siege all night, but some of the more artful of her excluded guests bribed the servants to let them down the area steps, and by passing through the offices and up the kitchen stairs they gained access to the drawing room. At this point Harriot thought it better to surrender and let everyone in.

In 1835 and 1836 there were frequent accounts of Harriot's attempts to vie with the hospitality of Mrs Wyndham Lewis (afterwards Mrs Disraeli). The latter's mansion in Grosvenor Place was described as 'the most perfect lady's house in London'.[17]

In June 1836 the Duke and Duchess gave a fête at Holly Lodge to commemorate the Restoration of Charles II. A magazine article gave an account that showed the manners of the 'Fashionables' left a lot to be desired:

> ...at the sound of a deafening gong the whole five hundred guests darted into the house, tents, and temporary rooms in which the breakfast-dinner was laid, and the scramble for places was something perfectly ludicrous among such high-bred persons long accustomed to similar entertainments... Every luxury was of course in profusion, but it was often to be wished that the champaigne [sic] had not been so plentiful. It is said that there were a certain set of dowagers of high rank who were proverbial for sitting at more than one of the tables. Thinking that no one's attention was called they have been seen to take two repasts in different rooms, departing with a look of inquiry towards a quiet tent, perhaps hoping for a third.

---

[17]Charles Pearce, op. cit., 1915, p.311.

Yet the newspapers were taking less interest in Harriot, not surprisingly considering that she had been constantly in the public eye for twenty years, and had often been the most talked-about woman in London.

In any case, Harriot was spending more time in Brighton. Augustus Sale remembered that as a child he attended, with his mother, Harriot's Twelfth Night party in Brighton in 1835,

> I have no hesitation in admitting that the strongest impressions in connection with this grand Twelfth night are connected with the cake and the supper. The cake itself... was ornamented with a vast number of musical instruments in miniature, and I brought away the models of an ophicleide[18] and a kettle-drum, the principal parts of which I devoured before I went to bed.[19]

The Duke treated Brighton to many falconry displays, in Regency Square, on the downs by the racecourse, and at Devil's Dyke. When the field sports were over, the invited spectators returned to St Albans House, where there was a champagne party and sideboard supper, with a firework display and dancing far into the night. As usual, the amusements were not of an intellectual kind, since Harriot took more delight in disguises, comic recitations and songs, jugglers and ventriloquists.

Harriot's second marriage was generally considered one 'of convenience', but this is not borne out by the correspondence. When the Duke was mildly ill with smallpox early in 1836 he stayed at Stratton Street and Harriot stayed for safety at the Clarendon Hotel. They wrote to each other regularly for 'a mutual sense of comfort and consolation' and on 15 January the Duke spoke of 'the loathsome disease I am slowly recovering from' (probably smallpox) and signed himself, 'your affectionate blotched-faced husband'.[20]

His letter on 16 January gives his view of the marriage and of his wife. First, he tells Harriot that he is happier with small gifts from her, rather than large ones, and that it was her letter he really

---

[18] An obsolete brass instrument with keys.
[19] M W Patterson, op. cit., 1953, p.40.
[20] Coutts Bank Archives, 1321.

appreciated. He speaks of Thomas Coutts's good fortune in having her for a wife, and Coutts's good judgment in leaving her his fortune and banking interests. In unromantic but realistic fashion he says they have borne with each other as well as most married people would, and had their ups and downs. He refers to quarrels with his family, and the calumny poured on both of them, then writes of Harriot's constant acts of charity. He tells her a parable about the ostentatious use of riches exciting envy, but using them to alleviate the needs of the under-privileged is Christian and ultimately rewarding – which suggests he had a kinder heart than many of his peers. In a note at the end of the letter he calls Harriot his Better Half, his Rib, and tells her he remains most faithful and affectionate. The letter is not passionate, but it reveals that the Duke had sincere affection for Harriot after nine years of marriage, which was uncommon amongst upper-class spouses then.[21]

The letters show that in 1836 Harriot was meeting members of the St Albans family again, and that Lady Guilford and Lady Burdett were writing 'affectionate' notes to the Duke. The Duke asked his wife on 20 January to give his sister Louisa and her husband wedding presents of their own choosing,[22] mentioned on 21 January a letter from his brother Augustus, asking to borrow a horse,[23] asked Harriot how his sister Georgina had got over the operation on her throat, and mentioned that he had ordered a new wig because his head has been shaved.[24] On 29 January he said he had heard his brother Frederick had drunk five bottles of wine when dining with Harriot, and commented, 'I would put a stop to this excess or decline the honour of his company'.[25] On 30 January he wrote that he was giving up sending a statement of his expenditure to his Uncle and brother Frederick, but would send Harriot a copy for her private inspection. He asked her to read over to Frederick the list of his Bills (debts). His brothers were obviously scrounging from him, and in the following year

---

[21]Coutts Bank Archives, 1322
[22]Coutts Bank Archives, 1325.
[23]Coutts Bank Archives, 1323.
[24]Coutts Bank Archives, 1329.
[25]Coutts Bank Archives, 1330.

relations between Harriot and the St Albans clan were fractured for ever.

On 3 February the Duke said, 'The hesitation that I have at times in my speech is not as bad now as it was before my illness, and I think it proceeds from nervous agitation'.[26] On 4 February he moved to Berkeley Square from Stratton Street[27] and the last letter says,[28] 'I burnt the letters you wrote me, but kept a copy of mine, and a note of the substance of yours... I will not send any letter to the Hotel from myself. I have been told my blotch marks will remain'. Presumably Harriot was afraid her letters had been contaminated with the smallpox, and asked for them to be destroyed.

The Duke's letters show how far from the truth *The Age*, scurrilous to the last, was when it wrote of their marriage,

> [Of] her long negotiations, her trial tours, her ultimate purchase of that living nonentity the disconsolate Duke of St Albans... suffice it for the present that she used to say that 'he was a bad bargain – she bought him too dear, it cost her so much trouble to keep him in order, and as for his ducal honours he derived them from a source no higher or better than herself'.

There is no evidence in the archives or the memoirs of her friends that Harriot ever said any of these things.

In February 1837 Harriot gave a St Valentine's Day ball and supper of which *The Court Journal* reported,

> Nothing could exceed the beauty of the designs and tasteful decorations emblematical of the occasion. Hearts of every size and colour united by love knots, with garlands of flowers, were suspended in festoons around the spacious apartments, which were lighted up in the most effective and brilliant manner'.

By that date, King William IV had been declining in health for some time. Harriet Martineau noted:

---

[26]Coutts Bank Archives, 1336.
[27]Coutts Bank Archives, 1337.
[28]Coutts Bank Archives, 1338.

> The old King was manifestly infirm and feeble when I last saw him in the spring of 1837. I was taking a drive with Lady S-, when her carriage drew up at the roadside and stopped, because the King and Queen were coming, He touched his hat as he leaned back, looking small and aged'.[29]

On 20 June 1837, just after two o'clock in the morning, the King died; at 6 A.M. the young Queen Victoria was awakened and told the news. The throne of England had been successively occupied by 'an imbecile, a profligate and a buffoon', to quote Sir Sidney Lee, and the change was generally welcomed. The Queen was proclaimed from an open window in St James's Palace on 21 June. Harriet Martineau said some relatives of hers went to the park and stood in front of the Palace window, though 'scarcely half-a-dozen people were there; for very few were aware of the custom'.[30]

Harriot did not long enjoy the young Queen's reign. She and the Duke were back at Holly Lodge in March 1837, when she fell ill and a series of summer fêtes had to be cancelled. Shortly after this she was so weak that she had to be assisted in and out of her carriage. She was driven round the grounds of Holly Lodge in her pony chair whenever she could stand the fatigue, but she became weaker every day. Visitors were excluded, and it was guessed she had cancer of the stomach, though the obituary in *The Gentleman's Magazine* said 'the disease was paralysis of the limbs'. Her appetite had gone, and she subsisted for two months on arrowroot and a little brandy. She was taken to Stratton Street in June and lay in the great dining room for two months, 'quite tranquil and without pain'. Then she asked to be carried to the room where Thomas Coutts had died. She died on 6 August 1837, clutching his pillow. The English stage, the City, and the nobility had lost a colourful member.

When she died, *The Brighton Gazette* and *The Brighton Guardian* each devoted four lines to her memory. *The Brighton Guardian* remarked that 'she will be much missed by the poor' – a meagre tribute to one who had formerly been of such importance in the

---

[29]Harriet Martineau, *Autobiography*, 1983, vol. II, p.118.
[30]Harriet Martineau, op. cit., p.119.

town. *The Age*, vindictive to the last, felt obliged to defend its persistent attacks on her:

> During her life, and particularly since her marriage to the Duke of St Albans, we have occasionally indulged in some harmless pleasantries upon her vagaries, more with a view to correct her ridiculous exhibitions of pride and folly, than with any desire to annoy the feelings of the woman... When she ceased to advertise her ostentatious almsgiving and theatrical mummeries at Holly Grove [sic] and elsewhere, we ceased to notice her.

The yellow press was as malignant then as now.

Harriot's funeral was conducted with pomp and ceremony, after a long journey to Redbourne Hall, seat of the St Albans family in Lincolnshire, which involved various stops for the night at roadside inns. The Duke, Sir Francis Burdett, and 'most of the noble relatives of her Grace' were present at the funeral. The procession was followed by all the Duke's tenantry 'who were anxious to pay a last tribute of respect to one who in the hour of need, and in the time of distress, had always proved their best friend and benefactress.' The inscription on the coffin gave only her name, rank and date of death – not her age, on which Harriot had always been sensitive. If it is true she was born in 1777 (and not two years earlier, as some thought), she was only 60 when she died. But even in death Harriot, as we shall see, was to spring her greatest surprise.

Chapter XV
THE WILL[1]

Harriot's Revenge

When Harriot St Albans's Will was published on 16 February 1838, some of those who had scorned and mocked her had cause to regret it. Apart from two large, but by comparison with her wealth, modest legacies to her husband the Duke and to her stepdaughter Lady Burdett, plus a number of small legacies or annuities to friends and servants, she left the whole of her vast fortune in trust to the youngest granddaughter of Thomas Coutts, Angela Burdett. Far from being the social butterfly and giddy-headed spendthrift painted by her enemies, Harriot had proved to be a superb manager and business woman and, despite her extravagant lifestyle and immense generosity to the family of Thomas Coutts, her charity to the poor, and her aid to beneficiaries most of whom were unknown to the public, she had built up one of the largest fortunes of the nineteenth century, said to be twice the amount left to her by Thomas Coutts.

The details of the Will demonstrate what a masterly woman of business she was. She set out to control the destination of this great mass of capital from the grave, in the way Thomas Coutts would have wished her to do, and to ensure that it did not fall into the hands of those who had reviled her, or whom she suspected would squander it. Almost every bit of it was tied up in trusts, so that the beneficiaries could enjoy the fruits but not uproot the tree.

Harriot left her husband, the Duke of St Albans, £10,000 a year, but only for his lifetime, together with £2,000 worth of plate

---

[1] A play by Frederick Reynolds in which Harriot appeared as Cicely Copesley in January 1798.

of his choice, and the use for life, together with their contents, of the great house at number 78 Piccadilly, and of Holly Lodge 'as being what I loved best of all I possessed'. She also left him £10,000 to furnish the Piccadilly house, formerly occupied by the Burdetts and Lady Guilford. Harriot empowered the trustees of her Will – Sir Coutts Trotter, Bart, Edward Marjoribanks, Esq., Sir Edward Antrobus, Bart, and William Coulthurst, Esq., (her partners at the Bank), William George Adam, Esq., accountant-general of the High Court of Chancery, and John Parkinson of Lincoln's Inn Fields (her solicitor) – to renew the leases of Stratton Street and Piccadilly, or 'purchase them for fee-simple and inheritance thereof'. The Duke could also use the suite of rooms set aside for Harriot in Coutts Bank in the Strand. Upon his death all these benefits were to revert to Angela Burdett.

The Duke's subsequent history was that in 1839, two years after Harriot died, he married a wealthy Irishwoman named Elizabeth Gubbins, and he died in 1849 of an epileptic fit, at the age of forty-eight. He and his wife had a son, William Amelius Aubrey de Vere, who succeeded to the title as 10th Duke of St Albans, and a daughter, Diana. When the Duke died, the income from Harriot died with him.

The family of the Duke of St Albans was explicitly excluded from benefiting in any way from her Will, so much so that if the Duke entertained his uncle, Lord Aurelius Beauclerk, or either of his brothers, Lord Frederick and Lord Charles Beauclerk, in his house for so long as a week in any year, he was to lose his annuity and everything else Harriot had left him. This was the only mention of the Beauclerk family in the lengthy Will and testament. Not a single memento was left to the Ladies Beauclerk, the Duke's sisters, who had previously been Harriot's good friends. Harriot also showed her continuing hostility towards Alexander Trotter and his descendants, by stating in her Will that they should be permanently excluded from partnerships in Coutts Bank.

Harriot's legacy of £20,000 to Lady Burdett – over and above the carefully accounted £118,602. 15s. Harriot had already given her since Thomas Coutts's death in 1822 – was held in trust by the Executors. Harriot heartily disliked Sir Francis Burdett, and the money was left to 'the said Dame Sophia Burdett, for her sole use and benefit exclusively of any husband of the said Dame Sophia Burdett, and I do hereby declare that the same shall not be subject or liable to the debts, control, power inter-meddling, or engagements of any such husband.' After Sophia's death, the money was to go on the same terms to her surviving daughters, 'share and share alike', and if only one of them survived, to her alone.

Before her death in 1832, Lady Bute had received from Harriot the same amount as Lady Burdett. There was no mention in the Will of Lady Bute's son, Dudley Coutts Stuart, or his sister Frances. Harriot was not generous to the other surviving daughter of Thomas Coutts; neither Lady Guilford nor her daughters were mentioned in the Will, though Harriot recorded privately that since Thomas Coutts's death in 1822 she had voluntarily given Lady Guilford £108,500, plus £10,000 each to the Ladies North, her two daughters. Harriot neither forgot nor forgave Lady Guilford's violent attacks on her good name.

Harriot left lump sums of £5,000 each to the son and daughter of her partner Edward Marjoribanks, and to the daughter of her partner Sir Coutts Trotter. There were small annuities of between £50 and £500 a year to fifteen women and five men, including friends, her ex-companion Eleanor Goddard, and some of her servants.

The residue of the estate, all the properties and houses, her jewellery and plate and personal effects, she left to the sixth and youngest child of Sir Francis and Lady Burdett, Angela Georgina Burdett. Technically, the bequest was left to the trustees, who were to pay an annual income to Angela. Neither she nor her parents, nor any future husband, could touch the capital. On Angela's death, the estate was to go to any son of hers 'in the event of his attaining the age of twenty-one years, but not otherwise', then, failing sons, to her elder sister, Johanna Frances Burdett and her eldest son, and failing them, to another sister, Clara Maria Burdett and her eldest son, under the same restrictions as Angela. Failing all the named Burdetts, and surprisingly by-passing any daughters they might have, the estate was to go to the son of Edward Marjoribanks. If Dudley Coutts Marjoribanks had no surviving son, it would go to Harriot's godson Coutts Lindsay, grandson of Coutts Trotter. If all these failed, then the fortune was to revert in trust to the partners for the time being in the Bank.

Harriot further provided that any person coming into the inheritance should within six months take the surname of Coutts. Thus Angela became Angela Burdett-Coutts; under that name she became the greatest philanthropist of the nineteenth century, and was created a Baroness in her own right. One other restriction Harriot placed on the bequest, surprising at first sight but probably intended to prevent the takeover of Coutts Bank by foreign interests. If Angela (or any of the reversionary legatees) should marry an alien by birth, whether or not that person had become a naturalized British citizen, 'immediately after such marriage... the trusts and powers shall cease, determine and become utterly void... as if such person were actually dead... and the fortune will go to the person being next in remainder...'. Angela was to fall foul of this clause when she was 67 years old, by marrying a much younger man, William Ashmead-Bartlett, her secretary who had been born in the U.S.A. More will be said about this later.

The Will was proved on 16 February 1838. Personalty was sworn under £600,000, which at that time excluded real (landed) property. The full value of the estate was not known, but the fortune was said to amount to £1,800,000 – worth at least £100 million at today's prices, or twice the amount left to Harriot by Thomas Coutts. Angela was in modern terms a multi-millionaire. It was by no means the largest fortune of the age: between 1809, when probate valuations began to be recorded, and 1858, when they were removed from the two consistory courts of Canterbury and York and taxed by the state, the deaths of eight millionaires (excluding landholdings and settled property) were recorded, and the Duchess of St Albans was recorded as a half-millionaire. To put her fortune in perspective, Nathan Rothschild, banker, died in 1833, estimated to be worth £5 million, and the first Duke of Sutherland, who died in 1836 and was known as 'the Leviathan of wealth', was said by Greville, the diarist, to be 'the richest individual who ever died', though most of it was in land.

Nonetheless, Harriot's fortune was great enough for *The Morning Herald* to try to visualize it in concrete terms,

> Miss Angela Burdett's fortune is said to amount to the sum of £1,800,000. The weight of this enormous sum in gold is 13 tons, 7 cwt, 3 qrs, 12 lbs, and would require 108 men to carry it, supposing that each of them carried 289 lbs (equivalent to the weight of a sack of flour). This large sum may be partially guessed by knowing also that, counting at the rate of 60 sovereigns a minute, for ten hours a day, and six days a week, it would take ten weeks, two days and four hours to accomplish the task! In sovereigns, by the most exact computation, each measuring in diameter 17/20th of an inch, and placed to touch each other, it would extend to the length of 24 miles, 260 yards, and in crown pieces, to 113 and a half miles and 240 yards!

Unlike Harriot, Angela was not to be a partner in the Bank, nor to interfere in the running of the business. Yet she always considered herself the head of the bank, and so did the world, though according to Edna Healey, the modern historian of the bank, she was neither as rich nor as influential as people imagined. She could not touch the capital or anticipate the interest.[2]

Why Harriot left the bulk of her fortune to one person, with reversion to one heir and no more, she never explained. She may have felt that a unified great estate was more visible, gave greater power and status, and enabled the holder to do more not only for her or himself but for the whole family, friends and dependants. But why Angela, the youngest and, by all accounts, least importunate of all Harriot's step-grandchildren? Her youth and modesty may be one answer. Unlike her older Burdett siblings and even grander Stuart and North cousins, she had not offended Harriot with aristocratic pretensions. And she had been a favourite from childhood.

Angela was born in 1814 at 78 Piccadilly. She was only a year old when her grandfather married Harriot, so she remembered nothing of the family storms that then raged, culminating in Lady Guilford retreating to Putney, and her parents the Burdetts

---

[2]Edna Healey, *Coutts & Co: The Portrait of a Private Bank*, 1992, p.285.

leaving the Piccadilly house in 1818. Sir Francis Burdett said he 'owed nothing to Coutts and wanted nothing' – which was grossly untrue on both counts, but he took a house across the road from Stratton Street, at 23 St James's Place, and his family was reconciled with Harriot in 1819. Harriot even offered to pay the cost of his parliamentary election campaign at Westminster in 1837.

Angela had a restless and rootless childhood, her mother being constantly on the move between their London and country homes or living abroad. Her father was usually absent on his political campaigns, and all the world knew that from 1798 he was the lover of Lady Oxford – he found marriage stifling, and in a letter to Thomas Coutts called it 'the grave of love'. Sophia Burdett was gentle and virtuous but also plaintive, demanding and a hypochondriac. Angela grew up in a female world with four sisters; her brother was usually away. Like most upper-class girls, Angela was educated at home; in 1821, when she was seven years old, Hannah Meredith of Lancashire came as her governess and remained to become her friend and companion for nearly sixty years, during which time they were rarely separated.

Harriot took a great fancy to Angela, who ignored family differences and took pleasure in the company of a kind woman who sent her and her sisters gowns for the theatre, and bonnets decked with primroses. Parcels from Harriot were always arriving at their home, containing a length of lace, peppermint drops, silks, chintzes and ribbons, as well as boxes of books. Once Harriot sent Angela a piano from Bath. She took the young girls on trips to Holly Lodge, where she played games with them, told them the romantic story of her life, and opened up her old theatrical costume boxes. In 1826 Angela went abroad with her mother for three years, and when she came back, Harriot had married the Duke. The young woman often stayed with Harriot in the following years, and accompanied her on many driving tours around Britain, in a great procession of coaches, wagons, couriers, liveried servants and armed outriders. During these trips, Harriot instilled into Angela her deep concern for the sufferings of the poor, but she also indulged her constantly. It was to Angela that Harriot wrote one of the rare non-business letters that survives:

> My dear Angela: I knew you would all be famished when I left therefore I have ordered a Pie for you with Mulligatawny what a long word and some Grapes... all of which I hope will arrive good Carriage paid... Mind you all behave properly till I return, Mama and all, she really is too frolicsome. I beg you consider my writing to you as a great favour; what a beautiful day we had yesterday. Arrived at half past two [at Holly Lodge] and ah such primroses and daffodils.
> Love to all,
> Your affectionate Harriot St Albans[3]

As she grew older, Angela was often invited to balls and dinners at St Albans House in Brighton, and to hawking parties on the South Downs. Augustus Sale recalled in 1882 how Angela had been favoured:

> Among the ladies who were especially kind in patronizing and befriending my mother, I remember, first, the Duchess of St Albans, the once fascinating actress Harriot Mellon... To me, the Duchess comes back stately, benignant, in black velvet and diamonds... but more distinctly do I remember a young lady who always accompanied her and who, in 1837, was to inherit her vast wealth. This was Miss Angela Burdett... It must have been in 1835 that, as a little urchin, I went with my mother to a grand Twelfth Night entertainment at the Duchess's house in Brighton... I can recall clearly that when the Twelfth Cake was cut, the slice which fell to Miss Angela Burdett contained a magnificent diamond ring.[4]

To the solemn young Angela, whose mother was loving but frequently prostrated with grief or illness, Harriot opened up a world of warmth, gaiety and life. But Angela also saw the aristocratic smiles that turned to sneers as the Duchess passed by, saw the toadies and hangers-on, saw the vulgar cartoons and heard the vicious gossip. She thought Harriot's charitable efforts were undiscriminating and attended by too much publicity. She heard that Harriot's gifts to the starving Irish peasants often ended up in the pockets of unscrupulous agents. If in later life Angela was

---

[3] Edna Healey, *Lady Unknown*, 1978, p.45.
[4] M W Patterson, *Angela Burdett-Coutts and the Victorians*, 1953, pp.39–40.

obsessively anxious to be an anonymous donor to charity lists, and to make sure her money reached those she intended it to reach, it was because she never forgot the way Harriot's largesse was treated.

Harriot observed all Thomas Coutts's grandchildren as they grew up, with the shrewd eye of someone who had made her own way in the world and learned to judge character. If she had ever thought of Dudley Coutts Stuart, son of Lady Bute, as her heir, she ruled him out when he married Napoleon's niece, Christina (daughter of Lucien Bonaparte, Prince of Canino) who was a pathological spendthrift, and French to boot! Lady Bute's daughter, Frances, who married Lord Sandon, later Earl of Harrowby, had made no effort to conceal her disdain and disapproval of Harriot, and had discouraged her visits, so she was cut out of the Will.

As far as the children of Sir Francis Burdett were concerned, the only son, Robert, was excluded from the Will because, according to *The Gentleman's Magazine*, he had already been provided for, with securities payable to him on his father's death. Robert was taken away from school at Eton in 1810, and became a shadowy figure; at Oxford he took to heavy drinking and when he joined the army he virtually cut himself off from his family. Later he became Colonel Sir Robert Burdett, and inherited his father's estate of 20,984 acres; he died unmarried in 1844, when his sisters inherited as his coheirs. The baronetcy went to Francis Burdett, son of a younger brother of the famous Sir Francis. Sophia, the eldest daughter, was rejected because she married the Irish M.P. Otway Cave, and Harriot did not think the other daughters – Susan, Johanna and Clara – had the qualities she was seeking. So Angela, the youngest daughter, came before her older sisters and got everything. She soon left her father's house and moved to Stratton Street with her governess; she was determined to be independent, which was a courageous step at the time. She gave her mother £8,000 a year and settled allowances of £2,000 a year on each of her sisters. Her sister Susan Trevanion was the most difficult family member she had to deal with, for Susan married a man who twice ruined himself financially, and Angela refused to bail out the husband.

Harriot Mellon had really enjoyed being rich, whereas Angela Burdett-Coutts once wrote that her wealth brought her little real happiness. She was besieged by suitors offering marriage; one suitor, a bankrupt Irish barrister named Richard Dunn, pursued her for eighteen years with an insane persecution which neither policemen nor bodyguards were able to prevent. For the rest of her life she was afraid to be alone. She travelled in great style but did not give extravagant parties and balls as Harriot had done, though she loved giving concerts and play readings in her drawing room, and received the artists as friends rather than performers. She did not patronize painters, but collected pictures, china and rare manuscripts. Her father said her 'great means' demanded a great cause, and this she found in charity, becoming the greatest philanthropist of the Victorian age. In 1871 she became the first woman to be made a Baroness in her own right. In the citation, her aid for sufferers in the Turkish war, her 'efforts to relieve the sufferings of lower animals', her building and endowing of churches, and her aid to the poor were mentioned. It also said, 'If, like other philanthropists, she has sustained disappointments, she has never allowed them to arrest the progress of her generosity'. Harriot would have been very pleased to hear that, since it echoed her own behaviour. Unlike Harriot, Angela was neither mocked nor satirised by the press but lauded for her efforts to help the poor.

Angela remained unmarried until she was 67, and then she echoed Harriot's life again, by marrying her 26-year-old secretary, William Bartlett, an American by birth. Efforts by Queen Victoria and the bank officials (who pointed out that under the terms of Harriot's Will she would forfeit her inheritance if she married a foreign-born man, even though he was a naturalized citizen) failed to change her mind, and they married in 1881.

Was the marriage a success? Enemies of Bartlett said he destroyed her happiness and wasted her inheritance, and that Angela's useful life ended with her marriage. She did forfeit the right to her inheritance, though to avoid a legal battle an agreement was reached with the Bank whereby she took one-third of the income (£16,000 a year), the other two-thirds going to her sister Clara Money. Angela gave Bartlett the share in the

Burdett fortune she received when her brother died, transferred her stocks and shares to him and bought Holly Lodge for him from her sister. Harriot would not have approved of this transfer of assets to her husband. By 1903 Bartlett found it necessary to mortgage Holly Lodge; he was not skilful in financial affairs and his tastes were expensive. In 1885, having taken the name William Lehman Ashmead Burdett-Coutts-Bartlett-Coutts, he became Conservative M.P. for Westminster. He is remembered for having introduced into Parliament, under Angela's direction, the Hampstead Heath Act which preserved Parliament Hill and 300 acres of Hampstead Heath as an open space for the public.

Angela lived on to the age of 92, celebrating 25 years of marriage before she died in December 1906. She was buried in Westminster Abbey. In her Will she left £78,000 gross, over £63,000 net, which was only a tiny fraction of her original inheritance. Her husband was a womaniser but Angela never believed it, so she remained reasonably happy. In her marriage partner she was not so fortunate as Harriot Mellon had been. The 'little player girl' was a better judge of a husband than she, a better businesswoman, and more determined than Angela to control her own property.

Harriot Mellon's career was in striking contrast to the reputedly scandalous lives of most late eighteenth-century actresses. She remained chaste until in her late twenties she became the protégée of a rich married man. He always affirmed, even in private letters to Harriot never intended for other eyes, her 'purity' during a ten-year extra-marital relationship. Harriot, with no advantages of birth, upbringing or education, had a natural talent for business, pleasure and friendship, and far outshone all her rivals. F W A. Lingard wrote of her later:

> To rise from the position of an actress in receipt of thirty shillings per week [he did not know she started as a child actress on 4s.6d.], and become the wife of a great banker, and subsequently a duchess, is a curious turn of 'Fortune's Wheel'... What a romantic career, I think my readers will say. It began in rain, and

ended in glorious sunshine.[5]

There were, however, heavy showers along the way. Harriot was a strong and independent woman, but her one weakness was a desire to be accepted by the *Haut Ton*, which was extravagant, arrogant, snobbish, exclusive, and with few exceptions totally uninterested in those less advantaged than themselves. They looked down on those who made money by trade, the *nouveaux riches*. To be of the *Ton* was the height of every social climber's ambition, the final seal and hallmark of fashion. Yet although Harriot was an excellent mimic and so could have copied the formality and artificial graces of the society lady of the period, she never pretended to be what she was not. As long as her low-born mother and stepfather lived, she was a generous and caring daughter. As the wife of the wealthy Thomas Coutts, Harriot refused to fade into the conformity – as did other actresses like Elizabeth Farren who married up the social ladder – which might have made her more acceptable to the élite. She preferred to hold the stage and astonish everyone in the magnificence of her entertaining; everyone flocked to her parties, but made fun of her behind her back. She became the target of satirists; as she grew older she increased in weight and size, and she was cartooned as a big, fat melon nursing a baby-sized duke. Her trials in society showed the difficulty of getting into the inner circle, but also the power of riches to overcome it; the Royal Dukes, sons of George III, were regular guests at her table. She was not accepted at the Court of George III, but was invited there by George IV, and more reluctantly by William IV, guilty about his treatment of her colleague and mentor Dorothy Jordan. Though Harriot was never completely accepted by the nobility, she could not be ignored; at the Coronation of William IV, Harriot as consort to a duke of royal, if illegitimate, descent stood third lady in rank after the Queen.

Harriot was a mixture of realism and romanticism, common sense and sentimentality, warm-heartedness and vulgarity, reticence and ostentation. Her contemporaries reacted to her in

---

[5] F W A Lingard, n.d.

different ways. She was always popular with the poor and common people, to whom she was a Cinderella figure and unfailingly generous. Anne Mathews said, 'She could not stir abroad but like a shining comet she was wondered at, and men would tell their children, 'This is She!'...'[6] She was the sort of woman one loved or hated, but to whom one could not be indifferent. Sir Walter Scott liked her, saying she was 'kind and friendly, without either affectation or insolence in the display of her wealth, and most willing to do good if the means be shown to her.' To Henry Fox she was 'vulgar and purse proud', though not lacking in 'a sort of frank good humour and hearty gaiety, which alone makes her sufferable.' Wellington nicknamed her Queen Mab; at a breakfast she gave in July 1835 he found her with Lady Aldborough, the Duchess di Camizaro and Lady Stepney, and called them 'all the demi-reps in town'. *The Biographical Keepsake* on the other hand said, 'She has virtues that far surpass those of thousands who have been her most wanton and bitter assailants'.[7]

After she died, her obituary in *The Gentleman's Magazine* said hundreds of theatre people could testify to her kindness, and commented, 'Whatever may have been the faults of the late Duchess, it is certain that we may look far and wide ere we find one who ensured to others so much happiness or effected so much good.' Actor-manager Tom Dibdin commended Harriot's partiality for ostentation, since one should not hide one's light under a bushel! He remarked that many actors had become rich, and some actresses had married noblemen, but few had afterwards remembered their poorer colleagues in the theatre, as Harriot had always done. Her generosity to the two Theatrical Funds was well known. Sir Walter Scott said she always spoke entertainingly and without scruple of her stage life. When Horace Smith proposed the health of the Duchess at one of her birthday parties in Brighton, she replied, 'Ladies and Gentlemen, unaccustomed as I am to public speaking – since the days when everyone who chose could come and hear me for 6d. in the gallery...'.

Margaret Baron-Wilson, a sympathetic biographer who knew

---

[6]Coutts Bank Archives, 7991.
[7]Coutts Bank Archives, 7985.

Harriot personally, said her life had been 'a romance from beginning to end', and Harriot's career 'perhaps the most varied and fortuitous of any female of modern times'. Harriot was warm-hearted, unaffected, generous and virtuous, but also proud, quick to take offence and unguarded in her expressions, hasty in temper and credulous. She loved a facetious anecdote, a jest or *bon mot* with more gusto than most people, her laugh being described as 'prompt and hearty'. She was in every respect 'the Merry Duchess'.

Though none knew the full extent of her kindnesses, from the evidence of correspondence to, from and about Harriot in the archives of Coutts Bank, Harriot was more generous than even her friends suspected. Despite her reputation for capriciousness and her hasty temper, most of her domestic servants remained in her service for many years; she knew how to keep their loyalty.

Harriot Mellon's life was bizarre, spanning as it did the whole of Georgian society from the world of the lowly strolling player through the *haute bourgeoisie* to the highest ranks of the nobility. More than the triumphs and disasters of one woman's life, it demonstrates that acting was a more lucrative way for a woman to earn a living than almost any other occupation, since it could provide a prudent woman with comfortable savings and income. Harriot showed, twice over, that marriage could be happy and successful even when the world judged the partners mismatched in age and unsuited to each other. She had the good fortune to be found and loved by a wealthy man who appreciated her humble origins, gave her sound financial training and paid her the supreme honour of leaving her all his enormous wealth, to dispose of as she pleased. Despite what critics said about marrying for money, Harriot genuinely loved Thomas Coutts, made him deeply happy, and after his death grieved for him for the rest of her life. She was promiscuously generous with her wealth, yet as the senior partner in Coutts Bank she was an excellent business woman and doubled its capital in fifteen years. Thomas Coutts would have been proud of the way she handled the inheritance, and the way she dispersed it in her Will.

As to her second marriage, it is true that she 'bought a Duke', but the English aristocracy would 'marry anyone for her money', trading social position for great wealth. The Duke of St Albans, in a letter to Harriot after nine years of marriage, said, for what it was worth, that he was sincerely devoted to her.

This is the story of an original, a woman of independent character and sound common sense as well as charm and, in her early years, beauty, who overcame the disabilities of most women in that unemancipated era, and rose triumphant to the zenith of wealth and influence. She was a credit to the high station in society to which she was raised. She unashamedly loved life and making people happy and, seizing fortune by the hand, shared her good luck with everyone around her. The young woman whom, rather than her husband, she chose as her heir became the greatest philanthropist of the Victorian age. Thus Harriot Mellon, darling of the frivolous Georgian stage, became against all odds, fairy godmother by proxy to the Victorian poor.

BIBLIOGRAPHY

Archival Material: the letters, accounts and other unpublished sources cited are from the Archives of Coutts Bank in the Strand, for permission to quote them I am grateful to the Bank

The Plays: the authors of the plays used as chapter titles were identified in Van Lennep, Avery, Scouten & Stone, eds., *Index to the London Stage, 1660 to 1800*, 11 volumes (compiled by B R Schneider), Carbondale, U.S.A. Southern Alliance University Press, 1979

Anonymous References

A Tale of the Last Century, The Secret Memoirs of Harriet Pumpkin, a celebrated actress, London, J Cahuac, 1825

An Amateur, Real Life in London, 2 vols., London, Jones & Co., 1821–1822

Authentic Memoirs of the Green Room, London, 1801

Biographical and Historical Addenda to life of Thomas Coutts, London, John Fairburn, 1822

Epistle to Harriot, Duchess of St Albans: the first Lash of Nemesis, London, James Ilberry,1828

Fine Acting, Or A Sketch Of The Life Of Harriet M- and T.C- Esq., Banker, London, 1815

Life of Frances Abingdon, London, 1816

A Person of the First Respectability, *Life of the late Thomas Coutts, Esq., Banker in the Strand*, London, John Fairburn, 1822

A Person of the First Respectability [alias Percy Wyndham], *Strictures on a Slanderous and Indecent Book* (n.d.), Homerton, J S Turner

A Person of the First Respectability, *Authentic Memoirs of Mr and Mrs Coutts' in Lives of Malone, Coutts, Parnell, Ward and Curran*, London, J Fairburn, 1819

Thespian Dictionary, London, Dundee, 1805

Other References

Airlie, Mabell, Lady, *In Whig Society, 1775–1818*, London, Hodder & Stoughton, 1921

Airlie, Mabell, Lady, *Lady Palmerston and Her Times*, London, Hodder & Stoughton, 1922

Anderson, W E K, ed., *The Journal of Sir Walter Scott*, London, Oxford University Press, 1972

Arbiter, Petronius, *Memoirs of the Countess of Derby*, 1797, London, H D Symonds

Aspinall, A, *Mrs Jordan and her Family*, London, 1951

Baker, Michael, *The Rise of the Victorian Actor*, 1978, London, Croom Helm

Bamford Francis, *The Journal of Mrs Arbuthnot*, 1820–1832, London, Macmillan, 2 vols, 1950

Baron-Wilson, Margaret Cornwell, *Memoirs of Harriot, Duchess of St Albans*, 2 vols., London, Henry Colburn, 1839,

Bell, John, *British Theatre*, London, 1791

Bernard, John, *Retrospections of the Stage*, London, Colburn & Bentley, 1830

Berry, Miss Mary, ed. *Lewis, Journal & Correspondence*, London, Longmans, 1844

Bleackley, Horace, *Ladies Fair and Frail: Sketches Of The Demi-Monde During The Eighteenth Century*, London, John Lane, 1909

Boaden, James, *Memoirs of Mrs Siddons*, 2 vols., London, Henry Colburn, 1827

——, James, *Life of John Kemble*, London, Longman Hurst, 1828

——, James, *Memoirs of Mrs Inchbald*, London, Richard Bentley, 2 vols., 1833

Bonfield, Lloyd, *Marriage Settlements, 1601–1740: The Adoption of Strict Settlement*, Cambridge University Press, 1983

Broughton, Lord, *Recollections of a Long Life*, 6 vols., London, John Murray, 1909

Butler, E M ed, *A Regency Visitor*, London, Collins, 1957

Burnett, T A J, *The Rise and Fall of a Regency Dandy*, London, John Murray, 1981

Coleridge, E, *The Life of Thomas Coutts*, Banker, 2 vols., London, John Lane, Bodley Head, 1920

Colquhoun, Patrick, *A Treatise on Indigence*, London, J Hatchard, 1806

Cunningham, P, *The Story of Nell Gwyn*, London, 1903

Dejardin, I, *The Images of Mrs Jordan, Mrs Jordan: The Duchess of Drury Lane*, English Heritage, 1995

Dewar, P and Adamson D, *The House of Nell Gwyn*, London, William Kimber, 1974

Dibdin, Thomas, *Reminiscences of a Literary Life*, London, Henry Colburn, 1837

Ffrench, Yvonne, *News From The Past*, London, Gollancz, 1934

Forster, J, *Life and Times of Oliver Goldsmith*, London, 1855

Fulford, Roger, *Royal Dukes*, London, Duckworth, 1933

Fothergill, Brian, *Mrs Jordan: Portrait of an Actress*, London, Faber & Faber, 1965

Frampton, Mary, *Journal*, London, Samson Low, 1885

Genest, J, *Some Account of the English Stage From 1660–1830*, Bath, H E Carrington, 10 vols., 1832

George, M. Dorothy, *Catalogue of Prints and Drawings in the British Museum: Division l, Political and Personal Satires*, vols. 5–11, 1949–1952, Oxford University Press

Gore, J, ed, *Thomas Creevey's Papers, 1793–1838*, London, Penguin Books, 1948

Haight, G, ed, *The Portable Victorian Reader*, London, Penguin, 1985

Healey, Edna, *Lady Unknown*, London, Sidgwick & Jackson, 1978

——, Edna, *Coutts & Co: The Portrait of a Private Bank*, London, Hodder & Stoughton, 1992

Holcroft, Thomas, *Memoirs*, London, Longman, 1816

Holland, Lady Elizabeth, *Journal, 1791–1811*, London, Longman, 1908

Holland, Lady Elizabeth, ed. by Earl of Ilchester, *Lady Holland to Her Son*, London, John Murray, 1946

Howitt, William, *Northern Heights of London*, 1869

Hunt, Leigh, ed. R Ingpen, *Autobiography*, London, Constable, 1903

Kelly, Michael, *Reminiscences*, 1826

Leslie, C R, *Autobiographical Recollections*, 1860

Lingard, F W A, 'Actress, Millionairness and Duchess', unpublished, handwritten 4-page document in the personal file for Harriot Mellon at the Theatre Museum of the Victoria & Albert Museum in London

Lockhart, J G, *Memoirs of the Life of Sir Walter Scott*, 10 vols., London, Black, 1892

Longford, Elizabeth, *Queen Victoria: Born to Succeed*, London, Weidenfeld & Nicolson, 1964

Marshall, Dorothy, *Eighteenth-Century England*, 2nd edition, London, Longman, 1974

Martineau, Harriet, *Autobiography*, 2 vols., London, Smith Elder, 1877

Masters, Brian, *The Dukes*, London, Blond Briggs, 1975

Mathews, Anne, *Memoirs of Charles Mathews*, 4 vols., London, Richard Bentley, 1838/9

——, Anne, *Anecdotes of Actors*, 1844

——, Anne, *Tea-Table Talk, Ennobled Actresses and other Miscellanies*, 2 vols., 1857, London, Thomas Cautley, Newby

Oxberry, William, *Oxberry's Dramatic Biography and Histrionic Anecdotes*, London, George Virtue, 1825–1827

Patterson, M W, *Angela Burdett-Coutts and the Victorians*, London, John Murray, 1953

Pearce, Charles, *The Jolly Duchess*, London, Stanley Paul, 1915

Perkin, Harold, *The Origins of Modern English Society*, London, Routledge & Kegan Paul, 1969

Perkin, Joan, *Women & Marriage in Nineteenth-Century England*, London, Routledge, 1989

——, Joan, *Victorian Women*, London, John Murray, 1993

Pückler-Müskau, Prince, *Tour of Germany, Holland and England, 1832*, New translation by Flora Brennan, London, Collins, 1987

Raikes, T, *Journal*, London, Longman, 1856

Rigby, Elizabeth, *The Quarterly Review*, 84167, London, December 1848

Rubinstein, W D, 'The Structure of Wealth-holding in Britain, 1809–1839', *Historical Research*, February 1992

Sale, Augustus, *Life and Adventures, 1829–1895*, 1882

Smith, J T, *Joseph Nollekens and His Times*, 1828

Stirling, Edward, *Old Drury Lane*, 1881
The Political Register, ed. William Cobbett, 1817
Tomalin, Claire, *Mrs Jordan's Profession: The Actress and the Prince*, U.S.A. Knopf, 1995
Villiers, Marjorie, *The Grand Whiggery*, London, John Murray, 1939
Walpole, Horace, *Letters*, 9 vols., R. Bentley & Son, London, 1891
Wilkinson, Tate, *The Wandering Patentee*, 1795, York, Scolar Press edition, 4 vols., 1973
Wollstonecraft, Mary, *A Vindication of the Rights of Women*, 1792, 1891 edition, London, Fisher Unwin

INDEX

A

Adelaide, Princess of Saxe-Meiningen, Duchess of Clarence, later Queen to William IV, 71, 195–98, 223
Ashmead-Bartlett, William, 216, 221–22

B

Bibby company, 19–20, 24
Burdett, Angela (Baroness Burdett-Coutts), 112, 114, 221
   dies, 222
   life, 219
   marries (Ashmead-) Bartlett which excludes her from legacy, 221
Burdett, Sir Francis and Lady (Sophia Coutts), x, 75, 100, 107–9, 112, 114–15, 181–84, 214, 107–9, 217–18, 220
Bute, Lady Frances (Fan), later Lady Sandon and then Countess of Harrowby, 180–81, 215
Bute, Marchioness of (Frances Coutts), x, 73, 75, 95–96, 113, 119, 180

C

Caroline, Princess and Queen, 137–40, 155
Charles II, xi
Charlotte, Princess, 135
Charlotte, Queen, 117–19, 125
Clarence, Duke of, King William IV, ix, 49–50, 71, 73, 78, 136, 154, 193, 195–98, 210–11, 223
Coutts Bank, x, 68–70
   archives, 225
   Harriot's control of, 202–3
   income but no partnership left to Angela Burdett, 214
   inherited by Harriot, 144–45
   partners, 200
   survives 1825 c, 164
Coutts, Susannah, 74–75
   dies, 91, 95–96, 135
   insanity, 82
Coutts, Thomas, ix, 54, 66–67, 68–81
   85th birthday, 140
   becomes Harriot's 'protector', 77, 79
   determines to leave fortune to Harriot, 110–21
   dies, 141
   funeral attended by royal dukes, 142–43

marries Harriot, 97, 100–102
　　marries Susannah, 74
　　pre-marital relations with Harriot, 82–96
　　reaction of daughters, 99–109, 110–21
　　Will, 144
Creevey, Thomas, 109, 159, 178–79, 196
Cruikshank, George, 155, 172–73

D

Dibdin, Charles, 22
Dibdin, Thomas, 23–24, 92–93, 204
Dickie, Andrew, 136–37, 146, 181, 194
Duchess of Devonshire, Georgiana, xii, 43, 70, 78

E

Entwisle, Thomas, 18–20, 24–25, 26–27, 39, 64, 65, 103–6
Erskine, Lord, 112

F

Farren, Elisabeth (Countess of Derby), 50, 52, 54, 92, 98
Fitzherbert, Maria Anne, 78, 138
Foster, Lady Elizabeth, 63
Fox, Charles James, 25, 73

G

George III, 60, 70, 111, 137

George, Prince of Wales, George IV, x, xi, 66, 71, 77, 78, 81, 110, 137, 138–40, 155, 169–70, 195, 196–97
Goddard, Eleanor, 128–29, 146, 215
Guilford, Countess of (Susan Coutts), x, 73, 75, 93, 99–100, 106, 112, 117–18, 181, 209, 215
Gwyn, Nell, xi

H

Hamilton, Emma, xii, 111
Holly Lodge, x, 123, 127–28, 177, 193, 195

J

Jordan, Dorothy, ix, xi, 23, 49–50, 51, 53, 55, 59, 60–62, 78, 92, 150, 193, 195–96, 223

K

Kemble, John, 53, 60, 61
Kena company, 13–14, 16, 18–19
Kent, Duke of, 72, 125, 136

L

Lawrence, Sir Thomas, 200–201
London life, 41–47

M

Macaulay, Thomas B, 154

233

Mellon, Harriot, Mrs Thomas Coutts, Duchess of St Albans
  allows most of her income to stepdaughters, 148, 182
  appointed to Drury Lane, 48
  attacked by press, 132–35, 149–56, 159, 166–68, 172–75, 178–80, 190, 193
  birth, ix
  charity, 59, 123–25, 130, 140, 147, 165, 203–4, 225
  child actress with Bibby company, 20–23
  first appearance, 51
  generous hostess, 151, 177, 193–94, 206–7
  goes to London, 39
  her Will, 213–14
  illness and death, 211–12
  inherits Bank and Coutts's fortune, 144–45
  investments, 58, 83–87
  joins Stanton company, 24
  married life, 174
  marries duke, 171
  marries Thomas, 97–98, 101–2
  meets Lord Burford, heir to dukedom of St Albans, 153
  meets Thomas Coutts, 66–67
  performs before Sheridan, 38
  presented at Court, 177
  protégée of Thomas, 82–96
  refused at court, 117–19
  relations with Beauclerk in-laws, xi, 196, 209, 214
  story of lottery ticket, 87–88
Mellon, Lt. Matthew, 16, 27

Mellon, Sarah (Mrs Entwisle), 13–20, 24–25, 26–27, 29, 31–32
  to London with Harriot, 39, 50, 64, 65, 79–81, 102–4
Money, Clara (Burdett), xi
  inherits Harriot's fortune by Angela's exclusion, 221

P

Pitt, William, the younger, 73

S

Sale, Augustus, 208
Scott, Sir Walter, xi, 160–64, 168, 173–74, 224
Sheridan, Richard Brinsley, MP, 38–39, 48, 72, 90
Siddons, Sarah, xii, 49, 53, 54, 61
St Albans, 9th Duke of (William A D V Beauclerk, Lord Burford), xi, 153, 156–57
  courts Harriot, 158–69
  dies, 214, 224
  Hereditary Grand Falconer, 188–89, 191
  left Stratton Street House and income for life, 214
  marriage to Harriot, 171
  married life, 171–84
  praise of Harriot, 208–9, 225
  remarries, 214
Stanton company, 24, 26–33
Stephenson, Sally, 128
strolling players, 14
Sussex, Duke of, 146, 178, 198

T

Trotter, Alexander and family, Harriot's antipathy towards, 201–2

Trotter, Sir Coutts, 144–45, 183, 194, 200, 214, 215

V

Victoria, Princess and Queen, xi, 72, 195, 211

W

Walpole, Horace, 44
Wollstonecraft, Mary, xii
Wright family, Stafford banker, 33, 36, 38, 48, 59

Y

York, Duke of, 119, 127, 135, 145, 150

Printed in Great Britain
by Amazon